ENDORSEMENTS

Many believers will fall away in these last days, but God has given us a secret weapon. This book will activate the difference maker in you—the gift of discernment. It could save your life!

SID ROTH
Host, *It's Supernatural!* television

Rebecca Greenwood is a seasoned and trusted intercessor, teacher, mentor, prophetess, and apostolic leader. I respect and honor deeply and highly recommend her timely book for the body of Christ, *Discerning the Spirit Realm.*

PATRICIA KING
Author, minister, television host
www.patriciaking.com

Discerning the Spirit Realm is an extraordinary book! The revelation it contains will open your eyes to strongholds that have led to defeat in your life. It is full of keys that will open doors of victory to help you lead an overcomer's life, to pray victoriously and to discern and welcome history-making moves of the Holy Spirit.

CINDY JACOBS
Generals International

We are living in a momentous new era in the spirit. Now more than ever, it is time for the Church to fully awaken and identify how God is moving across the earth. In her new book, my good friend Rebecca Greenwood opens up a unique door for believers to enter into greater discernment in the spirit realm, as she shares biblical principles and powerful stories that will spark your faith to grow more in this gift. *Discerning the Spirit Realm* imparts valuable insights as you are guided through different layers of tapping into your God-given spiritual senses and aligning with the ways of God. I believe God is raising up change agents who can discern the times and seasons and shape history even in the midst of unprecedented global shaking. Take these words to heart and let the Holy Spirit transform your prayer life!

DR. CHÉ AHN
Founder and President, Harvest International Ministry
Founding and Senior Pastor, Harvest Rock Church
Pasadena, California
International Chancellor, Wagner University
Founder, Ché Ahn Ministries

Angels, demons, principalities, four living creatures—what do they have in common? They are all created beings with distinct purposes. What else? They are all spiritual beings that can be perceived, distinguished, and discerned by believers in Christ Jesus through the gifts of the Holy Spirit. Becca Greenwood is a biblically sound prophetic teacher of the Word of God who demystifies the unseen realms and makes flowing in the supernatural very natural. You hold in your hand a stick of dynamite to blow up the powers of darkness! Read and act!

JAMES W. GOLL
Founder of God Encounters Ministries
GOLL Ideation LLC

DISCERNING THE
SPIRIT
REALM

DISCERNING THE
SPIRIT
REALM

THE KEY TO POWERFUL PRAYER
AND VICTORIOUS WARFARE

REBECCA GREENWOOD

DESTINY IMAGE® PUBLISHERS, INC.

P.O. Box 310, Shippensburg, PA 17257-0310

"Promoting Inspired Lives."

This book and all other Destiny Image and Destiny Image Fiction books are available at Christian bookstores and distributors worldwide.

Cover design by Eileen Rockwell

Interior design by Terry Clifton

For more information on foreign distributors, call 717-532-3040.

Reach us on the Internet: www.destinyimage.com.

ISBN 13 TP: 978-0-7684-5487-1

ISBN 13 eBook: 978-0-7684-5488-8

ISBN 13 HC: 978-0-7684-5490-1

ISBN 13 LP: 978-0-7684-5489-5

For Worldwide Distribution, Printed in the U.S.A.

1 2 3 4 5 6 7 8/24 23 22 21 20

CONTENTS

FOREWORD

What an honor to be able to write the foreword for Rebecca Greenwood's book, *Discerning the Spirit Realm*. I've had the privilege of knowing her and her husband Greg for several years. They are great people, down to earth, fun, and like family. But also very gifted!

I've sat back and watched Becca, as she is affectionately called by close friends and family, over the years develop from a simple yet powerful prayer and deliverance ministry to an exploding international ministry that very much touches discerning the spirit realm. Yet the totality of her gift and ministry is much larger than this. I watched her develop grace, not just experience, as she's advanced, and she's a delight to work with.

How we need to understand the whole realm of discerning! I'll never forget when I stumbled into this realm and with shocked awareness thought, *What in the world just happened to me?* I was a graduate student and had recently been baptized in the Holy Spirit. Walking past the student center, I looked through the window to where students were sitting at tables eating as well as walking around. Suddenly, they were no longer people but they were white forms. They were in the form of a person yet they obviously were not flesh and blood. They were moving about as these white, formless bodies. In one sense they looked like ghosts that were in the form of a person. I knew they weren't ghosts; I'm simply trying to describe what I saw. They looked like walking spirits.

I returned to my apartment and thought, *What in the world just happened to me?* I called a woman who was much more mature than I in spiritual matters to see if she could explain to me what just happened. She confirmed that yes, I was seeing spirits and they were human spirits. I had suddenly entered a realm that was both totally new and quite shocking as well as intriguing. My spiritual senses were being enlarged to see in to the spirit world. I had just experienced the discerning of spirits.

To discern in its simplest form is to see. I learned that there are three realms in which the Holy Spirit pulls back an invisible curtain so that we can see this spiritual realm, not with our natural eyes but through our spiritual eyes. There are basically three rooms to discerning of spirits. We see human spirits, angels, and demonic spirits.

This realm became essential to understand when I was a young pastor. The only resource I knew of at that time to understand it was Kenneth Hagin's book on the Holy Spirit and His gifts. Since then I've experienced God walking me through strategic prayer for people by seeing into the spirit realm. They didn't need to be present for me to experience this. People have been healed from cancer because God showed me pictures of what was keeping that cancer in place. I would pray through the picture until the entity I saw was totally removed. (I usually saw those spirits in the form of gorillas or monkeys.) When that entity was removed, the people were completely healed or released from the cancer.

Discerning of spirits is the most dangerous and has been the most misused gift of the Holy Spirit. Many people believe that it's limited to the demonic realm. When they see a demon, they immediately use it to accuse or label a person. But God shows us things so that we know how to pray for and help people. In prophetic churches it can be the most damaging gift because people's spiritual senses are heightened yet they lack knowledge. Both knowledge and experience are necessary to correctly interpret what one is seeing. When this is lacking, people can get hurt and at times even leave a church because of what someone has "seen" concerning them. Why? Because it's used to label and accuse a person rather than set them free. There's been a dearth of books serving as resources to understanding this area of discerning of spirits. People have desperately needed knowledge, experience, and wisdom in this realm from someone who is experienced and mature.

What a blessing for the body of Christ to finally have a resource to use in this area. Rebecca's book is timely because we've never needed to understand this realm more. She deals with not only the realm of seeing but other gifts of the Spirit that release supernatural knowledge to help us understand what is happening. The gift of knowledge often imparts a different type of discernment to us.

I found it very significant that, upon reading this book, I had a very unusual and intimidating encounter with a demonic force. That encounter literally made me ill. Because I had just completed reading this book and was preparing to write the foreword, I was alerted to the need for discernment. I was able to tease apart some of the aspects of what I'd experienced. The encounter had to be discerned so that I could then move on into devising and then implementing a strategy to overcome.

Becca's book is totally down to earth yet detailed and extremely helpful. I can hear her in the book. I hear her voice. It doesn't simply impart knowledge, but her book is wrapped in the warmth with which she ministers. We're in a season when we need help. It seems the whole world and the nations of the earth are in an uproar. And that uproar or rage is a complex intertwining of multiple factors, societal and individual hurts and wounds. We need love and we also desperately need discernment.

May your discernment be multiplied through reading this book. And may God give you His heart as you interpret what you're seeing and feeling so that you can advance with great victory and deliverance. This is an amazing day that calls for great people with a great heart that is both informed by and wrapped in the love of God!

BARBARA YODER
Lead Apostle, Shekinah Regional Apostolic Center
Breakthrough Apostolic Ministries Network
www.shekinahchurch.org

INTRODUCTION

Have you ever been in a room where others are rejoicing, yet you are not? Or have you watched as doors are flying open for someone, meaning others are promoting this individual, but you do not feel at ease with this particular person? Have you felt the presence of angels? Have you felt the presence of demons? Are you able to know a person is demonized just by looking at them? Are you able to know the Lord's purpose for an individual? Do you hear, see, or feel angelic activity? Maybe you hear, see, and feel demonic activity. Are you able to know who or what is influencing the spiritual atmosphere of a city or region? Can you feel the direction the Holy Spirit is moving in a meeting? Allow me to personally share that I often experience the majority of the above-mentioned spiritual encounters, which are all encompassed in the gift of discernment.

Discernment is a gift that has not been widely taught in the Body of Christ, often because of lack of understanding of the gift. That being said, there are many who operate in this revelatory gift but find it hard to communicate what they are encountering, experiencing, or what is being revealed to them in the realm of the spirit. As one who functions highly in discernment, I understand the difficulty when the gift is in operation, yet those with whom I am attempting to communicate the spiritual reality I am experiencing stare at me with a blank or perplexed look.

Often conversations between me and my husband will go as follows.

Me: "Do you feel that?"

Greg: "Feel what?"

Me: "That heaviness in the atmosphere. It is overwhelming."

Greg: "No, I am not feeling the heaviness."

Or another scenario:

Me: "Do you hear that?"

Greg: "Hear what?"

Me: "That sound of worship in the atmosphere."

Greg: "Is someone worshiping? I'm not hearing it."

Me: "Yes. I hear the angels worshiping as we pray."

Or maybe some have experienced this:

Me: "That person is tormented by a spirit of fear."

Greg: "How do you know?"

Me: "I see it on his countenance. I hear the lies it is speaking to him in the spirit."

There are many key words or phrases that are used by those who function in the gift of discernment. *I hear, I see, I feel, I know, I smell.* Or another common statement: "I am not able to explain how I know what I know, but I know what I am sensing, hearing, seeing, and feeling is real." The truth is, those who function in this gift are legitimately having these experiences. But often they have learned not to share what is being revealed due to previous times of being shunned or misunderstood.

Allow me to share a testimony that is common in our world. I had just returned from a powerful time of ministry in a particular nation that will remain unnamed for security purposes. I love the church and the friends we work with in this nation as they are ones who are on fire and have learned to follow the Lord through extreme situations of persecution. In fact, the government sends agents into Christian church services in order to listen to what is being shared to ensure that there are no "rebellious" mindsets being perpetuated that would threaten or challenge their government. When these agents come into the service they dress in civilian clothes and record what is being shared. They then will share the recording with government officials. Therefore, while ministering I am keenly aware of the fact that I am being watched, listened to, and recorded. Even so, I have yet to feel unsafe.

As I said, I had just returned home. Greg and I, along with our three daughters, decided to have a fun family night. We enjoyed a nice dinner and spontaneously decided to go to a movie. Upon arriving at the theater, I quickly began to experience alarms going off in my spirit. I felt a looming sense of danger in the atmosphere. My husband could see that I was apprehensive. He asked, "Are you okay?"

In order not to alarm our daughters, I calmly replied, "No, not really. Greg, I just returned from meetings where government agents came for the sole purpose of recording my messages. I knew that if I had said something the government deemed out of line I would have been taken by the authorities and questioned and possibly arrested, yet I never felt unsafe while ministering. But at this theater, I feel a looming sense of danger. It does not feel safe."

After sharing this discernment with my husband, immediately two of our daughters began to chime in: "Dad, she is right! We feel it too. Maybe we should leave."

Greg has proven to be a voice of wisdom in the midst of these situations. He patiently inquired, "Do you feel we are in danger now, or are you discerning something in the spirit realm concerning the atmosphere of the area and region we are in? Why don't we ask the Lord for clarity?" He then prayed a simple prayer, "Lord, if we are in danger and need to leave, we welcome You to speak to us now. Or if this is discernment in operation concerning the spiritual atmosphere or a demonic presence in this area and region, reveal it to us. Lord, are we in a dangerous location? Should we leave?"

We stood in a close huddle as a family and listened to the Lord. Quickly, we came to place of unity. We were not in danger but were indeed discerning a demonic strongman in the region, resulting in a tangible feeling of endangerment. Once we gained this understanding, we were able to watch the entire movie in peace and to continue our family night of fun. We do not need to run and hide just because we find ourselves in the presence of evil. We can discern and yet remain in peace and joy. Through the blood of Jesus, we have the victory.

Maybe many of you reading this story can relate. Some might be rejoicing to realize you are not alone in this world of discernment. Actually, I believe many are functioning in this gift without full understanding because of lack of training. I also feel strongly that discernment can be taught and activated in many by natural observations of people, situations, and regions. It is my prayer that as we delve into this teaching, great truth and wisdom on how to discern the times and seasons will be imparted to help you navigate this gift. May you feel empowered and be activated in your ability to distinguish in the realm of the spirit. Most importantly, may each of you reading experience a release to be yourself and no longer feel a need to apologize for this gift. It is time for Holy Spirit-anointed permission and freedom to discern.

Chapter One

DISCERNMENT DEFINED

*Every believer has received grace gifts, so use them to
serve one another as faithful stewards of the many-colored
tapestry of God's grace. For example, if you have a speaking
gift, speak as though God were speaking his words through
you. If you have the gift of serving, do it passionately with
the strength God gives you, so that in everything God alone
will be glorified through Jesus Christ. For to him belong the
power and the glory forever throughout all ages! Amen.*
—1 PETER 4:10-11

Every believer has received abilities, administrations, enablements, functions, and gifts of the Holy Spirit. The beauty of this truth is that each gift and ability is given for the profit of all. You see, the Church is a living being, a body, which is to function in a cooperative manner as a coalition and network to benefit and profit each other and influence and disciple culture. I appreciate how this is clearly explained in Romans 12:4-5: "In the human body there are many parts and organs, each with a unique function. And so it is in the body of Christ. For though we are many, we've all been mingled into one body in Christ. This means that we are all vitally joined to one another, with each contributing to the others." Peter Wagner defines a spiritual gift "as the special attribute given by the Holy Spirit to every member of the Body of Christ, according to God's grace, for use within the context of the Body."[1]

You and I are a part of a living body with Jesus as the head. As further discovered in Romans, "God's marvelous grace imparts to each one of us varying gifts and ministries that are uniquely ours" (Rom. 12:6). How awesome is it that our heavenly Father has created a many-colored tapestry of grace gifts that we are to faithfully steward. While this book is not a teaching on all the spiritual gifts, abilities, and functions, I do believe it is important to understand that we are all uniquely created and graced to be a part of the living Body of Christ. It is also vitally important to understand and to know how God has gifted each of us individually so we can learn, grow, function in, and mature in the giftings and abilities He has bestowed to benefit the corporate body. But in this message, we are going to focus on thoroughly outlining a particular gift that is not often considered or taught—discernment. What is discernment? How is it defined according to the Word of God? How am I to grow and mature in this Holy Spirit-given ability? These questions, along with many other topics, will be clearly discussed and explained.

THE ABILITY TO DISCERN

A spiritual gift is given to each of us so we can help each other. To one person the Spirit gives the ability to give wise advice; to another the same Spirit gives a message of special knowledge. The same Spirit gives great faith to another, and to someone else the one Spirit gives the gift of healing. He gives one person the power to perform miracles, and another the ability to prophesy. He gives someone else the ability to discern whether a message is from the Spirit of God or from another spirit. Still another person is given the ability to speak in unknown languages, while another is given the ability to interpret what is being said. It is the one and only Spirit who distributes all these gifts. He alone decides which gift each person should have (1 Corinthians 12:7-11 NLT).

Discernment is a revelatory gift. It is one of the nine gifts given to us through the Holy Spirit. It is a gift that has rarely been taught. For those who function in discernment, many have walked for years without teaching and training, feeling alone in their revelation. There are those who have misused the gift. And there are many believers who shun or do not accept the discernment of those who clearly function in this ability because it is difficult to lead, make decisions, and understand times and seasons based off revelation in the spirit realm that is not visible or tangible in the natural.

The ability to discern is very real and biblical. Several times people have asked me, "Can't you turn that off or shut that down?" The question does make me laugh because, for the most part, those who have posed this question are coming from a genuine place of trying to understand. However, others have asked because they truly don't want to hear what is being discerned. All of that being said, the reality is—no, I can't. To ask someone who functions in the ability to discern if they can stop discerning is like asking someone who has the gift of faith to quit believing. It is real and functioning and is one of the ways the Lord has knitted me and countless others into the tapestry of the living being of the Body of Christ.

The Greek word for discernment is *diakrisis* (see 1 Cor. 12:10). It means the ability to judge or decide, the ability to judge the genuineness of gifts that come from the Spirit and those that do not, the gift to differentiate the Word of God proclaimed by a true prophet or that of a satanic deceiver (Strong's #G1253). In this First Corinthians passage it is also used to describe one of the gifts or enablements of the Spirit and refers to the supernatural power of spiritual insight to know what is from the Lord and to detect and expose demonic and false strategies, teachings, and activities. A more simplistic explanation is the differentiation between good and bad and the discerning of spirits.

I am sure some of you reading this can relate to these definitions. There have been numerous times I have heard someone speak and minister and I have absolutely no peace. Or I am watching a governmental leader, media anchor, businessman or woman, even ministry leader or fellow believer speak and everything inside of me is telling me what is being spoken is not truth but deception and a lie. Then there are those times I hear an individual speak and I know that everything that is being said is coming from truth, a genuine honesty, or a pure and true revelation of the Lord. We will discuss this later, but it definitely takes time to mature in this area so as not to cross over into a critical or judgmental spirit that is not from the Lord or to try to force someone to fix an unrighteous area in their lives when they are not ready to do so. When I was younger in the Lord and new in discovering and operating in this gift, I had to go through many lessons on how to maneuver in wisdom with the revelation I was hearing and receiving.

A PERSONAL LEARNING LESSON

As I listened to the prophet speak revelation to the group, I was extremely troubled. Many were listening, certain that what was being shared was a message from the Lord. As the ministry time progressed, I could not understand how those receiving were not able to recognize the subtly controlling, demeaning tone of the words being released and the power play occurring through this individual. I could see in the near future great division coming to the prayer group if this individual was allowed to continue down this vein of ministry. Suddenly, in the midst of his corporate ministry, this individual turned to me in front of the entire prayer team and called me out, "The Lord says you are still in fear! He has told me to ask you how long you will hold on to this demonic spirit in your life!" He then abruptly turned and proceeded to the next person in a demeaning, intimidating, and divisive manner. All the words being given were totally off and inaccurate. Not only did this occur publicly, but there were also many private divisive conversations about the leadership of this network.

This individual decided to become a very active member in this prayer ministry. It became apparent to me that they were aiming extreme jealousy at me and several others. I decided to try to remedy this situation. Against the wisdom of my husband, I met with this person in a sincere attempt to work through the jealousy and negative prophetic words that they continued to aim toward me. I thought to myself, "I am being overly judgmental and critical. Certainly, this person's motives aren't as bad and divisive as I feel they are."

We planned a private meeting at a public location. I wanted to inquire if I had done something to cause this person to view me as fearful and as a threat. The response was, "You are jealous of me."

I gently replied, "No, I am not jealous of you. But if I have given you that impression I apologize, and I ask you to forgive me."

As soon as this statement came out of my mouth the reply was, "Thank you for sharing that. I receive it. But let's not tell anyone about this conversation. I don't want the leaders of this group to view you in a more negative light because they have confided in me that they already do. If you tell them you came to me, this might harm your relationship with them and your position in this group." Instantly, red flags sounded the alarm in my spirit man and I knew this was not an acceptable response, but in my lack of experience I did not know how to maneuver this situation and I agreed to the terms.

Within 48 hours, this individual decided to share with the leaders and others in the prayer group that I had admitted my jealousy. As a result, I was thrown into a season of having to lay low and pray that this divisive spirit would be fully exposed. Soon, this person overplayed their hand, and exposure did come. I was invited into a leadership meeting and asked, "You have been very quiet about this person; what have you been discerning?" I shared what I had discerned through revelation of the Holy Spirit, and within a short amount of time this individual was brought into a meeting and offered help to receive freedom and training in order to move beyond these divisive ways. Unfortunately, the person chose not to and left the group. What proved heartbreaking was the number of other individuals hurt and falsely accused during this short time. It took many several months to recover from the chaos and confusion released.

THE WISE IN HEART ARE CALLED DISCERNING

The one with a wise heart is called "discerning," and speaking sweetly to others makes your teaching even more convincing (Proverbs 16:21).

I cannot express enough the need for wisdom when operating in discernment. In my personal testimony above, my discernment was correct, but my lack of wisdom in handling this situation set me up for a season that proved to be difficult. We will discuss maturing in this gift later, but our foundation here is an important truth in the Word: "*Solid food is for the mature, who because of practice have their senses trained to discern good and evil*" (Heb. 5:14 NASB). When discerning, wisdom and maturity to handle and share the revelation must be an intentional goal.

As also exemplified in the above testimony, the individual functioning in division was not using words of love and caring to bring wise instruction but was purposely acting in a divisive manner in order to be the one heard and in control. This is a clear example of manipulation in action—when someone is attempting to operate in prophecy and a gift of discernment but is either not gifted or is gifted but does not carry the depth of purity or maturity necessary to function in the wisdom of the Lord.

WE ARE CALLED TO CAREFULLY EVALUATE THINGS

This is what we speak, not in words taught us by human wisdom but in words taught by the Spirit, explaining spiritual realities with Spirit-taught words. The person without the Spirit does not accept the things that come from the Spirit of God but considers them foolishness, and cannot understand them because they are discerned only through the Spirit. The person with the Spirit makes judgments about all things, but such a person is not subject to merely human judgments, for, "Who has known the mind of the Lord so as to instruct him?" But we have the mind of Christ (1 Corinthians 2:13-16 NIV).

People often ask me, "Can all believers discern?" My answer to this question is yes. While some might not function in this ability on a regular basis, I do believe people can learn how to discern and can mature in it. The Greek word in this scripture for *discern* is *anakrino*. It means "to examine, evaluate carefully, investigate, interrogate, determine, and judge" (Strong's #G350).

Paul is teaching here that all believers are being taught by the Spirit. As sons and daughters of God, we are no longer taught by the ways of the world but by the Holy Spirit. We are spiritual beings. As representatives of His Kingdom we must know and understand the vocabulary of His Kingdom. This also includes the realities and vocabulary of the Spirit. Just as an engineer, a teacher, a doctor goes to school and has to learn the vocabulary and ways of that trade, we too must learn the vocabulary and ways of the spirit realm. Hear me—the spirit realm is more real than the physical realm. The physical will pass away, but the spirit lives eternal.

As believers, we have now entered the plane of the spiritual. We are now able to live in the realm of the Spirit. Therefore, we all must grow in this reality in our lives. The unsaved cannot understand or comprehend the things of the Spirit. However, you and I can and must.

One of the marks of growth and maturity in our spiritual lives is discernment. While it might look different for each of us, there is a divinely given ability to be able to examine, evaluate, and judge in order to see or penetrate beyond the surface of life and the natural world to see, perceive, and understand the way things truly are. You see the unsaved walk by sight and yet they really see nothing; they lack depth of sight because they are spiritually blind. Paul clearly states:

> *Beware that no one distracts you or intimidates you in their attempt to lead you away from Christ's fullness by pretending to be full of wisdom when they're filled with endless arguments of human logic. For they operate with humanistic and clouded judgments based on the mindset of this world system, and not the anointed truths of the Anointed One* (Colossians 2:8).

The maturing believer grows in discernment and the ability to understand more and more the ways of God, the Word of God, and the realm of His Kingdom. Maturity positions us for victorious insights and solutions to issues that can only effectively be resolved through understanding and wisdom in the realm of the Spirit.

SALVAGING THE GOOD AND DISCARDING THE USELESS

> *And this is my prayer: that your love may abound more and more in knowledge and depth of insight, so that you may be able to discern what is best and may be pure and blameless*

until the day of Christ, filled with the fruit of righteousness that comes through Jesus Christ—to the glory and praise of God (Philippians 1:9-11 NIV).

Let's investigate this scripture further. In this scripture, the Greek word for *discernment* is *dokimazo*. It means "to approve or the testing process that salvages the good and discards the useless" (Strong's #G1381). It signifies the ability to regard something as genuine or worthy on the basis of testing. This is exactly what Solomon prayed and asked the Lord to bestow on him.

Most scholars believe that Solomon was twenty years old when he began his reign. His words express his feelings concerning his lack of experience in order to fulfill this new position. It seems evident that it was weighing heavily on him to be able to function effectively as the vice-regent of Yahweh. We read that the Lord came to him in a dream and gave the following instructions: "Ask for whatever you want me to give you" (1 Kings 3:5 NIV). As we continue to read, we learn what transpired.

> *"Now, Lord my God, you have made your servant king in place of my father David. But I am only a little child and do not know how to carry out my duties. Your servant is here among the people you have chosen, a great people, too numerous to count or number. So give your servant a discerning heart to govern your people and to distinguish between right and wrong. For who is able to govern this great people of yours?" The Lord was pleased that Solomon had asked for this. So God said to him, "Since you have asked for this and not for long life or wealth for yourself, nor have asked for the death of your enemies but for discernment in administering justice, I will do what you have asked. I will give you a wise and discerning heart, so that*

there will never have been anyone like you, nor will there ever be" (1 Kings 3:7-12 NIV).

I can imagine the overwhelming weight of following in the footsteps of his father David. And even though he had reached manhood, he was still younger in years. We see the awesome exchange between him and the Lord and the promise of destiny released. Solomon asked for a discerning heart to govern the people. The Hebrew word for *discern* in this encounter is *habin,* also stated as *biyn.* It means "to understand, pay attention, examine, realize, hear, and pay attention to information; have specialized knowledge that is effectively implemented; teach, perceive, look closely, see with the eyes, cunning; and to have perception and judgment about what is seen" (Strong's #H995).

It is evident from his reign that wisdom and discernment were indeed bestowed on Solomon. He was able to build the temple and return the Ark of the Covenant to its divinely designed home. He built his palace, he attained great wealth, he traded with nations. His fame spread wide because of the gift of wisdom conferred on him by the Lord. However, Solomon did not listen to the Lord concerning his wives and concubines from the nations He had previously warned the children of Israel about. The Lord said that if they lay with them in sexual relations, they would succeed in turning their hearts away from the God of Israel and toward their gods. That is exactly what happened to Solomon in his later years. Therefore, when his son became king, the kingdom was torn out of his hands due to the sin of his father.

What is the lesson here? We must ask the Lord for increased wisdom and discernment, but also learn to walk in obedience with the Lord and allow His purifying work in our hearts so that we will not bow our knee to idols of our culture. Even the wisest are able to stumble and be lead astray by the desires of the flesh and the seduction of worldly and impure cultures.

BUILDING AN ALTAR THAT BROKE OFFENSE

As I travel and minister throughout the nations, there is a consistent prayer I voice to the Lord: "Lord, give me Your heart, discernment, wisdom, presence, message, and strategies for transformation." For several years, I visited a particular city and region in Mississippi. We watched the Lord move miraculously in tangible breakthrough and victory leading to transformation, which I will share in Chapter Eight. On this visit, the Lord spoke to us to go to a location where there had been hurt and offense from the white man to the First Nations people of our land.

As we stood in on-site intercession and worship, the Lord moved powerfully. We engaged in effective repentance and true intercession, healing a divide. As we were completing the time of intercession, all on the team felt we were to do a prophetic act on the land. It was an act of building an altar to the Lord, dedicating this land to Him. When the Lord moved powerfully on behalf of the children of Israel, altars of covenant and dedication were erected. Likewise, when it was mentioned we all agreed, including me.

As we gathered stones to build the altar of covenant, I quickly felt a check and uneasiness in my spirit. I stopped and engaged the Holy Spirit. "Holy Spirit, why am I uneasy? Is there something we need to know?" I quickly heard Him and gained wisdom I would not have known in my own understanding. As I approached the team I shared, "The Lord just spoke to me. He said we are not to build an altar made of stone with our hands on this Native land. If we do, it will be another act of the white man enforcing our ways and spirituality on their sacred places. He revealed that we are to form a circle, kneel on our knees, and lock arms. We are to build a human altar of love and blessing for our Native brothers and sisters and their land." As soon as I voiced His Kingdom strategy, the glory presence and anointing enveloped the entire group. We fell to our knees in a circle and locked arms, establishing a covenant of love, acceptance, and blessing. It was a weighty and powerful moment. When we shared it with leaders from the tribe, they were beyond blessed. From that act that night, the beautiful people of this First Nations tribe blessed me as one of them and said, "You are truly one of us."

Friends, I had no understanding in the natural that this would bless my Native friends to the degree that it did. This is what occurs when we ask for an increase in discernment and wisdom. Our hearts become so in tune with Him that we are able to maneuver in ways beyond our own knowledge to see deliverance, healing, breakthrough, and victory.

MOVING ON

As we have discovered, discernment involves words that carry much weight and responsibility—words such as examine, test, evaluate carefully, to know if a message is true or false, to judge, to know if one is a true or false prophet, the differentiation of good and bad, to discern spirits in operation, and to salvage the good and throw out the useless. All of us as believers are to discern or approve what is good and what is useless. But we must be sure to do this with the heart of love. This is something I want to ensure from the beginning—to invite and welcome His heart of love so that as we learn to function in this ability we do not cross into critical judgment, which then becomes sin in our own lives. This is the point of caution. God is not giving us this gift so we can be critical or judgmental. He is not licensing us to glorify the demonic and get our focus out of balance. He is not bestowing this ability for us to use our discernment as a gossip session or as an invitation to think or operate in a rebellious way. Operating in this realm is to be done in love, wisdom, maturity, and revelation from the Holy Spirit. This gift is bestowed because it is a key to powerful breakthrough prayer and intercession, clear prophetic words, and victorious warfare for individuals, churches, cities, regions, and nations. The truth is, discernment is to be used in beautiful ways that bring victory over death and healing over wounds that have existed for hundreds of years. So let's advance in our journey to understand how learning to hear and receive the voice of the Lord causes our discernment to mature and increase.

NOTE

1. C. Peter Wagner, *Discover Your Spiritual Gifts* (Ventura, CA: Regal Books, 2002), 15.

Chapter Two

THEY WILL HEAR MY VOICE

My own sheep will hear my voice and I know
each one, and they will follow me.
—JOHN 10:27

It was my Sunday night off from serving on the worship team. I was looking forward to a time of refreshing in the Holy Spirit in our corporate gathering. A time to worship and to be filled and refreshed. The added bonus was worshiping and sitting with my husband. A few minutes into the worship service, I felt a tap on my shoulder. I turned and saw one of the pastors of the church standing next to me. He whispered, "Becca, we need your help. Can you come to my office? It is a deliverance crisis that has been going on now for almost 18 hours and we are at a loss of what to do." To be honest, I did not want to say yes, as it had been a very busy week of deliverance ministry sessions, but my pastors very rarely interrupted me in a service unless there was a serious situation. So I obliged and followed him to the office.

As we entered the room, there was a woman sitting in the chair trembling uncontrollably in utter fear. Several of the trained deliverance ministry team members were seated in front of her. It was quickly explained to me that she had called the pastor at 3:30 a.m. that morning in great fear and unable to function. Her husband was out of town on business and they had small children. They quickly drove to her home to try to calm the crisis. But after three hours of ministry, the manifestation increased with no relief. The pastors called friends to take care of her children and took her to their home in the hopes of helping her. Unfortunately, they had not been able to bring her any reprieve. They felt bringing her to the worship service that evening would help. Unfortunately, it only further aggravated this demonic manifestation. I asked her and the pastor what was causing this torment. Her explanation: "I just woke up like this."

Allow me to explain—I was newer in deliverance ministry, but God had been using me to see people radically set free. One of the reasons I believe this was and is the case is because of the giftings I operate in—prophecy and discernment. Often when I minister in deliverance, I am able to prophetically see and hear the root issue or demonic open door quite quickly through hearing the voice of the Lord. Also, through the gift of discerning of spirits I am more often than not able to identify the demonic spirit that has gripped the individual. In other words, this gifting allows me to hear, see, feel, and perceive in the spirit realm. So when it was explained to me that she "just woke up" in this great fear-based torment for no apparent reason, multiple red flags and spiritual alarms began to be resound. I was not buying that explanation. Quietly in my spirit, I spoke to the Holy Spirit, "Holy Spirit, direct me on what to do."

He answered me, "Ask her the following questions as I speak them to you."

In obedience, I turned my attention back to her, all the while listening to the Holy Spirit in an inner dialogue. I asked her if I could ask a few questions before praying. While trembling excessively she replied, "Yes."

First question: "Your husband is out of town and you were in bed alone?"

She replied, "Yes."

Second question: "Did you have a bad dream or a nightmare? Did a demon visit you in a dream?"

"No."

Third question: "But you woke up suddenly in unexplainable torment?"

"Yes."

Now at this moment the Holy Spirit opened my spiritual eyes to see a vision. I saw her wake up, yet she was calm and fully able to function. She then walked over to a desk in her bedroom and sat in the chair. She turned on the computer and went to a website. The Holy Spirit did not show me the website but instructed me to tell her the vision I was seeing and then to ask her to identify the website that she had intentionally chosen to visit.

Shocked, she quickly blurted out, "He is showing you that?"

Calmly, I replied, "Yes. Can you please share with us the website you visited this morning at 3:00 a.m.?"

She began to weep uncontrollably and between sobs shared, "I have been going through deliverance for pornography and compulsive masturbation. I have received tremendous freedom. I woke up and was missing my husband so I decided to visit a porn site one more time. When I did the demons came back and they came back seven times worse. I was so ashamed to admit that I had fallen back into sin." Turning to the pastor she explained, "I just could not tell you the truth, pastor. I was so ashamed and embarrassed. This torment is unbearable! I want these demons out of my life for good."

Without any coaching, she began to repent to the Lord and to the pastor for not sharing the truth. And friends, she really meant it. As soon as she repented, I was able to cast out the spirits of perversion and fear that had been welcomed back in, and the unbearable demonization and torment instantly left her. She has walked free since that day. You see, hearing the voice of the Lord and paying attention to the red flags and alarms resounding in my spirit were the keys for this breakthrough, deliverance, and victory.

THE LORD'S VOICE IS POWERFUL

It is evident from these testimonies that the Lord uses many ways to speak to us. As we begin to learn His ways of discernment communication, a key point I want to emphasize is the voice of the Lord is powerful, and when we learn how to recognize the different ways He is speaking to us we can obtain wisdom to see breakthrough and victory. Hear me in this word of encouragement and exhortation—He has not left us alone or without spiritual foresight, language, or gifts. He is more than able to give us what we need at the exact right time. Jesus too was able to perceive and discern in the midst of many situations as He maneuvered in His ministry on earth.

> *And some men were carrying on a bed a man who was paralyzed; and they were trying to bring him in and to set him down in front of Him. But not finding any way to bring him in because of the crowd, they went up on the roof and let him down through the tiles with his stretcher, into the middle of the crowd, in front of Jesus. Seeing their faith, He said, "Friend, your sins are forgiven you." The scribes and the Pharisees began to reason, saying, "Who is this man who speaks blasphemies? Who can forgive sins, but God alone?" But Jesus, aware of their reasonings, answered and said to them, "Why are you reasoning in your hearts?"* (Luke 5:18-22 NASB)

What an insightful example of Jesus being aware of the thoughts of others. Some translations use the words, "But Jesus, knowing their thoughts"; other translations say, "But Jesus perceived their thoughts." The root Greek word for *aware* in this scripture is *epiginosko*. It means "to know, recognize, perceive, be aware, and to have full discernment" (Strong's #G1921). Therefore, here in this moment of the religious leaders yet again inaccurately questioning and judging Jesus, His teachings, and actions, He fully discerns what they are reasoning in their hearts and begins to teach them based off this supernatural gift "to know, perceive, recognize, and fully discern." The results are powerful lessons and truths spoken in such a way that it can only come from supernatural, spiritual insight.

Some of you might be reasoning, "Well, this is Jesus and of course He could do this, but this level full discernment is not for us." However, the truth is it is available and many function in this same manner that Jesus modeled. God wants to work with and through each of us the same way He worked with and through Jesus. He is our example and model to follow. The Word also tells us that we will do greater things than He did (see John 14:12). His voice is powerful. It is His desire and divine design for us to understand and to be equipped and operating in hearing His voice and discerning in the realm of the Spirit. Not only is it a divine design, but, friend, it is one of the most necessary gifts we must begin to understand, activate, and maneuver in. We are in the most historic time of Christianity in the world. To extend His Kingdom in the earth, it is imperative that we learn the moves of the Holy Spirit; the deceptions, traps, and schemes of the enemy and His army of darkness; and also the times and seasons in which we have been we born.

Allow me to pose a question—how can we leave our mark on this earth, the lives of others, and spheres of influence if we shun the ability to discern in this crucial time? It is my belief that our influence to transform will not fully be reached if we do not discern and move in His wisdom and strategies to see breakthrough and victory.

HIS VOICE IS CREATIVE

In the Genesis creation account, we see repeatedly that God's voice was creative. He created the heavens and the earth. He spoke and there was light. He spoke and there was night and day. He spoke and there was separation of land and water. He spoke and there was vegetation. He spoke and the creatures of the water, sea, and land came into being. Then from the ground He formed human beings. The power of His voice created all the beauty of the canvas of the earth and the heavens, which is now our inheritance as His sons and daughters and Kingdom ambassadors. You and I and our very existence are a product of His creative voice and foresight.

We think of a voice as something that is spoken out audibly, and this is correct. However, the voice of the Lord speaks in many different ways and it is important to learn how to recognize His voice and His Kingdom and to become familiar with all the different creative dialects used in the language of heaven. Key ways He communicates with us are prophecy and prophetic words spoken through others, spoken or taught words, dreams, visions, impressions, a knowing or perceiving, the Word of God, angels, a message the pastor or minister is speaking, signs in the natural, circumstances, our five senses, discernment, and the discerning of spirits.

Prophecy

Prophecy is one of the most familiar ways many of us in this age and time have become familiar with hearing the voice of the Lord. A scriptural promise that speaks of the times we are in is Acts 2:17-18:

> *This is what I will do in the last days—I will pour out my Spirit on everybody and cause your sons and daughters to prophesy, and your young men will see visions, and your old men will experience dreams from God. The Holy Spirit will*

come upon all my servants, men and women alike, and they will prophesy.

Propheteuo is the Greek word used in this text. It means "to speak or make inspired utterances, to declare the will of God, sometimes with regard to what is to happen in the future, to speak under divine utterances, to exercise the prophetic office" (Strong's #G4395). As the Holy Spirit is poured out and is welcomed, for many the revelatory gift of prophecy is awakened and activated. Often those who have a strong and maturing gift of prophecy will also function in the gift of discernment and discerning of spirits.

A Spoken Word

While this obviously can occur in a prophetic word, it often can come innocently in a conversation with a friend, through a pastor who is speaking a message, through a spoken prayer released during an intercession time, through a news broadcast, a Christian radio or television show, a book being read, or the Word of God. There have even been times when a lost person has innocently spoken words to me that have confirmed the discernment of a situation at hand. As a mentor and dear friend, Alice Smith, always expresses, "In God's Kingdom, any old donkey will do." While this statement makes us chuckle, in reality it is profoundly true. God can use creative ways to confirm revelation and discernment even through those in the world.

Learning His Voice Through the Word

For we have the living Word of God, which is full of energy, and it pierces more sharply than a two-edged sword. It will even penetrate to the very core of our being where soul and spirit, bone and marrow meet! It interprets and reveals the true thoughts and secret motives of our hearts (Hebrews 4:12).

We find great supernatural help and advantage from the Word of God to strengthen our faith and motivate our persistence. The Word is quick, very lively, and active. It convicts of sin, transforms the mind and thoughts, brings comfort, and binds up the wounds of the soul. It is full of life and is compared to the light. It is vital to bring full, free, victorious, and abundant light. As stated above, God's voice is powerful, and I want to add here that His Word is all-powerful. It is so powerful that it pulls down strongholds, raises the dead, and makes the deaf to hear, the blind to see, the dumb to speak, and the lame to walk. It is powerful to batter down satan's kingdom and to set up the Kingdom of Christ. It is sharper than any two-edged sword. It enters where no other sword is able and makes a more critical separation. It penetrates and pierces to the very core of our being where the soul and spirit meet—where those sinful habits that have become natural to the soul, rooted deeply and at home in it, are separated and cut out and off. It cuts off ignorance from the understanding, rebellion from the will, and hostility from the mind and thoughts. This sword divides between the bone and marrow, which are the most secret, close, and intimate parts of the body. Praise God, this sword cuts off the lusts of the flesh as well as the lusts and vain imaginations of the mind. We rejoice that it snatches us out of sin into a transformed life. It is a discerner and interpreter of the thoughts and intents and secrets motives of the heart. His Word brings life, hope, joy, passion, faith, encouragement, and divine direction. Friends, how necessary it is to intimately acquaint ourselves with this living Word so vital to life.

Knowing and studying His Word is one of the most essential and imperative ways to learn His voice and increase in discernment. Why? Because at the basic level of functioning in this gift we must discern the "wiles of the enemy," who always seeks to appeal to our emotions. While we will discuss sensing and feeling to help us grow in this gift, we also must realize that the enemy seeks to entangle us by enticing and seducing us through our "feelings." We need to discern from an objective perspective and a neutral standpoint by keeping before us the original blueprints of the Word of God and prophetic revelations the Lord has given us. We discern by the Spirit of the Lord and move strategically in alignment with His Word. All is not implemented simply by emotions.

Dreams

Throughout the Word we read of men and women who experienced life-changing revelation and direction in their dreams. One instance occurred when the angel of the Lord appeared to Joseph in a dream telling him to take Mary as his wife because what was conceived in her womb was by the Holy Spirit (see Matt. 1:20). Other instances include Solomon, Pharaoh, numerous kings, and prophets.

A dream is revelation that is released while our physical body and mind are at rest. Sometimes this is the best and most effective way for God to get a message through to us. I believe dreams are one of the most significant ways the Lord speaks to bring clear revelation and discernment. Here is a beautiful testimony from our oldest daughter, Kendall:

> The ways the Holy Spirit speaks to us—alerting us that we need to pay attention to our surroundings and the people in them and things in ourselves—are immeasurable. In the Bible, the Lord tells us that we'll feel the Holy Spirit's guidance through His intercession over us (Rom. 8:26), His actual voice (Acts 13:2), in signs and wonders (Mark 16:17-18), and more. But my favorite way to hear the Lord's voice and feel His guiding, reassuring hand comes during the hours of the day when I'm the least alert—when my eyes are closed, my mind is wonderfully blank and my body is almost completely still.
>
> I absolutely love it when He speaks to me with dreams. You see, discernment doesn't sleep.

I get giddy even typing about it now because in my adult life this is a new part of our relationship. The first time I remember feeling that the Lord was talking to me this way was when I was about seven or eight years old. My family, living in Texas at the time, was potentially going to move to a new town or state because my dad was looking for a new job. One night, I had a dream of mountains and snow (I can still picture the scene today) and woke up telling my parents that Jesus said we are going to move to Colorado. Guess what's been home for the last 20 years?

About three years ago, after a slow and quiet dream life through my teens and early adulthood, a prayer brought it all back. I was reminded in a teaching that we can ask the Lord for anything, and anything we ask, the Lord wants to give us (Matt. 7:7-8). I'd really been missing having Him in my dreams, so I started asking. As I prayed, my request got confirmed through others' prayers over me. I so eagerly waited.

And sure enough, I woke up one morning to a detailed, completely lucid memory of the previous night's vision and a loving little twinge on the right side of my chest. No one get concerned—there is no need to call a doctor! This is how I feel the Holy Spirit a lot of times—I'll get this burning, twinging sensation opposite from where my heart is, and I just know it's Him.

Since that night, the Lord has talked to me about my heart, my fears, my family, my career, my prayer group, and the spiritual atmospheres I'm in while I sleep. I have learned quite a bit about interpreting dreams (though not enough to do it completely on my own just yet), but what I've heeded even more is the sharpening of my discernment in speedy circumstances.

If discernment is gut (or rather, for me, chest) instinct, then walking through a dream with the Lord is, to use one of my mom's phrases, a gut instinct on steroids. When I think I feel the Holy Spirit tell me something when I'm awake, there are often worldly thoughts and distractions I have to contend with in the midst of determining if that inkling is from Him; and I'll sometimes take too much time to figure it out. But in the short moments when I am just waking up from my usual seven hours—those seconds when any dreams you had suddenly come flooding back—thoughts about my to-do list, people I need to text back who I didn't have time to respond to the day before, work deadlines and so on aren't there. For a split second, the only thing that's real is the urging I get in my spirit as to whether or not the midnight showing that just happened in my mind is from the Lord.

And to know the answer to that question, I have to listen to that urging just as quickly as it happens. I need to recognize it and remember it; it needs to stick in my spirit. And then I need to act on it.

At the start, my feet were so unsteady in knowing if a dream was from the Lord. But the more He brought them, the more I could identify that fast feeling and the more convinced I became. The ultimate result of all of this— my relationship with the Lord has grown more special and intimate. When I feel the Holy Spirit jump up inside of me to give me a loving insight—no matter the time the clock reads—I'm finding it easier to humble myself to His direction.

The Lord doesn't sleep, which means our discernment—our literal direct connection to the God of heaven and earth—doesn't have to either.

Such a powerful testimony of what dreams are able to activate. I love and appreciate Kendall's statements, "Discernment doesn't sleep" and "If discernment is gut (or rather, for me, chest) instinct, then walking through a dream with the Lord is, to use one of my mom's phrases, a gut instinct on steroids." The following are a few key areas in which dreams empower us to discern even while we sleep.

- Dreams can reveal events and discernment that will lead the dreamer to make the right decision for his or her future.
- Dreams can reveal discernment for intercessory prayer assignments.
- Dreams can reveal discernment and victorious battle plans for intercessors.
- Dreams can bring revelation and discernment concerning future events.
- Dreams can bring a warning.
- Dreams can bring us into beautiful heavenly encounters with the Lord, angels, and His heavenly Kingdom.
- Dreams can identify areas in need of deliverance and healing.

Visions: Seeing in the Spirit Realm

A vision is like a dream. However, you are awake when it occurs. The apostle Peter's commission to eat with and minister to the Gentiles came in a vision (see Acts 10:9-23). C. Peter Wagner shares the significance of this type of communication:

> God knew that ordinary communication processes would not be adequate to move Peter in the radical direction He wanted him to go. So God did an extraordinary thing and gave Peter the famous vision of the unclean food in the sheet. Peter's background had personally prepared him to receive visions. For one thing, it would fit his world-view. Unlike many today, Peter believed that one of God's normal ways of communicating from time to time was through visions and dreams. He was praying at the time, so his heart was open to God. He may have been fasting, too. Luke doesn't say he was, but we read that Peter *became very hungry* (Acts 10:10). Prayer along with fasting removes obstacles to hearing God's voice.[1]

We read in scripture where there were visions of angels, the angel of the Lord, fire, an army of horses and chariots, and numerous other spiritual encounters. There are two types of visions—open and closed. In an *open vision* spiritual objects or beings are seen with the physical eyes. Sometimes objects that are not yet built, but will be in the future, can be seen with the physical eyes as if they already exist. Or they may be visions of future or past events. A *closed vision* is seeing something play out in the theater of your mind or your spirit much like a dream. There is also the operation of discerning of spirits in which you can see an individual's countenance and see the beauty and presence of the glory of the Lord or the shadow of darkness of emotional distress and demonic strongholds. We may also see moving shadows or glimpses of light in our peripheral vision. Allow me to share an experience in which perceiving, seeing a vision, and hearing were all in play.

An Open Door

Many years ago, Greg and I were in a church membership situation where things seemed to get increasingly more difficult every time we attended a service. What do I mean by difficult? This is where discernment begins in the impression and your "spiritual knower" realm. For several months, when we would attend a service I would feel confusion, unease, and a heaviness/darkness looming in the spirit. I was unable to fully enter into worship even though the other ten thousand in attendance were engaged. I felt a deep knowing of great caution and that something was not acceptable. Many times, I would begin to feel agitated while attending. That being said, I was not hearing specifically from the Lord what the issue at hand was, but I undeniably continued to feel the caution He was placing in my spirit. Not only was this occurring, but at this time the leader of the church had approached my husband about the possibility of a job on staff. This undeniably caused a hard to ignore uneasiness. I felt this leader could not be trusted and that we definitely could not put any real hope or consideration in this offer. As I prayed and sought the Lord, He did not tell me the moral issue occurring with the pastor that was revealed several months later, but He did reveal a clear vision. I saw the face of this pastor looking directly at me and out of his mouth came the word, "No!" I instantly knew we were not to continue down this path and that whatever he was saying he was going to offer my husband, the answer was to be no.

In time it was revealed that this leader totally misrepresented the possible staff position and was not truthful with us in the process. Within several months we attended a service in which the spirit realm was very active. I was uncomfortable and highly in tune, hearing in the spirit realm clearly. Honestly, it was one of those times I wish I could not hear what I was hearing. It was as if a multitude of demons had been unleashed and their mocking, demonic laughing and sneering of hatred toward the believers was beyond active. I knew at that point that some-one in leadership had opened a demonic door of sin.

Greg could see that I was clearly perceiving, hearing, and discerning. As we made our way out that night, I explained to him, "It is as if a por-tal to the demonic realm has been opened. Someone is in sin. I cannot go back and won't go back. What I was hearing in the spirit is demonic, unpleasant, and beyond unacceptable." From that night, I spent much time in intercession for the church and the leadership. Sadly, this leader was exposed in a moral failure very soon after this encounter.

Hearing in the Spirit Realm

This is the ability to hear what is occurring in the spirit realm. Often it can be the sound of angels worshiping. It can be the sound of angelic activity in the room. It can also be the sound of the demonic. Personally, I regularly and consistently hear in the spirit realm. It becomes a pow-erful weapon in deliverance ministry and while praying on the land for cities and regions. There is also the supernatural ability to discern sounds being released through music, voices, instruments, words spo-ken, and spiritual atmospheres. What do I mean by this? There is an ability to hear and perceive if music being played is spiritually accept-able or demonic. When someone is speaking it is possible to sense a pure anointing or a tainted message. The spiritual atmospheres in cities and regions also have a sound that can be heard in the spirit for those gifted in this ability.

Is the Sense of Smell Used to Discern?

The answer is yes, the sense of smell is often active with those with the gift of discernment. Scripture speaks of the pleasing aroma and fra-grance that would come from the sacrifices in the temple. And there are those scriptures in which Jesus is also referred to as a pleasing aroma and fragrance. Paul teaches a powerful truth concerning the fragrance that we carry:

> *But thank God! He has made us his captives and contin-*
> *ues to lead us along in Christ's triumphal procession. Now*
> *he uses us to spread the knowledge of Christ everywhere,*
> *like a sweet perfume. Our lives are a Christ-like fragrance*
> *rising up to God. But this fragrance is perceived differently*
> *by those who are being saved and by those who are perish-*
> *ing. To those who are perishing, we are a dreadful smell of*
> *death and doom. But to those who are being saved, we are a*
> *life-giving perfume. And who is adequate for such a task as*
> *this?* (2 Corinthians 2:14-16 NLT)

It is evident that there are fragrances and aromas in the spiritual realm. For instance, there have been many times when there is a weighty presence of the Holy Spirit and angels and fragrances of sweet myrrh and roses can be tangibly detected. In the Word of God, death is described as a foul stench. And even though demons and the demonic are alive and active in the spirit realm, they are doomed to eternal torment and spiritual separation and death. To those who walk in spiritual sensitivity, fragrances, aromas, and odors are important. When a strong demonic presence is manifest, those who are spiritually sensitive can smell death, decay, sulfur, or even odors similar to nicotine.

Impressions, Feelings, Discernment, the Sixth Sense

Eddie Smith terms discernment "the sixth sense." While this does sound mystical, I assure you he is not meaning it that way, I completely agree with and appreciate this description. Discernment is something that is not experienced in the natural, as seen in my testimony of the church we were attending many years ago. When someone has an impression or a revelation in their "knower," the one experiencing this will "know that they know" what they are prophetically hearing or perceiving. However, often there is no sign or indication in the natural of what is being encountered in the spirit. Below is a powerful testimony shared by my dear friend Becky Albert about the importance of not ignoring the impressions in our "knower":

> My firstborn son had left the nest and moved away to college and my momma's heart was missing him. His first semester of college at Oral Roberts University had gone well. However, semester two brought some challenges. Too much fun and not enough studying seemed to be the biggest challenge.
>
> He had found a part-time job and met a new friend. In the summer they decided to rent an apartment together. I was uneasy about it from the beginning, but my husband and son convinced me to "let go a little," so I agreed. About four weeks into this new living arrangement, I could not shake feelings of dread, feelings of darkness, and feelings of "something is just not right" about my son. I was praying for him daily, but the feelings persisted. I attributed it to empty-nest and being overprotective.
>
> I had only been Spirit-filled for about five years and had come from a Baptist background. I was still learning about the gifts of the Spirit and how they functioned. Honestly though, at that time in my life, I had never heard a teaching on discernment and its operation in our lives.
>
> A couple of weeks passed, and the "feelings" persisted. One morning I woke up just before dawn almost unable to breathe with such a sense of dread about my son. I ran to my prayer room and hit the floor praying in tongues. It was all I knew to do. I cried out, "What, Lord? What are these

feelings, what is this dread? I need to understand! Is my son in trouble or am I just being overprotective?" After an hour the Lord spoke to my heart very clearly and strongly. He gave me specific instructions to wake up my husband and explain to him all that I had felt for the last few weeks. He said we were to get in the pickup truck, drive straight to our son's apartment, and move him home before the end of the day! He told me specifics about the roommate/friend selling drugs from the apartment while my son was at work. He said the police were staking out the apartment and an arrest of the roommate was imminent.

God bless my husband, he listened carefully and knew by the intensity of my words that this was the Lord. We did exactly as the Lord had instructed. We arrived at the apartment complex to a very sleepy and surprised son by 8:00 a.m. that morning. I told him everything the Lord had said to me. He sat down with his head in his hands and began to weep. He knew what had been happening but did not know what to do to get out of the situation. He had felt ashamed and trapped. By the end of the day, my son was moved home. There was such a sure word from the Lord, we all knew it was right and true.

Within three days, the roommate was arrested and charged with selling drugs. My son gave a statement but was not charged with any involvement. The important thing you should know is that at the age of eight my son had heard the voice of the Lord calling him to be an attorney. Had he been caught in those felony drug charges, his dreams of being an attorney would have been thwarted by the enemy.

After all the dust had settled, my pastor helped me to understand that what I had "felt" had been the gift of discernment operating through me. All those feelings and senses of dread and darkness were Holy Spirit showing me what was surrounding my son and trapping him.

Needless to say, this incident changed my son's life, my life, and our family. What an incredible gift from Holy Spirit we have been given in the gift of discernment. It is a gift to be embraced and to learn to cooperate and flow with. I have walked in this gift now for over 20 years. It is not always a feeling. I now know discernment as "red flags" in my spirit. Sometimes it is a sense or feeling, sometimes it is an unusual smell, a chill up my neck, or a tightening around my head. But I now recognize it is Holy Spirit putting up a flag saying, "Pay attention, I want to show you something." I immediately engage in the spirit and ask, "What, Lord?" He shows me and tells me what to do or what to pray. I am so thankful and grateful for all the gifts of the spirit, and the gift of discernment is invaluable to our lives. It is time for more teaching, more understanding, and more cooperation with this powerful gift to the body of Christ!

DISCERNMENT CAN CAUSE CONFUSION

The truth is discernment can be confusing to those who are gifted in this arena. It can be confusing to believers and non-believers. Allow me to explain. Those who function in discernment can see, hear, feel, perceive, and sense. For many of us, it begins at a young age. For me, this was the case. I began to see in dreams and visions, seeing both the good and pure and the demonic and evil. It became a point of fear for me from a very young age. I was raised in a wonderful and loving Christian home, but there was no gauge for the dreams I experienced and the nightmares and visions that brought great fear and torment. Praise God, in my early twenties I was set free and my life radically changed.

I am going to make a rather controversial statement. I believe and know that there are many discerners—those who see, hear, feel, sense, and perceive in the spirit realm—who have been diagnosed with some sort of mental disease or handicap. Not all mental illness is spiritual or derived from heightened spiritual sensitivity. But when a young child or any individual shares that they are seeing, hearing, feeling, and sensing demons, dead people, or angels and this is shared with those who lack spiritual insight and understanding—the next step is often a visit to a psychologist or psychiatrist. Soon, this child or individual is labeled as paranoid, one who hallucinates, or one who hears voices—bipolar or schizophrenic.

Remember, discernment can often feel so real that the one discerning believes he or she is dealing with a mental or emotional instability or problem. If this one is a feeler, the diagnosis or label might be that of manic depression or bipolar. Another label might be one who struggles with anxiety and panic attacks. Hear me—I am not stating that all of these issues are caused by discernment. I am not a medical doctor nor do I claim to be, nor will I ever make a diagnosis or suggest someone quit taking medications. If the doctor prescribes the medicine, it is between the individual and the doctor to make the decision to stop the medication. I am giving a perspective that we have seen several times. When the issue is spiritual or lack of knowledge concerning discernment and this is realized and instruction and wisdom given, then growth in the gift and freedom can be achieved. The following is a true testimony written by my friend Tonya in which this was part of the issue at hand in a life gravely impacted by abuse and trauma.

Throughout a life of abuse and trauma, I was diagnosed with major depression, anxiety disorders, eating disorders, multiple personality disorder, struggled with addictions, and had numerous suicide attempts. I had hallucinations and heard voices, which only intensified my desire to escape and harm myself. Taking 15 prescriptions per day resulted in weight gain, and I reached 270 pounds. After many years of therapy and hospitalizations, at age 24 I was declared permanently mentally disabled and plans were being made to have me court committed to the state mental institution for the rest of my life.

I accepted Christ as my Savior at age 12 and even felt called to ministry. I had a genuine love for God and for people and continued to serve in the church as often as possible. I memorized scriptures and did everything religion had taught me, until I could no longer function and my only hope was heaven. After each failed suicide attempt, the pastor scheduled for hospital visitation would come and encourage me to get better. Three weeks later, I would be back at church and no one ever said a word.

I knew it was one thing for the world to say I was hopeless, but their lies were reinforced when the church had no other solutions. In my desperation to not be locked up for life, I discovered Mercy Multiplied. Through a process of discipleship, counseling, and deliverance, God began to restore my life. For the first time, I was discovering my identity in Christ and how to apply the authority He has given me. As I renewed my mind with His Word, I learned how to take my thoughts captive and to control my flesh. I realized that I had a voice and I could choose life!

Within that year, I stopped taking all medication and lost over 100 pounds. I was connected in a life-giving non-denominational church and learning to worship and cultivate a relationship with God. Being filled with the Holy Spirit was a game changer for me. I say speaking in tongues is my super-power! The mystery of supernatural things was a new revelation after previously judging everything weird as demonic.

I would never have chosen to participate in something demonic, yet I cannot deny the bondage that controlled my life. I do not believe all mental illness is demonic or discernment in action, but I know from experience that demons will take advantage of mental illness and intensify the battle raging in the spirit realm to cause heightened confusion. Satan is a legalist and seeks opportunity for an open door. If we're not aware of the spiritual realm, then we try to explain it in the natural.

After psychological testing, the doctor told me, "You have the most creative imagination and the most active fantasy life of anyone we've tested in our 20 years of practice." I've always been creative. Imagination was an escape for me. Dealing with multiple personality disorder, I discovered that it actually begins as a means of protection during trauma. It's during the trance-like state of switching where demons take advantage and pose as other personalities. In my case, I needed inner healing to deal with each trauma in my soul. I recognized any remaining personalities as evil spirits and commanded them to leave. If I had not learned about discernment in the spiritual realm, I would not have complete freedom. Why? Because much of what

I was experiencing required discernment to know what was demonic, my flesh, or emotion. And what was also key to learn was that a great deal of what I was discerning in others and in the spirit realm, I thought was my own issue, which added to my confused state.

Because of my history with physical and mental illness, I've had to learn not to automatically accept what I'm seeing, hearing, thinking, and feeling as my own personal issue. It's easy to be deceived and think, "Oh no! I'm dealing with this again." I now realize discernment can often be a call to intercede for someone else experiencing that same thing. It is now an honor to know and discern how to pray specifically.

As I grow in spiritual discernment, I can recognize I've always had an eye for detail or see words as pictures. I love receiving dreams and visions. Even in mental institutions, I was encouraging others and speaking life over them. Though I had little knowledge of the spiritual realm, something in me would rise beyond my emotional struggle to challenge others. No amount of medication could keep it suppressed. Ironically, celebrating imagination, which I now realize was my gift of discernment in action, and having permission to dream has brought great peace and mental health.

In this powerful testimony, Tonya obviously had several issues empowering her mentally tormented state. Yes, there was abuse, which caused great trauma and resulting demonic oppression. But throughout all of this and still to this day she functions in a high level of discernment. The demonic voices Tonya heard and the demons she felt and saw in the spirit realm in those hallucinations, she believed and embraced as her own issue. Therefore, she was labeled as hearing voices and suffering from hallucinations. The truth is, it was the spirit realm in action adding to the torment, not a mental illness. Once she received freedom, she was able to quickly discern the enemy's voice and lies and also recognize that what she was feeling was not her own issue but activity in the spirit realm. Trust me, when you are with Tonya now there is no shadow lingering over her from this troubled past. She is a free and victorious woman of God birthing her own deliverance ministry, training and encouraging others in how to function in their gift of discernment.

IS WHAT I'M PERCEIVING TRUE AND ACCURATE?

A key question I am asked frequently is, "How do I know that what I am perceiving is true and accurate?" This is an important question. It is imperative to try to recognize and be with those who function in this revelatory gift and who can mentor and impart wisdom. Read books and try to locate teachings on the topic. Obviously, this is a clear reason for this book. It is my prayer and desire to impart wisdom on how to maneuver. We will continue to discuss key ways to grow and mature, but I want to give a word of encouragement to you who are discerners—do not shun, sluff off, or ignore this revelatory gift given by the Lord. It is a vital and necessary gift in the days, times, and seasons we are in.

NOTE

1.   C. Peter Wagner, *Acts of the Holy Spirit: A Modern Commentary on the Book of Acts* (Ventura, CA: Regal Books, 2000), 228-229.

Chapter Three

MATURING IN HEARING
AND DISCERNMENT

We've been learning the different dialects of heaven and how the Lord speaks. Now we must begin to dive into the importance of maturing in hearing His voice and how to operate with discernment revelation evident in our walk. Personally, I believe the content of this chapter is some of the most crucial information on this topic. We are going to discuss some of the hard questions concerning discernment. We must learn and know what His Word says concerning discernment, and we must, to the best of our ability, understand what He is saying concerning how to handle discernment with great maturity, humility, holiness, and wisdom. It is my prayer that this message will bring people out of impure and immature operations into mature, holy, and wise function.

Let me state right now that there is therefore no condemnation for those who are in Christ Jesus (see Rom. 8:1). Are we all going to get things right 100 percent of the time? The answer is no. But I do believe we can mature to the point where our accuracy is sharper and sharper and is handled to bring victory and breakthrough. Hear me—it is our personal responsibility to guard and steward that which has been entrusted to us. That being said, let's begin this portion of our discussion with one of the most frequent questions I receive: "How do I discern and not enter into a judgmental and critical spirit?"

MOVING BEYOND JUDGMENTALISM AND A CRITICAL SPIRIT

I wrote you in my previous letter asking you not to associate with those who practice sexual immorality. Yet in no way was I referring to avoiding contact with unbelievers who are immoral, or greedy, or swindlers, or those who worship other gods—for that would mean you'd have to isolate yourself from the world entirely! But now I'm writing to you so that you would exclude from your fellowship anyone who calls himself a fellow believer and practices sexual immorality, or is consumed with greed, or is an idolater, or is verbally abusive or a drunkard or a swindler. Don't mingle with them or even have a meal with someone like that. What right do I have to pronounce judgment on unbelievers? That's God's responsibility. But those who are inside the church family are our responsibility to discern and judge. So it's your duty to remove that wicked one from among you (1 Corinthians 5:9-13).

These are very direct and powerful words spoken by Paul to the Corinthian church. Obviously, we are to reach those who are lost and trapped in bondage of sin. This is the heart of Jesus, and He sacrificially and victoriously died that all may have the opportunity to come to the saving knowledge of Jesus. But sadly, not all people will come to this vital, life-altering decision. Therefore, absolutely continue to pray for, witness to, and love the lost with His heart to see them brought to the beautiful gift of salvation. That said, let's study the words used in verse 13, where Paul plainly states it is our job to discern and judge those in the church family.

Krino is the Greek word used in this scripture and it means "to judge, distinguish, prefer, decide, evaluate, make a legal decision, rule over people, govern, condemn, or punish" (Strong's #G2919). Very powerful words. But these actions are to be based in the knowledge of the Word of God and the context of scriptural protocol. This scripture is not giving all who operate in discernment the license to become the Holy Spirit for the Body of Christ. However, we are not to ignore certain behaviors and sweep them under the rug as if they do not exist. It is very evident that we are to deal with these sins and not entertain them in our midst.

It is a leadership responsibility to deal with moral issues at this level, and it is my prayer that more in the Church will begin to rise up in obedience to the Word of God. During this time, we are seeing more and more churches not only tolerating perversion, homosexuality, lesbianism, and same-sex marriage, but pastors who are openly teaching that this lifestyle is acceptable for Christians. Many leaders themselves are walking in this sin. Of course, if someone involved in these activities is approached and does repent, then absolutely we want to see people turn from their sin and embrace the process of deliverance, healing, discipleship, and restoration. The point is, we are called to discern and judge those who are falsely misrepresenting the Word of God and the Kingdom of God.

> *Constantly be on your guard against phony prophets. They come disguised as lambs, appearing to be genuine, but on the inside they are like wild, ravenous wolves! You can spot them by their actions, for the fruits of their character will be obvious. You won't find sweet grapes hanging on a thorn bush, and you'll never pick good fruit from a tumbleweed. So if the tree is good, it will produce good fruit; but if the tree is bad, it will bear only rotten fruit and it deserves to be cut down and burned. Look at the obvious fruit of their*

*lives and ministries, and then you'll know whether they are
true or false* (Matthew 7:15-20).

The key here is we will know if they are true or false by the fruit
in their lives and ministries. I believe the following example will
help illustrate.

AN IMPURE PROPHET AT THE WRONG PLACE AT THE WRONG TIME

I was privileged to be invited to be a part of an international team on a
strategic prayer assignment at a key location in the nations. Each team
member had been chosen carefully through interviews and prayer. The
team was formed a year before the scheduled dates of the planned initia-
tive. We had spent months in preparation. The day arrived to leave on
the long journey and to pray for transformation in the nations.

I traveled with an intercessor friend of mine. We will call her Judy.
Thus far, it has been a very long and tiresome thirty-six hours of flight
time. We were finally on the final flight to our destination. After boarding the plane and taking our seats, we patiently rested while the other
passengers made their way onto the aircraft. I often enjoy people-watch-
ing as the boarding process ensues and quickly noticed a gentleman
boarding the plane who caused an instant red flag and check in my spirit.
Judy recognized him as one who had been invited to minister in our home
church on a weekend Greg and I were out of town. She recalled how he
caused problems and an uproar as a result of his ministry. My first inward
thought was, "Oh my, why is he on this flight to such a remote nation?"

Soon the plane was full, the door shut, and it was time to take off.
Once in the air, Judy and I were enjoying a nap. We were awakened by a
man's voice: "Excuse me." It was the gentleman. He curiously inquired,
"Are you ladies team members on the international strategic prayer

assignment occurring over the next two weeks? I am curious because I was invited at the last minute to be a team member as well."

Now this instantly did not sit well with me. This nation was not friendly to Christians, and we were told not to mention what we were sent to accomplish. At that point in time, those who were believers living in this nation suffered great persecution. Not only was he asking us, but he was intentionally speaking loudly, purposefully projecting his voice where many on the plane could hear the conversation. I abruptly ended the conversation by stating, "We were told not to mention that to anyone in our travels." It felt as if a thousand alarms were echoing out "DANGER" in my spirit.

Sure enough! He ended up at the same hotel and informed our team leader that the leader over the entire international team had, a month prior, invited him to join our team and assignment. This was done without informing any of the other team leaders or team members. The leader of the entire international team was already in a remote location in the nation and had been for three weeks. Finally, we were able to make contact and it was confirmed the invitation to this man had been issued. This caused the entire team to be uneasy with this sudden change, and the majority of us felt great concern regarding the spirit operating through this man. To be honest, everything about him screamed impure prophet controlled by and operating with a spirit of perversion and a religious spirit.

It soon became clear that he felt he was there to "correct" and "teach" our team. As he plainly stated, "You all are full of pride and don't know how to hear God or pray to bring breakthrough." I finally decided one day to begin to ask the questions that would reveal his lone ranger, loose cannon and impure motives. The conversation went something like the this:

"What church do you belong to?"

"I don't belong to any church. No one wants me and I am usually such a threat to the pastors and leaders, I am asked leave." This had occurred multiple times now. "Churches don't like me."

"Are you in relationship with any other believers on a regular basis? Do you have anyone you are in a relational alignment with?"

"No, I just need God. The Lord told me a long time ago that I don't need anyone but Him. I am a lone ranger prophet. And to be honest people don't like me and don't want me around. And I don't want to be around people."

"Then why are you here?"

He then answered, "I am here for (he stated the name of the international team leader). She is an angel and I am sent here to be her angel on this assignment and in her calling to the nations. God revealed secrets to me about her that only she and the Lord know. I tracked her down in the hotel she was staying in before she left the U.S. for this assignment. I found she and her husband in the hotel restaurant and revealed to her the secrets I had received. She instantly expressed to me that I was angel sent by the Lord to her and invited me to be involved. We had never met before that day. I really don't care about being here with you all or for the assignment. I just want to be here in support of her."

When the entire team was finally united in one place, his motives for being with us became visibly evident. He was attracted to the international team leader, who was not picking up on the not-so-subtle comments, flirtatious moves, and come-on lines and actions. This was proving to be beyond torturous for the rest of the team leaders and team members.

As the trip progressed, one afternoon he was able to corner me and the international team leader by ourselves. It was just the three of us. He was very condescending, attempting to label me as the impure false prophet. Trying to sway the leader to his point of view, he stated, "She has hated me since day one. I've done nothing but try to be nice to her. But she dislikes me!" The leader was puzzled by this comment and said she did not see this in me. But he had already convinced a good portion of the members of a team from another country that I was jealous of him and I was the one who was off spiritually. One of the intercessors on a team from another nation was so convinced concerning his accusations that she bluntly stated, "God will deal with your religious and impure heart."

At this point the other team leaders had decided enough was enough. A meeting was called with all the leaders and they insisted on his instant removal, which he begrudgingly adhered to. Although he did show up the final night at our departure hotel. He had showered, was attired in dress clothes, and was wearing a cheap cologne; the scent greatly overpowered the entire room. He instantly sat next to the leader with her spouse sitting on the opposite side and began flirting again, showing absolutely no regard for the spouse's presence.

Obviously, this man was impure, religious, and I will venture to state a false prophet. I learned a great deal from this experience about how to investigate and ask questions for confirmation. Most importantly, there is the crucial ministry lesson of protocol and having history with those who are involved in significant ministry assignments.

Dutch Sheets said, "There are those you go to lunch with and those you go to war with." Hear me, because I am going to take it a step further—know those you live life with and who sit at the table of friendship, and know those you go to war with. This is always our protocol in our ministry. If we do not know a person, have history with them, or there is not alignment or relationship with a reputable leader, we do not go to war with this person.

THE ORIGIN AND MOTIVE OF THE JUDGMENT

So yes, we have the understanding that the Word of God does indeed encourage us to discern and judge someone by their fruit. We also have the following words by Jesus in Matthew 7:1-4:

> *Refuse to be a critic full of bias toward others, and judgment will not be passed on you. For you'll be judged by the same standard that you've used to judge others. The measurement you use on them will be used on you. Why would you focus on the flaw in someone else's life and yet fail to notice the glaring flaws of your own? How could you say to your friend, "Let me show you where you're wrong," when you're guilty of even more?*

Jesus is identifying the wrong motive of a critical spirit. You will be judged, *krino*—judged, evaluated, condemned—by the same standard that you've used to judge, *krino*—make a decision about, evaluate, judge, or condemn others (Strong's #G2919). The standard by which you are evaluating, making decisions about, and condemning others will also be used on you. Judgments made in a critical or wrong spirit come from motives such as bitterness, unforgiveness, hatred, a holier-than-thou mindset, enjoying finding fault in others for the sake of feeling better about yourself, a spirit of competition, feeling elite and above all in your knowledge, a divisive spirit, a religious spirit, a defensive spirit, or one who has not welcomed a purifying work of the Lord. If the judgment is shared in a way to bring harm—through bitter unforgiveness, as a gossip session, to undermine in order to gain position, or in order to be heard for popularity—then the door is open for that same type of judgment to come back on the originator.

I shared in Chapter Two how the Lord led me in discerning a sin issue in a church many years ago. Not one time did I make what I was hearing into a gossip session. First and foremost, I took the discernment and revelation to intercession because I am a firm believer in this statement by Oswald Chambers: "Discernment is God's call to intercession, never to faultfinding."[1] Yet the spiritual alarms, red flags, and concern continued to increase and escalate.

In my intercession time, I felt the Lord leading me to schedule a time to speak with a leader who had been in a ministry alignment with the pastor and whom I also had relationship with. However, the sin was exposed before the meeting occurred. Here is key word of wisdom—I did not go to anyone outside the right and appropriate leadership channels to voice my concern. Going to other members of the church, staff members, or random people is not appropriate and is out of protocol. But I will add—when someone is being treated in an abusive, sinful manner by a leader or another member of a corporate gathering, it is a must to reach out for help and not remain silent. Going to trusted leaders to share and to ask for wisdom is the correct avenue.

When you are discerning something about someone, do not judge them from your own flesh and emotions. While I realize this can be easier said than done, ask the Lord to help you intercede and to handle this situation with His heart and with purity, truth, and wisdom. You love people but hate the sin. In operating in discernment this is a vital Kingdom principle to understand and to exercise.

DISCERNMENT SEES WITH THE EYES OF THE FATHER

The carnal man is not able to judge a spiritual man or things of the Spirit because he does not know our heavenly Father or the things of the Spirit, as taught by Paul: "We join together Spirit-revealed truths with Spirit-revealed words. Someone living on an entirely human level rejects the revelations of God's Spirit, for they make no sense to him" (1 Cor. 2:13-14). However, we as believers and sons and daughters of our heavenly Father are to discern all things and to do so in the sight of our heavenly Father. Allow me to explain by sharing scriptural examples.

Samuel Learns to See with the Father's Sight

We are all familiar with Samuel the prophet and his role with Saul. After Saul's disobedience to God and the Lord's rejection of him as king due to his rebellion, Samuel was given instruction to anoint the new king. Let's look at the encounter when the Lord spoke to him to go to the house of Jesse to discover and anoint the one chosen by God to be the future king of Israel. The encounter occurs in First Samuel 16.

He held a sacrifice, inviting Jesse and his sons to come. During this consecration time, all of Jesses' sons passed before Samuel. As Samuel looked upon Eliab, he thought, *Surely he is the anointed one of the Lord* (see 1 Sam. 16:6). But let's look at our heavenly Father's response, "Do not look on his appearance or on the height of his stature, because I have rejected him. For the Lord sees not as man sees. For man looks on the outward appearance, but the Lord looks on the heart" (1 Sam. 16:7 MEV).

Powerful words and a great teaching moment for Samuel. The Lord Himself was teaching him that man will *nabat*—judge, see, a judgment made on perceptions of physical sight (Strong's #H5027). But our heavenly Father doesn't *yireh*—approve, judge, discern, evaluate—as man does based on the appearance (Strong's #H7200). He does so by looking and seeing at the *lebab*—the mind, soul, spirit, and source of inner life of a person with the focus of this action being on feelings, thoughts, and volition (Strong's #H3824). What a great scriptural example of a prophet being taught directly to hear the Lord and perceive. What was it he was being taught? How to discern who Jesse's sons were not and to see who David was. We all know the story. When he saw David, he discerned he was the one and anointed him with oil in preparation for his calling to be king.

Jesus with Peter

Now let's examine Jesus in a teaching and revelatory moment with Peter. It was evident through Jesus' ministry that the religious leaders and many others did not have the discernment to know who He truly was—the Son of Man and the Son of God, the promised Messiah. He asked His disciples, "Who do people say that I am?" and they replied, "Some say Elijah, some say Jeremiah, some say a prophet." You see, many were not able to discern correctly who He truly was. Then He asked the disciples another question: "Who do you say that I am?" And praise God, Peter "got it" and discerned correctly. "You are Jesus the son of the most high living God" (see Matt. 16:13-16). Peter had the revelation and discernment to know the true identity of Jesus.

In spite of Peter discerning the true identity of Jesus, he still needed to mature. For example, in the next biblical encounter, Peter, out of his sincere love for Jesus, spoke out of emotion, stating that Jesus should never suffer at the hands of man. Jesus rebuked him: "Get behind Me, satan." Why did Jesus give such a harsh rebuke? Because even emotions can prove to be a snare if they are not lined up with God's Kingdom plan. We discover that Peter had other moments. He cut the ear off the servant of the high priest who was part of the large detachment sent to arrest Jesus in the Garden of Gethsemane. He denied Jesus three times when Jesus needed unwavering support of faithful friends. It is evident that Jesus discerned Peter's carnal nature and the areas in which he must continue to grow and mature, yet He looked beyond Peter's carnal nature and chose to see him with the sight of our heavenly Father. This should be a great encouragement to each of us as we are all still in the process of growth and maturity. Not only should it be an encouragement to us personally, but also a model to follow as we discern and perceive concerning others.

Jesus Could Perceive Beyond the Darkest of Strongholds

Remarkably, Jesus was able to perceive beyond the utterly evil and depraved condition of the Gadarene demoniac. He discerned, cast out the army of demons, and this man was victoriously set free. He perceived and saw a man whose freedom struck great fear in an entire region through the victory ordained by His Father. We can continue to read numerous encounters throughout the Word where in His earthly ministry He saw beyond sin and powerfully transformed many—the woman with the issue of blood, the woman at the well, the Roman centurion whose child had died, the criminal who hung next to Him on the cross.

One beautiful encounter that pierces my heart each time I read it is found in Luke 7:36-50. Jesus saw beyond the lifestyle of the prostitute who humbly, beautifully, and sacrificially anointed His feet with costly perfume and wiped them with her tears and hair. This pure act of devotion and surrender brought her into glorious freedom. And highlighting one more significant event, He even saw beyond the hatred of those who savagely crucified Him when He cried out, "Father, forgive them for they know not what they do."

Jesus Perceived the Hearts of the Sadducees and Pharisees

> Then Jesus addressed both the crowds and his disciples and said, "The religious scholars and the Pharisees sit on Moses' throne as the authorized interpreters of the Law. So listen and follow what they teach, but don't do what they do, for they tell you one thing and do another. They tie on your backs an oppressive burden of religious obligations and insist that you carry it, but will never lift a finger to help ease your load. Everything they do is done for show and to be noticed by others. They want to be seen as holy" (Matthew 23:1-5).

In Chapter Seven, we will discuss a religious spirit and how to see, hear, feel, and sense when it is in action through an individual or region. Suffice it to say, Jesus had watched, perceived, discerned, and understood the heart motives of these religious leaders who were fiercely jealous and envious of Him and who engaged in conversation and plots to have him killed. He used them and their poor behaviors as an object lesson to His disciples and those He taught. He spoke with wisdom and truth, clearly stating they were not to follow what had been modeled by those religious leaders, but to follow His lead of humility and service.

What About Others?

What about others in the Word of God? Peter discerned through a vision he encountered while in a trance. As a result, he did the unthinkable in Jewish culture and preached the Gospel to Gentiles, which forever changed the tapestry and history of Christianity. Saul was spiritually blind and satisfied to kill those who believed in and lived a life surrendered to Jesus. But God! He then encountered the radical, life-transforming moment on the road to Damascus and received spiritual sight. He stepped into his true Kingdom identity as Paul. He transformed from Christian-killer to the most influential apostle at the foundation of Christianity spreading throughout the nations of the world. He boldly became one who turned the world upside down for the Kingdom of God.

Paul discerned the spirit operating in the slave girl and cast it out. As a result, the entire city of Philippi began to experience salvation and transformation. He did not preach in Turkey when instructed by the Lord not to. Instead, he ministered and had great impact throughout other regions of Asia. Paul, discerning the will of the Father beyond human concern and emotion, chose to go to Jerusalem even when others begged him not to out of genuine and great concern. He still went, even knowing it could cost him his life. And we could continue to share many other testimonies from others who learned to hear the voice of the Lord and to discern the correct path to follow.

Greg and I recently watched the movie *Tortured for Christ*, the powerful and true story about Richard and Sabina Wurmbrand, who lived in Romania during World War I. He was a Christian pastor who refused to quit speaking the truth of the Gospel even in the face of severe persecution at the hands of Russians. He spent 14 years in prison suffering unimaginable interrogation and torture. At the end of the movie they shared this piercing quote he made after their time in unthinkable circumstances, "I love the Russians and the Russian prison guards, while I hate the Communist system." You see, Richard could perceive men beyond the darkest of strongholds. It is good to study these examples and learn to glean what was modeled.

LORD, IS THIS ME OR YOU?

One of the key concepts we have to be intentional to mature in is separating what is the Holy Spirit and our own thoughts, opinions, and emotions. At a personal level, you might be seeing, hearing, and discerning correctly, yet the Lord will not or does not release you to share the revelation for great periods of time. It is a Kingdom principle; He will take us through testing times before He allows us to share. He deals with our character and takes us through circumstances and situations to ensure our motives are pure and emotionally we are healed. This is done so we will function in a mature manner and not the motives of a critical mindset or wounded soul.

As stated above, the measure that we judge will be how we are measured. Unhealed trauma attached to our soul will cause our discernment and spiritual hearing to be off. We must get healed from past wounds. We must be healed from a critical mindset and spirit. *Critical* means inclined to find fault or to judge with severity, often too readily. Someone who is ready to judge with severity and do it quickly and readily is not seeing, hearing, or discerning as the Father sees. All wise and mature sons and daughters will weigh things carefully before the Lord.

At other times, some things should be shared quickly and right away to avoid severe or traumatic wounding in individual lives. If discernment is operating from hurt feelings, woundedness, and fleshly opinions, welcome the Holy Spirit to bring healing and deliverance to those areas and to release purity to the gift. Trust me, He will aid us in this process. The good news is, as we draw closer to Him we learn that our thoughts, words, and actions begin to line up with His and we grow in recognizing the difference between His voice and our own.

LEARNING FROM EXPERIENCE—SPEND TIME NURTURING THIS GIFT

Frankly, if a person has no intention of developing intimacy with the Father and allowing Him to transform them from glory to glory, then they should not release discernment concerning others. Yes, the gift is without reproach, but character is more important than the gift. I have witnessed many who have a strong gift, but they abuse the revelation in a power play or competition. When the fruit of their lives reveals the motives of their hearts, often there is impurity and the desire to be heard before the growth, discipleship, and maturity has transpired.

There is a vast difference between impurity and immaturity. Those who desire to be teachable will grow to be trusted. The Lord will graciously take each of us through seasons of discipleship and growth. Once He knows hearts can be trusted and motives are being led in obedience to Him, He will entrust more. Remember, He reveals His secrets to those who abide in Him and are vitally united to Him, who have learned to move in obedience to Him instead of over-zealousness to be heard and known. I fully believe God does not have *favorites*, but He does have *intimates*. His desire is that each of us would be intimates.

Make time to know the Word and to study it. Make time to worship Him until His presence is increasingly manifest. Be intentional about spending time in His throne room glory presence. Learn to set aside quality time with Him even in the midst of all the busyness and distraction of our culture. Build a personal relationship with the Holy Spirit. Welcome Him to transform you from glory to glory. And grow in an intimate friendship from an abiding place.

ABIDE IN HIM

I thoroughly explain this truth in my book *Glory Warfare*, but I feel the urging of the Lord to share it here again as we learn how to know His voice.

> *Dwell in Me, and I will dwell in you. [Live in Me and I will live in you.] Just as no branch can bear fruit of itself without abiding in (being vitally united to) the vine, neither can you bear fruit unless you abide in Me* (John 15:4 AMPC).
>
> *If you live in Me [abide vitally united to Me] and My words remain in you and continue to live in your hearts, ask whatever you will, and it shall be done for you* (John 15:7 AMPC).

Upon hearing the word *abide*, our minds quickly go to the normal steps we have been taught and know to be true. However, let's take a closer look at this word, *abide*. The Greek word is *meno*. It means "to remain, dwell, continue, endure, not to depart from, to continue to be present, to be held and kept" (Strong's #G3306). In other words, when we abide we become so in tune with His presence from the dedicated times of entering in beyond the veil and encountering Him in His glory that we grow into the ability to remain in existence with Him. We know who we are in Him. He is very real and close to us. We are not separate or apart, but vitally united. The following is an incredible promise that Jesus shared:

> *No one has greater love [no one has shown stronger affection] than to lay down (give up) his own life for his friends. You are My friends if you keep on doing the things which I command you to do. I do not call you servants (slaves) any longer, for the servant does not know what his master is doing (working out). But I have called you My friends, because I have made known to you everything that I have heard from My Father. [I have revealed to you everything that I have learned from Him.] You have not chosen Me, but I have chosen you and I have appointed you [I have planted you], that you might go and bear fruit and keep on bearing, and that your fruit may be lasting [that it may remain, abide], so that whatever you ask the Father in My Name [as presenting all that I Am], He may give it to you* (John 15:13-16 AMPC).

Such an awesome Kingdom promise. He is stating that you and I can be vitally united to Him, His friends to whom He reveals everything, and we will grow in wisdom and discernment to see victorious answers to our prayers. I believe He hears all of our prayers. But the key is this—when we are vitally united to Him, our prayer burdens and assignments become those that He has entrusted to us. Praying in unison and agreement with His heart over a matter is key for breakthrough. And it is key in maneuvering in the gift of discernment.

Truthfully, to be vitally united to Him and effectual intercessors, warriors, prophets, believers, and people operating in discernment, we must know the realms of the glory. Otherwise, we live in the realm of man's understanding and spend most of our time thinking on, interceding, and warring over all the wrong things. When we move beyond the veil into the realm of His Spirit, He shows us what to target because the glory causes our spiritual eyes and ears to be opened to see, hear, and receive from Him. Therefore, we must be intentional in pursuing Him so this gift of discernment is used in a purity of heart and motives and the resulting actions and intercessions follow His plan to see the breakthrough come.

LEARNING TO ASK AND LISTEN

Not only do we want to learn to hear His voice, we want to mature in conversing with Him. When you discern a situation, begin to ask questions, from this abiding place, about how His design for handling the revelation. Trust me, if He reveals something, He will also help you maneuver in the revelation with wisdom and in the right timing. It is vital to engage Him in the complete process of the revelation you discern. Therefore, learn to ask and, most importantly, to listen. Listening is vital in spiritual growth. If you are constantly speaking at someone, it is impossible to develop an intimate relationship. To abide, to learn His voice and distinguish between our own voice and His voice, or our ways and His ways, we must learn to sit in His presence and listen.

Is This My Assignment?

Those who have heard me teach will be familiar with the principle that I am about to share. Just because I discern something does not mean it is my assignment to deal with it or fix it. We are not to spiritually take on, come against, or engage ourselves in everything we see or discern. Not every demonized or troubled person is my assignment. Not every unjust issue or righteous movement is my assignment. Trust me, if I addressed all that I discerned, I would be totally worn out. Seeing my zealousness and feistiness, C. Peter Wagner many times gently reminded me, "Choose your battles wisely, darlin'. Only fight the battles the Lord is calling you to fight." And I would add this—choose your ministry undertakings and involvements wisely.

This is such an important principle—knowing His assignments for the season we are in, especially those involving spiritual warfare. Why is this imperative? Being in the right assignment begets authority for victory and breakthrough. The truth is, if we take on assignments that have not been allotted to us, we can wear ourselves out by striving in order to make things happen and begin to feel worn down, battle weary. I have seen this happen to numerous believers and Kingdom warriors. They take on every assignment that they discern without seeking Him over the specific missions He is calling them to. They do not spend time in His glory presence to hear and receive clearly the marching orders to advance in order to achieve victory. We will discuss this further in Chapter Nine, but the most important model to follow in this is Jesus. Jesus did what He saw and heard His Father leading Him to see, hear, and ultimately do. Jesus intimately knew the voice of His heavenly Father, and it was the key voice guiding Him to stay within the assignments God was entrusting to Him.

Submitting Revelation to Those Who Function in Authority

Learn to gain wisdom and insight from those who speak into your life. If they advise you to share the discernment, then do so. If they say to hold it, then do so. I am an international minister. Last year I ministered in thirteen nations and over twenty cities in the United States. This year I will do the same. Yet when I am discerning something that will potentially influence many or strongly influence someone or a group of individuals, I will take the revelation to those who love me, believe in me, and have discipled me in the path I am on. Why? If what I am going to speak and release is going to reach and possibly influence multitudes,

I believe it is imperative to have the wisdom and agreement of those who have gone before.

Red-Light Revelation—Stop, Listen, Use Caution and Wisdom

First allow me to state that if someone functions as a lone ranger in the Body of Christ, the likelihood that they will receive discernment is minimal. If someone arrives on the scene with no relationship and begins releasing words of discernment, prophetic words, judgmental words, directional and correctional words, this will not be received. How relationship is established and the history of relational experience is valuable when sharing. When functioning in discernment, be cautious or avoid sharing sexual sin, adultery, and personal sin in a public forum. This should be done in a private deliverance session to bring freedom and victory. But in a corporate setting, take the revelation and pray into it and seek the Lord over the steps to initiate before blurting it out. Be cautious about sharing discernment that could cause confusion and harm if spoken and released too quickly.

Friends, I prophesy over multitudes, cities, regions, and nations. But these are the following principles I adhere to when discerning and releasing that discernment:

I do not engage in spiritual matchmaking. I am cautious and use time-proven wisdom on speaking out discernment concerning new jobs, moves, future pregnancies, and major life decisions. Even in the midst of prophesying, I am listening to the Holy Spirit on how to share, what to share, and when to share. Remember to engage Him in the full process of the discernment and the manner and steps taken to share it. How the discernment and revelation are spoken is at times as important or more important than the discerned revelation.

Here is a great scriptural example of how Nathan maneuvered with David in the discernment of his sin. It was a dark hour in the life of King

David. He had committed adultery with Bathsheba and then had her husband, Uriah, killed. God sent the prophet Nathan to tell David a parable of a rich man who passed over his own flock and took a poor man's beloved pet lamb to feed his guests. The parable aroused David's anger at the injustice of it all. Let's read further about the encounter:

> *And the Lord sent Nathan [the prophet] to David. He came and said to him, "There were two men in a city, one rich and the other poor. The rich man had a very large number of flocks and herds, but the poor man had nothing but one little ewe lamb which he had purchased and nourished; and it grew up together with him and his children. It ate his food, drank from his cup, it lay in his arms, and was like a daughter to him. Now a traveler (visitor) came to the rich man, and to avoid taking one from his own flock or herd to prepare [a meal] for the traveler who had come to him, he took the poor man's ewe lamb and prepared it for his guest."*
>
> *Then David's anger burned intensely against the man, and he said to Nathan, "As the Lord lives, the man who has done this deserves to die. He shall make restitution for the ewe lamb four times as much [as the lamb was worth], because he did this thing and had no compassion." Then Nathan said to David, "You are the man!"* (2 Samuel 12:1-7 AMP)

You see, Nathan did not come into David's presence and blurt out the sin the king had committed. He sought the Lord and came prepared to share the truth of David's sin in a manner that he could receive it. Now, I am not saying that there should never be an up-front conversation with someone who has been involved in sin. But in this case, as in some situations in our lives, how a matter is spoken and handled is as crucial as stating the obvious. What was the result of this encounter between Nathan and David? He confessed his sin: "I have sinned against the Lord" (2 Sam. 12:13 AMP).

Green-Light Revelations to Share

Let's end this chapter on those issues I term green-light discernment and prophetic revelation to share—words of exhortation, encouragement, comfort, confirmation, hope, Kingdom direction, words of destiny released in the right timing, and words of deliverance and freedom. Even words of transition or direction, if worded in a way that brings guidance, hope, and confirmation, are generally good words you can share freely. With discernment like this, it's always the right time!

NOTE

1. Oswald Chambers, *My Utmost for His Highest,* "May 3: Vital Intercession" (Grand Rapids, MI: Discovery House, 2018).

Chapter Four

DISCERNMENT AND PROPHECY WORK TOGETHER

*Now I'll listen carefully for your voice and wait to hear
whatever you say. Let me hear your promise of peace—the
message every one of your godly lovers longs to hear. Don't
let us in our ignorance turn back from following you.*
—PSALM 85:8

The phrase *I'll listen carefully* is also as stated in some translations, "I will listen intentionally." The desired outcome is to hear His voice. The Hebrew word for *hear* in this scripture is *shama*. It means "to hear intelligently, to hear attentively and obediently, to discern" (Strong's #H8085). David goes onto to say, "Let me hear [*shama*] your promise of peace." It is important to recognize how discernment and prophecy work together. The two partnered together cause us to speak the word of the Lord and engage in godly actions, but to also do so in wisdom. Let's investigate and learn how this works in operation.

DISCERNING SPIRITUAL CONDITIONS

I am a prophet and release prophetic words on a regular basis to individuals, churches, governments, spheres of influence, regions, and nations. It is important to not only release the true word of the Lord but to also learn to discern and perceive the spiritual condition of the individual church or region you are prophesying to. Why is this so crucial? Because their spiritual condition will also determine how the prophetic word will best be received and the level of preparedness to steward the word. So not only am I listening to and hearing the prophetic word from the Lord, I am also engaging the Holy Spirit on how to specifically share the word based on the condition and readiness of the ones I will be speaking into.

First and foremost, I am discerning what it is that they are in need of while I am ministering. Sometimes, people are certain they know what needs to be dealt with in a particular area when in fact the Lord is focusing on another topic or issue. There are times I have been asked to minister an exact word of destiny and the Lord is telling me to minister healing to the wounded emotions that have been ignored. Or then there are those who are running from their calling and the direction the Lord wants them to go, and He will lead me to release the word of the Lord to push them out of their comfort zone into more. So here is the inner dialogue I have as I minister in person or as I am preparing ahead of time in intercession: "Lord what is on Your heart for this person, church, governmental leader, region? What do You want me to share?" And after I hear from Him: "Lord give me wisdom and keen discernment on how to share the word that will bring this group into Your purposes and plans."

Then there are the more pressing times when I discern hardness in someone's heart or in a region and the Lord will assign me to be the one to break things open. Or I have come prepared to share one message and as I worship with the corporate gathering before ministering I can feel and sense that the message I am going to speak is not what the group is in need of. I will often hear the Holy Spirit directing me to go in another direction. You see, I believe the Lord wants a discernment and maturity level as we intercede and minister that will truly break people out of the old and into the new. Let me give a for instance at a regional level.

Church in Russia

I was invited to minister in a city in Russia and was asked to speak from my book *Let Our Children Go*, which in many settings is a great and appropriate message. However, as I met with the leadership team and heard their heart and learned the vast work they were engaging in throughout the nations, the Lord led me to speak a prophetic word to the leader, "It is time to go into cities and regions and to contend against principalities and territorial spirits to see transformational breakthrough and victory realized." Based off of this prophetic word, the entire pre-planned weekend agenda changed.

It proved to be a power-packed weekend with key strategies that were formed for the nation of Russia, which our prayer network has partnered with now for five years. The Lord led me to end the weekend with a message from Acts 2 when the Holy Spirit fell at Pentecost. In that Sunday service, many were healed, saved, delivered, and filled with the fire of the Holy Spirit. To this day, I am still hearing testimonies of breakthrough from that weekend of ministry.

NOT SPEAKING MORE THAN WE SHOULD

As stated above, I am in and out of a new region on a consistent basis. Each group and region I minister in has its own issues that require healing and destiny that the Lord is bringing them into. Therefore, as I am speaking to one church or region, in listening and hearing the Lord it is key to discern whether each group is ready for the fullness of the word concerning the strategy, outpouring, or move of the Spirit the Lord wants to release. These same principles can be applied to individuals as well.

On a personal level, if I am sensing that a person needs deliverance from a demonic spirit yet this person has not been saved, then I must introduce salvation first. If I see or discern a call to nations, yet this individual has only been a believer for six months, is still walking through deliverance, and is just engaging in discipleship, then I must discern if they are ready to hear the word. Why? Because a ministry to the nations involves navigating through spiritual warfare or battles that this individual might not be prepared to face. Is the individual at a maturity level to follow the direction of leadership, or do they have an independent or lone ranger mentality? Why is this good to perceive? Because the fullness of the prophetic word might encourage this lack of relational alignment and accountability. As we say in the South, will this empower their immaturity to cause them to "fly the coop" and launch out on their own too soon? Have I witnessed and discerned a teachable and hungry spirit in this individual?

As I am preparing to minister for a region, I ask—are they at the maturity level to handle the fullness of the revelation? Is this group relatively young in the Lord? If I am seeing the principality over the region and yet the group I am ministering to is barely practicing deliverance ministry, this is not a group who is ready to begin contending against principalities at a regional level. I also consider—is the church or region in an emotionally wounded place from trauma? Is there unity or division? Is the leadership of the believers in a level of maturity, established authority, and relational alignment to steward the fullness of revelation? Is the group on fire and hungry and pressing into the Lord? Is there Holy Spirit glory presence and activity in the gatherings? It is important to think long term—to have the mindset of relationship building and to continue the building process with them. Therefore, I seek wisdom from the Lord on what to share and release each time I am with a group.

Some of you might be pondering, "Is she saying that she does not always share what she is fully hearing and receiving?" My answer would be yes. At the direction of the Holy Spirit, some of what I am hearing I will share; some of what I am hearing I will not share. I am discerning the big picture, not just the immediate moment in front of me.

FAITH TO SPEAK OUT THE CREATIVE WORD

As we discussed in Chapter One, God's Word is creative. As we prophesy the word He is releasing, there is an agreement with His ordained agenda and it carries with it the power and creative anointing to see it come to pass. So while we discussed above discerning the condition of those we are prophesying to, we also must learn to discern when we are to speak the word to bring empowerment in that creative, supernatural atmosphere for it to bring life and come to pass. I will term these words *creative words* and *plowing words*. What does it mean to spiritually plow? Plowing is bringing the anointing of His Spirit and speaking out the word into the untilled spiritual soil of the individual, the corporate gathering, the sphere of influence, or the nation so it can create the Lord's intended purpose. Therefore, the word being spoken might take the hearers by surprise.

I was ministering in a conference in Houston. A pastor and his wife were attending from another state. I felt the Lord prompting me to prophesy to them. I quickly discerned in the spirit a demonic assignment of covenant breaking that had resulted in betrayals from several long-time church members and ministry friends. This assignment was a territorial spirit operating against the work of God and His move of glory in the region, and this couple was key to usher in awakening.

I shared the discernment and broke off the assignment that had come against them corporately and prophesied that within a short amount of time people would begin to return. Healing and restoration would begin for the corporate gathering and the region. Within two weeks, six couples who had been a part of the betrayal and exodus contacted them, scheduled a meeting, repented for the betrayal, and all the individuals returned to the church. You see, speaking the word out loud plowed the soil in the spirit and opened the creative atmosphere for the spoken and creative miracle to occur. The Lord's voice is powerful, and when we speak in agreement it carries the power and anointing to create the atmosphere for breakthrough and victory.

DISCERNING SOULISH DESIRES

What do I mean by soulish desires? Our soul is made up of our mind, will, and emotions. When there are soulish desires at play there will be a pull in the spirit from people and/or gatherings that feels like a forceful or impure fleshly pull instead of a purity of true hunger and passion. When asked to prophesy it will feel like a wrong demand and a pull of manipulation instead of a purity of hunger and humility. I am a lover of people. I enjoy being with people. When a pull is made on me with a manipulative and soulish bent, quickly a righteous indignation rises in my spirit. I still will respond out of grace, but that does not diminish the feeling of discernment. Usually my answer is a gentle, "No. But I will pray in agreement with you to hear the direction of the Lord clearly as you continue to pursue and seek Him." A scriptural example is found in Mark 10:35-40 when James and John ask for a favor from Jesus:

> *Jacob and John, sons of Zebedee, approached Jesus and said, "Teacher, will you do a favor for us?" "What is it you're wanting me to do?" he asked. "We want to sit next to you when you come into your glory," they said, "one at your right hand and the other at your left." Jesus said to them, "You don't have a clue what you're asking for! Are you prepared to drink from the cup of suffering that I am about*

*to drink? And are you able to endure the baptism into death
that I am about to experience?" They replied, "Yes, we are
able." Jesus said to them, "You will certainly drink from the
cup of my sufferings and be immersed into my death, but
to have you sit in the position of highest honor is not mine
to decide. It is reserved for those whom grace has prepared
them to have it."*

I believe this is an obvious request made from a soulish desire and
naïve understanding. They were evidently exaggerating their spirituality
and believing that they were more mature than they really were. In spite
of their soulish ambition and self-confidence, Jesus does express that they
will taste of the sufferings of Christ. But then to show His level of submission to the Father, He Himself expresses that He does not choose
who gets that honor of sitting at the right and left hand of the throne, but
only His Father in heaven determines who sits in this place of distinction.

DISCERNING HIS TIMING

There are many scriptural examples that direct us to the truth that God
is a God of timing. What do I mean by this? That there is the time to
hold revelation and a time to speak revelation, a time to wait and a time
to advance into a regional assignment. Discerning His timing of moving
forward empowers the victorious outcome. How do we know the timing
of when to speak? This might sound like a simplistic reply to the question,
but we ask Him, "Lord, is this Your timing for me to speak what I am
hearing and discerning?" Engage Him in conversation. He will answer.

Cindy Jacobs is a dear friend and mentor in my life. She had been
watching Greg and I serve in ministries for many years. One day she
phoned and asked to meet with me. As we engaged in conversation over
breakfast, it was evident that she came with an agenda and a prophetic
message and instruction. She began to tell me her story of her calling as

a prophet to the nations, the processes the Lord took her through, and many of the growth lessons she had to walk through. The difficulties of spiritual warfare she and Mike and their family pressed through, but also the glorious spiritual journey they had encountered and how faithfully the Lord had moved in their lives, ministry, and throughout the nations of the world.

To be honest, I was completely fixated on the conversation and gleaning all I could as she was sharing with me. She then began to shift the conversation to me. "Becca, where are you on this journey in your calling to the nations? How are you on this journey?" She brought me into a time of intentional examination. She spoke as a spiritual mother and encouraged me to run the race and to not shrink back. She shared that there were many women who felt the call but did not advance because of the cost and sacrifice required. "Becca, don't shrink back. Be the woman leader the Lord is calling you to be as a prophet to the nations." I was challenged in a beautiful way.

I was totally honored, humbled, and undone by her words, but also filled with a newfound impartation of faith and resolve to continue pouring into the nations. As we left the restaurant, I asked her, "Cindy, how long have you held off on having this conversation with me?"

She smiled and stated, "I have waited twelve years. If I had spoken all of this before now it would have been too soon. The Lord told me that now was the time." I was so beyond grateful for her wisdom in waiting to have this conversation until the Lord spoke to her and discerned the correct timing. If we speak too soon, we can abort or delay the victorious breakthrough the Lord has already intended to bring.

DISCERNING FALSE WORDS AND PROPHETS

We previously discussed knowing those who are true or false by the fruit of their lives and ministries. But in the discernment realm, what is transpiring for the discerner when in the presence of a false word being released or a false prophet speaking? There will be a feeling of being slimed in the spirit. An agitation in the spirit. A strong sense of distrust. A strong sense of knowing that what is being said is off or a lie. A feeling of wanting to protect those hearing this person. Sometimes it feels like a tight band around the forehead or an ache or pain in the heart. A feeling of being manipulated to do something or believe something that is totally against the Word of God. Others might be loving the moment and rejoicing, but everything in you is seeing, hearing, and sensing the false words being released. Don't put yourself in a place of questioning yourself. Remember converse with the Holy Spirit on what is occurring concerning these feelings and how to maturely handle the revelation. He will guide you.

DISCERNING THE ESTABLISHED DEMONIC STRONGHOLD AND THE STRATEGY FOR VICTORY

Hearing the sounds of the angels and demons in the spirit is a normal occurrence. I can honestly say sometimes when we are on site praying in a city, sphere of influence, region, or nation it sounds like a Frank Peretti book in action in the spirit realm. I will share further in Chapter Seven about discerning different strongholds. But I will state here, I often see the activity of the demonic stronghold in a person's life. I can sense and feel the spiritual atmosphere of bondage around an individual or established in a region. It is common for me to discern in a closed vision how the demonic stronghold established its grip, but also the strategy to see it broken. The following is an example that truly played out much like an encounter from a Peretti novel with angels, demons, and a clear open vision of a profound and distinct supernatural event.

It had been a power-packed weekend of ministry with the time of speaking and praying winding up in a Sunday morning church service.

Following the close of the meeting, we ministered to a precious woman whom we will call Laura. She was a mother of three beautiful children who came in great need of ministry. She was living with the shaman from her Native American tribe. He was practicing occult rituals in their home and had begun to turn against her in acts of abuse and violence. Three days prior she had to leave the home with her children to escape danger.

As the ministry time ensued, I explained we needed to break soul ties between her and her boyfriend. Laura gladly agreed. I discerned in the spirit that he would try to come back into her life and force her back into a relationship. I sensed great concern over this. I shared the warning with her and told her she must not fall back into his trap of deception because the harassment in the occult demonic realm would come back seven times worse and she and her children would be in danger. Little did I know how quickly that prophetic warning would come to pass.

It was time for lunch, so we all made our way to a local restaurant. Laura and her children accompanied us. The majority of the group had already arrived before me and the pastor of the church. As we entered the restaurant, it was busy that afternoon as many were out for Sunday lunch. Our crew was seated in the second room at a large table, and we began to make our way to them.

I had recently appeared on Sid Roth's *It's Supernatural!* for the first time, and there was a woman in the restaurant who recognized me and was extremely happy to meet me. I pleasantly greeted her with a warm, "Hello." As soon as I did, I saw a gentleman out of my peripheral vision moving toward the table with our church friends, including Laura and her children.

As soon as I caught a glimpse of him, something began to transpire that I had not experienced in many years. The room began to move in slow motion and went totally still and quiet. All in the restaurant were completely motionless and no one was speaking. It was as if for them time was standing still and silent. The only ones not impacted by this supernatural occurrence were the angry shaman, the woman who had seen me on Sid Roth, me, and the pastor who quickly whispered in my ear, "Becca that is him. The shaman." Then she realized that there was zero movement in the room and no one was making a sound, "Becca, are you seeing this? What is going on?" The woman who had seen me on Sid Roth continued to talk, but did not perceive what the pastor and I saw. She was very involved in the conversation and seemed to be oblivious to what was transpiring.

The shaman then spoke directly to Laura: "How dare you do this to me! How dare you humiliate me. You will come with me!" Laura, as if in a trance, stood up and began to follow him out of the restaurant while tears were streaming down her cheeks. He saw me and ensured he was a good distance from me as he made his exit out of the restaurant, feeling as if he had succeeded in intimidating her to follow and releasing his witchcraft spell in the atmosphere. Laura, however, walked only three feet from me as she was following him out. At that point, I gently pushed aside the woman speaking to me about the Sid Roth show.

I reached for Laura and swiftly pulled her toward me and exclaimed. "Laura, look at me! Look at me! I break all witchcraft control off of you right now in Jesus' name. You will not leave nor go back to him!" As I exclaimed this directive out loud in the atmosphere, she instantly fell into my arms weeping. I embraced her as I would one of my own daughters in the midst of a trauma. "Laura, I've got you. We are here for you, Jesus is here for you, He's got you. He loves you." I turned to see the shaman boyfriend staring at me in complete anger and disbelief. I shouted out to him as he quickly exited the restaurant in almost a full run, "And I am praying for you too. Jesus loves you and one day you will be saved!" As soon as those word came out of my mouth, the restaurant completely came back to life.

Wow. This truly was an unusual supernatural encounter. It was like a showdown between the sorcerers of Egypt and Moses and Aaron. The pastor and I were trying to process what had occurred. I was also in a state of questioning, "How did I know to do what I did in that moment?" To be honest, this is not something one prepares for. This is where abiding in Him and being vitally united to Him is so imperative. Frequently, there are encounters and confrontations that unfold in the supernatural realm in which I walk away asking the Lord, "How did I know how to do that!?" All the while rejoicing, "Thank You, Holy Spirit, for anointing me and causing me to respond in discernment and in sync with Your Spirit and wisdom!"

That night as I slept in the hotel room, the shaman astral projected into my room. I could hear him breathing at the side of my bed. I asked the Lord, "What do I do?"

He told me, "Go back to sleep. The angels will take care of the situation." As I closed my eyes, I could hear the dispatching of the angels and him leaving the room abruptly. It happened a second time, with the same scene playing out. And again, a third time. This final time the Lord released me to call the shaman out by name and to command him in the name of Jesus to leave. He left with the escort of the angels again and did not return that night nor any other time I have been ministering in that region. Laura and her children were free from the abuse.

Now this might sound a little out there for some of you, but it happened and I have 20 witnesses who were there in the restaurant in the midst of this showdown. The spirit realm is alive and active. Throughout the Word of God, we see multiple power encounters and engagement in the spirit.

- The eyes of Elisha's servants were opened to see that there are more for him than against him.

- Aaron's snake (rod) swallowed up the snakes (rods) of Pharaoh's sorcerers.

- Satan appeared to Jesus in the wilderness to tempt Him.

- Peter experienced a trance.

- Phillip translated.

- Jesus and Peter walked on the water.

- Elijah called down fire from heaven to consume the altar when encountering the prophets of Baal.

- Michael battled the Prince of Persia to release the answer of prayer to Daniel.

Suffice it to say the Bible is replete with supernatural encounters in the spirit realm. Trust me, it is more real than the physical. And we must not shun or ignore the reality of it nor the activity in it.

DISCERNING AND DISMANTLING HINDRANCES

There are churches and regions I am invited into in which there is a felt, tangible resistance in the atmosphere to a move of God. The people are visibly hungry and active in worship and intercession. Yet there is a hindrance to a move of the Spirit that they have been believing and contending for. Evansville, Indiana was one of those locations.

I had been invited by my dear friend Janet Douglas to minister in a weekend gathering at her apostolic center, CityGate Indiana. They are on fire for the Lord, faithful prayer warriors and worshipers cultivating an atmosphere for spiritual awakening. Following this time of ministry, I was invited to teach our Regional Transformation Spiritual Warfare School. I enjoyed and truly loved being with these awesome men and women from across Indiana and Kentucky. It was a dynamic time of training.

On the last weekend of this school, we go on site together as a group to key locations in the region to pray for breakthrough. The Lord had been revealing the strategic prayer locations. One was the Islamic Center of Evansville. We called and asked if we could have a tour of the center, explaining that we were Christian religious history students. We shared our interest to learn about their beliefs and to tour the center.

Now, before some begin to struggle with this, we were making this request in order to have an open door and access to get inside. We have learned from much experience over the past thirty years that when we are welcomed inside, we learn key information to pray into. And in this instance the added bonus was that we were able to meet the imam. This gives us a face and name so we can intercede for his salvation and of course, if the opportunity presents itself, a divine moment to show the love of Jesus. The center gladly granted our request and a tour was scheduled on our prayer journey day.

Upon arrival, the imam warmly met us at the entrance. He initiated the tour throughout the Islamic Center and asked if we would like to enter the prayer room where they gather five times a day to engage in the Muslim call to prayer. We agreed. Some of the older team members sat at the entrance of the door in chairs in order to listen as he continued to answer our questions over the microphone. They do not allow sitting on the floor of the prayer room by those who are not Muslim.

About twenty minutes into the interview, another gentleman joined us—a doctor from the town of Evansville, who is also a Muslim. They both engaged in conversation, sharing their beliefs and answering any questions we asked. The imam then began to tell us about his family in Syria and how they were in danger. The leader in the area of Bashan had initiated jihad and killing sprees in which he assassinated his own Islamic people. The imam genuinely made the following request, "Please, when you remember them, pray for the protection of my family in Syria."

I knew this was my open door. I inquired, "May we pray for them now?" The imam turned to the doctor as if they had to weigh this request. But quickly they both nodded in agreement and handed me the microphone. I gently asked, "Is it okay for me to pray in my Christian way to my Christian God?" Again, they both agreed! So now here I am, a Christian western woman in the prayer room of an Islamic Center. At this mosque, they only allow Muslim men to enter in order to pray during the Muslim call to prayer. I had been granted permission to pray and to pray to my Christian God on the microphone that will sound out through the entire Islamic Center. Woohoo!

Boy, did I pray! We prayed for the imam, the doctor, and for the imam's family in Syria. I prayed a sincere prayer of protection for the family. I entered into intercession for the family, the imam, and the doctor in which I invited encounters with the Father's heart of love. As the prayer time drew to an end, I stated out loud the following words, "And, Lord, we make all of these requests and stand in the truth that all these prayers will be answered in the powerful name of Jesus of Nazareth. Amen." When I opened my eyes to discern if I had crossed a line, the imam and the doctor, two Islamic leaders, were both fighting back tears. The presence of the Lord was tangibly resting in the center. To be honest, I was a little undone myself. They graciously thanked me and asked me to continue to pray for them and their families. The entire team agreed to do so. A sincere invitation was extended for us to visit again.

After making our way out to the parking lot, we broke out into pure rejoicing at what had just transpired. Rob Murphy, a pastor in Indiana, asked, "Becca do you realize what just happened?"

I enthusiastically exclaimed, "Yes. As a woman and a Christian woman on top of that, I was invited to pray on the microphone of the Islamic Center and to do so in Jesus' name. They don't allow their own women in that prayer room to pray. Even if they are praying to Allah!"

Rob then pointed out, "Becca, it was even more than that. Other Muslim men were waiting to enter that prayer room through another door. They were there for the call to prayer. Because we were in there with the imam, they waited to enter. When they allowed you to pray it was at the exact time of the beginning of their call to prayer. You just opened up their prayer time in Jesus' name and delayed them from praying at their scheduled time to Allah. A Christian western woman was granted permission by the imam to violate all rules in the Islamic Center and in their prayer room!" The entire team shouted in awe and joy!

That Sunday night in the church service, the tangible shift in the atmosphere was palpable. God's shekinah glory fell. People came from all across the region. Some were healed, some delivered, and some filled with the fire of the Holy Spirit. One person received salvation. Not only did this happen in the CityGate service, but churches across the region that were not a part of the prayer time reaped this glorious benefit as well. God's glory broke open in that region after that supernatural encounter in the Islamic Center. And as of the writing of this book, His presence is still moving in corporate gatherings. It has continued to increase since that weekend. Even typing this makes me want to release my Texan shout of praise, "Woohoo! Go God!"

DISCERNING OPENNESS TO A NEW MOVE OF GOD

When we view the lives of the apostles before the Upper Room experience, we see them in a process of asking questions, discovering, and learning. They were firsthand witnesses of Jesus. They observed and participated in many supernatural events, but they were not exhibiting Kingdom living. When the Holy Spirit appeared on the scene at Pentecost, these men and women were filled with His fire and great boldness. Their understanding of the Kingdom of God changed, and Peter—blunt, well-intentioned, all-too-human Peter—was no exception.

In truth, as we study Peter, we discover that he was often the first of the disciples to stumble into this new kind of living, although he sometimes took two steps forward and one step back. He was the first to realize that Jesus was the Son of God; he was the first and only one to walk on water; he was the first to deny Jesus; he was the first disciple to the tomb after Mary brought the news that Jesus had risen from the dead; he was the first to preach the Gospel message; he was the first to preach to the Gentiles. Peter was on the forefront of all that was happening.

When the Holy Spirit came on the 120, they began to operate under His guidance and anointing. They now had the power of the Holy Spirit available in their lives. Their focus shifted from lack of understanding, blind trust in tradition, and selfish thinking to a Kingdom Ekklesia mindset of saving souls and transforming society. At this life-transforming encounter, Peter never considered the idea of stopping and building a dwelling as he had done at the transfiguration, but instead he began immediately to declare the Gospel outside the walls of that room.

We see his changed nature in the story told in Acts 10 and 11 of how God used Peter to bring salvation to the Gentiles. Cornelius was a centurion in the Italian regiment in the town of Caesarea. The Bible tells us that he was a God-fearing man who gave generously to those in need. One afternoon he had a vision.

> *One afternoon about three o'clock, he had an open vision and saw the angel of God appear right in front of him, calling out his name, "Cornelius!" Startled, he was overcome with fear by the sight of the angel. He asked, "What do you want, Lord?" The angel said, "All of your prayers and your generosity to the poor have ascended before God as an eternal offering. Now, send some men to Joppa at*

once. Have them find a man named Simon the Rock, who is staying as a guest in the home of Simon the tanner, whose house is by the sea" (Acts 10:3-6).

Needless to say, following this encounter Cornelius dispatched two of his servants and a devout soldier who was one of his attendants to find this man Simon. As they were on their journey and nearing the city, Peter went up on the roof to pray. The Spirit caused him to fall into a trance and he, too, had a vision.

As the heavenly realm opened up, he saw something resembling a large linen tablecloth that descended from above, being let down to the earth by its four corners. As it floated down he saw that it held many kinds of four-footed animals, reptiles, and wild birds. A voice said to him, "Peter, go and prepare them to be eaten" (Acts 10:11-13).

Peter was aghast at the suggestion: "There's no way I could do that, Lord, for I've never eaten anything forbidden or impure according to our Jewish laws" (Acts 10:14). Peter was sensitive to the Spirit and the voice of the Lord, but his lifestyle of obedience to the Law was still in force, and it was overriding his discernment and resulting desire to obey. In his human thinking, it was difficult for him to believe the Lord would say this to him.

The voice spoke again. "Nothing is unclean if God declares it to be clean." The vision was repeated three times. Then suddenly the linen sheet was snatched back up into heaven (Acts 10:15-16).

The Lord was using this vivid picture to prepare Peter for his kingdom role of bringing salvation to the Gentiles. Peter had enough discernment to perceive and understand that the vision was symbolic and began pondering the interpretation. About that time the three men sent by Cornelius stopped at the gate of his house asking for him. The Spirit spoke to Peter: "Go downstairs now, for three men are looking for you. Don't hesitate to go with them, because I have sent them" (Acts 10:20). The vision required an act of obedience by Peter, and the Spirit led him step by step.

The visitors were welcomed into the home and they stated their business. The next day they all set out for Caesarea along with a group of men from Joppa. Peter knew he would be called into question for going to a Gentile home and so took witnesses he could depend on.

Now Cornelius was expecting them, even though he knew it was against Jewish law for a Jewish person to associate with a Gentile. Not only was it illegal, it was also an offensive and detestable notion to the Jews. I so love this about Cornelius and Peter—they could see and discern past the law of man and religious tradition to step into the new era of awakening. Cornelius sent for his relatives and close friends to be a part of the amazing thing that God was doing. As Peter entered the home and saw the crowd, he explained that God had told him to come, for he must no longer call any man impure. He then asked why he had been summoned.

Cornelius described the encounter he had experienced with the angel of God and explained that he, his family, and his friends were eager to hear everything the Lord had commissioned Peter to tell them. Peter shared a landmark message, one of the most strategic messages in the history of the Early Church. This sermon is important because Peter revealed that he now fully discerned and understood the meaning of the rooftop vision: God is no respecter of persons; He does not show favoritism or partiality.

When Peter recognized and discerned through the prophetic vision that God had sent him to share the truth of Jesus, he realized that his purpose was to be one to break cultural beliefs, traditions, and prejudices between Jew and Gentile and open the door for all mankind to hear the truth of the Gospel.

Peter discerned and knew he was operating under the mandate of the Lord, which went beyond the boundaries and restrictions of Jewish law. Because of his obedience there were powerful results. As he preached, the Holy Spirit came on all who heard the message.

> While Peter was speaking, the Holy Spirit cascaded over all those listening to his message. The Jewish brothers who had accompanied Peter were astounded that the gift of the Holy Spirit was poured out on people who weren't Jews, for they heard them speaking in supernaturally given languages and passionately praising God. Peter said, "How could anyone object to these people being baptized? For they have received the Holy Spirit just as we have." So he instructed them to be baptized in the power of the name of Jesus, the Anointed One. After their baptism, they asked Peter to stay with them for a few more days (Acts 10:44-48).

No one could doubt that God had been at work. When the Jewish believers heard the truth, they were able to discern this new era and had no further objections and themselves began to praise God that even the Gentiles could receive repentance unto life.

What a tremendous encounter! This incident changed the face of Christianity in the Early Church and, through those believers, throughout the world today. When we operate under the direction of our own understanding, traditions, and human desires and choose to shun prophetic revelation and the gained discernment, we can miss the big picture and God's designed plan. However, when we walk in step with Jesus, operate in the anointing of the Holy Spirit, and embrace His prophetic revelation and Kingdom discernment of the plan at hand, transformation and a new move of God will take place. So now let's move on to learn how discernment can be activated by observing in the natural.

Chapter Five

Learning to Discern by Observing in the Natural

The mind of the discerning acquires knowledge,
and the ear of the wise seeks it.
—Proverbs 18:15 HCSB

We can learn to discern. As we develop our natural discernment in practical ways, we will grow and mature into the spiritual gift of discernment to gain understanding of moves of the Holy Spirit, the truth of the Kingdom, and also uncovering the schemes of the enemy. Discerning the implication of behaviors, words, and situations and learning to detect and discern the long-term effects of decisions, behaviors, and actions are key focuses in this process. In fact, the FBI, CIA, and law enforcement officers identify and discern criminal activities by determining a pattern of behavior through an analysis of possible motives, means, and opportunities. These FBI and CIA people discern all different variables, traits, and factors that become a "sign" pointing to the answers. The following are interesting, real, and practical responses that these officers of justice are taught to watch for during interrogations in order to detect deception, discover truth, and to reveal possible guilt versus innocence. Below are portions of an article written by former FBI special agent Joe Navarro.

> In some respects, interviewing entails nothing more than "effective communication with a purpose." In a forensic setting, investigators search for information with general investigative value or something that may prove their case. That constitutes the purpose of the interview.
>
> Communicating effectively includes both verbal and non-verbal messages. It means that the interrogators must ask questions properly so as not to arouse behaviors that mask true sentiments. When an interviewer becomes suspicious of a statement or begins to accuse a suspect, a negative emotional response usually results—the kind most people feel when someone blames them for something. When stimulated this way, the interviewee's emotional state and nonverbal behavior become altered, masking true sentiments. This affects the innocent, as well as the guilty.
>
> If investigators ask questions with curiosity rather than suspicion or animosity, they will notice the suspect displaying nervousness, tension, stress, anxiety, fear, apprehension, concern, or dislike as a result of the substance of the question, rather than the tone. This proves critical to detecting deception because the interviewer's tone, attitude, demeanor, intensity, and manner all affect the emotions of the interviewee. It is better to be curious than accusatory. Once interviewers cross that line, the suspect's behaviors result from emotions, not guilt.
>
> When the suspect with guilty knowledge hears a question, survival instincts kick in, body movements can become restricted, and psychological discomfort may result.

Interviewers may observe these reactions as body tension, a furrowed forehead, immobile arms, disappearing or tense lips, and distancing by leaning away. At the same time, this person initiates pacifiers—any tactile self-touching, such as stroking the face, biting nails, licking lips, wringing hands, or tugging at clothing—to relieve stress.

As most parents know from caring for an infant who does not speak, the brain responds to the world around it in real time, which allows people to see or sense what others think or feel. However, each person physically responds differently to stressors. Some people show stress by excessively sweating, vigorously massaging their neck or forehead, blocking with their eyes, ventilating their shirt, or tightly grasping their legs. More subtle persons swallow hard, compress or lick their lips, conceal their neck dimple with a hand, or cover their thumbs with their fingers. Over 215 identified behaviors associated with stress and discomfort provide clues as to how a person feels when asked a question. Fear, guilt, shame, and excitement cause emotional responses that most people cannot control. These provide insight during the interview process.

Law enforcement officers must recognize the limits of lie detection. Deception can be identified only when all information is known, which usually is not the case. To guide them in their inquiries, investigators look for cues of discomfort or lack of confidence. If unknown issues or hidden information cause stress, interviewers must ask why. They should ascertain if the suspect is involved, lying, or not telling the entire story. Investigators should pursue all questions that indicate issues. A polygrapher cannot say definitively that persons have lied, only that they displayed indicators of stress when asked a question. Unfortunately, the same holds true for interviewers. That does not mean that interrogators stop asking questions. The interviewee's discomfort or lack of confidence during questioning compels knowledgeable investigators to look further.[1]

This provides powerful insight into how agents are trained to detect deception and to reveal the truth. They learn how to observe clues through gathering information and observing responses in the natural. We see this with men and women of law enforcement. What about in the Word of God?

JESUS ASKS QUESTIONS TO FURTHER DISCERN A DEMONIC ASSIGNMENT

We see throughout His ministry that Jesus functioned in a very keen ability to perceive and discern as we have already discussed and will continue to discuss throughout this book. Let's investigate a situation where He did investigative work and asked questions in order to understand fully what He was dealing with. It is the encounter with the boy who was bound by a deaf and dumb spirit that was causing violent and harmful manifestations.

> *"What are you arguing about with the religious scholars?" he asked them.*
>
> *A man spoke up out of the crowd. "Teacher," he said, "I have a son possessed by a demon that makes him mute. I brought him here to you, Jesus. Whenever the demon takes control of him, it knocks him down, and he foams at the mouth and gnashes his teeth, and his body becomes stiff as a board.*

I brought him to your disciples, hoping they could deliver him, but they were not strong enough."

Jesus said to the crowd, "Why are you such a faithless people? How much longer must I remain with you and put up with your unbelief? Now, bring the boy to me."

So they brought him to Jesus. As soon as the demon saw him, it threw the boy into convulsions. He fell to the ground, rolling around and foaming at the mouth. Jesus turned to the father and asked, "How long has your son been tormented like this?"

"Since childhood," he replied. "It tries over and over to kill him by throwing him into fire or water. But please, if you're able to do something, anything—have compassion on us and help us!"

Jesus said to him, "What do you mean 'if'? If you are able to believe, all things are possible to the believer."

When he heard this, the boy's father cried out with tears, saying, "I do believe, Lord; help my little faith!"

Now when Jesus saw that the crowd was quickly growing larger, he commanded the demon, saying, "Deaf and mute spirit, I command you to come out of him and never enter him again!" (Mark 9:16-25)

In this encounter, it is obvious that this boy was bound by a demon. We know this was something that all in proximity could see. We also read that the father had already explained about the boy's demonized condition. But still Jesus asked questions in order to gain necessary information. In verse 21, Jesus turned to the father and asked. The Greek word for *ask* is *eperotao*. It is defined as inquire, seek, and interrogate (Strong's #G1905). So here we see that Jesus inquired to gain necessary information in a situation to ensure supernatural breakthrough not only for the boy but to awaken the father and all those observing to a new level of faith.

MY TESTIMONY OF ASKING
QUESTIONS TO DISCERN

Pastor John called the U.S. Prayer Center office in Houston, Texas, where I served as assistant prayer coordinator, in urgent need of assistance. He had been ministering to a woman in his church by the name of Christina for five weeks. She was experiencing great torment, and demonic manifestations were occurring every night in her apartment. These visitations were frightening her and her three daughters. Being new to deliverance ministry, Pastor John had done all he knew in praying for Christina, but she could not gain freedom. He asked if I would help. I agreed, scheduled an appointment, and secured the team members. Pastor John and Christina arrived for the ministry session. Because the pastor and the church's deliverance team had been meeting with Christina for five weeks, I assumed that they had investigated all essential areas. Because of this, I did not ask some of the questions I normally do before agreeing to pray with someone. (I have since learned never to assume!) I did ask her to explain the torment she was experiencing. As I listened, I knew it was a stronghold of witchcraft with strong ties to voodoo practices.

The team began to minister to Christina. We prayed and asked the Lord to bring revelation of the root or pillar event that had opened a door to this stronghold of witchcraft. We asked Christina if she had been involved in witchcraft at any point in her life. What about past family members? We prayed through all these areas, broke ties, and renounced in Jesus' name, but this spirit was not budging.

Let me explain that I had assembled a power-packed team. We had all ministered together on a regular basis for several years, and it was not normal for spiritual freedom not to come quickly with this group. I could see it on the team members' faces, and I was beginning to feel it as well—we were stumped by this demon. It would not leave. I then heard the Holy Spirit speak to me. "Becca, as I instruct, ask Christina the following questions." After hearing each question in my spirit, I then voiced it to her. This had happened to me several times in previous deliverance sessions, so I knew the Lord was trying to expose something. The following dialogue transpired.

"Christina, what time of the night do these visitations happen?"

"Around midnight."

"They happen at the same time every night?"

"Yes."

"Are you and your girls asleep by this time?"

"Yes."

"Is there music playing in the house that would present an open door to these demons?"

"No."

"Are there items in your house that are attached to witchcraft or voodoo practices?"

"No."

"Christina, I will ask one more time—you have no clue why these spirits are tormenting you daily and entering your home every night and frightening your girls? You have not been in the past and are not presently involved in any type of activity that would allow this to be happening?"

"No."

"Well, Christina, the Lord wants you to tell me who is lying in bed next to you when the torment begins and the demonic visitations occur."

Christina's face instantly turned red. She raised her head, locked eyes with me, and answered, "My boyfriend."

I responded, "Christina, the Lord wants you to tell Pastor John, the team members, and myself how long you and your boyfriend have been living in sin. He also wants you to tell us the evil practices your boyfriend is involved with and performs in your apartment on a daily basis."

With an edge of defiance in her voice she replied, "We have been living together for two years, and he is a voodoo priest from Africa. He practices witchcraft in my apartment."

Needless to say, the group was stunned. I turned to the pastor and asked, "Pastor, did you have any idea this was happening?"

His face was nearly frozen in shock. "No, I did not."

"And how long have you been ministering to her?" I asked.

Now quickly growing agitated with Christina and the situation, he turned to look at her while answering my question. "Five weeks!"

I then confronted Christina. "You have abused five weeks of this pastor's time? You have taken two hours of my time? Do you know you are in blatant sin?"

"Yes."

"Then why have you submitted yourself for deliverance ministry?"

"Because," she said, "I was hoping to get breakthrough so I could continue to live with my boyfriend. He won't marry me, but I love him. I thought the deliverance might make my sin and the spirit of witchcraft easier to deal with."

I was truly shocked. "You have been using deliverance ministry to get enough temporary relief from the torment in order to go home and purposefully sin, opening yourself up once again to this demon of witchcraft?"

With a shrug she said, "Yes."

"Christina, are you willing to repent, get right with God, and break off the relationship with your boyfriend? You can do this right now.

We can then pray and get you free from this torment and a life with a voodoo priest."

"No," she said. "I will not repent, and I have no desire to break the relationship with my boyfriend. I love him."

I announced immediately that the deliverance session was over!

JOSHUA ASKED IN ORDER TO DISCERN THE ANGEL

Now when Joshua was by Jericho, he looked up, and behold, a man was standing opposite him with his drawn sword in his hand, and Joshua went to him and said to him, "Are you for us or for our adversaries?" He said, "No; rather I have come now as captain of the army of the Lord." Then Joshua fell with his face toward the earth and bowed down, and said to him, "What does my lord have to say to his servant?" The captain of the Lord's army said to Joshua, "Remove your sandals from your feet, because the place where you are standing is holy (set apart to the Lord)." And Joshua did so (Joshua 5:13-15 AMP).

Here we witness Joshua, the one anointed and appointed to lead the children of Israel to possess the promised land—the same one who led with Moses in the wilderness and who spent time in face-to-face encounters with the Lord in the tent of meeting during the 40 years of wandering in the wilderness. The children of Israel had been encamped at Gilgal, and all those who had not been circumcised during their journey through the wilderness, in a covenantal act of obedience, had fulfilled the Lord's direction to do so. They then set aside time to heal and observe Passover.

As Joshua approached Jericho, he encountered the armed man with his sword. Unaware of the stranger's identity, Joshua quickly engaged him. The word for *said* in the above scriptural reference is *amar*. It means to command or ask (Strong's #H559). It is apparent that Joshua was not discerning or perceiving the magnitude of who stood in front of him.

I find it interesting that as soon as the true identity was spoken out, Joshua did not hesitate in his response to quickly humble himself in honor of this angelic captain. This warring angel stood with him to prepare him for the battle by revealing the strategy that would secure ultimate victory. I must admit, I am a warrior. And I love that this captain of the Lord's army, in response to the covenant previously made through circumcision, was armed to show his agreement with and commissioning into battle and taking of Jericho. So here we see an example of an angel in human form and Joshua, a spiritually well-prepared warrior inquiring to discern correctly the true identity of this mighty warrior.

EVEN DEMONS CAN IDENTIFY THOSE WHO OPERATE IN THE SPIRIT OR THE FLESH

God kept releasing a flow of extraordinary miracles through the hands of Paul. Because of this, people took Paul's handkerchiefs and articles of clothing, even pieces of cloth that had touched his skin, laying them on the bodies of the sick, and diseases and demons left them and they were healed.

Now, there were seven itinerant Jewish exorcists, sons of Sceva the high priest, who took it upon themselves to use the name and authority of Jesus over those who were demonized. They would say, "We cast you out in the name of the Jesus that Paul preaches!"

One day, when they said those words, the demon in the man replied, "I know about Jesus, and I recognize Paul, but who do you think you are?"

Then the demonized man jumped on them and threw them to the ground, beating them mercilessly. He overpowered the seven exorcists until they all ran out of the house naked and badly bruised (Acts 19:11-16).

This is indeed a powerful story we are all familiar with. Let's investigate a little further for the sake of our study. The exclamation the evil spirit spoke out was, "Jesus I know and Paul I know." The Greek word for *know* is this scripture is *ginosko*. It means to be familiar with, acknowledge, or to perceive (Strong's #G1097). This is an important point to make in this study. We want to be known in the demonic realm, because if we aren't then it means we have not obtained to the authority bestowed to us as believers. Then there are those who claim to know the Lord or try to operate in authority in the flesh who have no intimacy or personal relationship with Him.

Hear me—true authority comes from a surrendered relationship with Jesus and the Holy Spirit, not just using formulas and techniques. Understand that the higher up you go on the mountain of the Lord, the closer you get to your assignment on earth. The closer you get to your assignment, the closer you get to invading that second-heaven realm of demonic resistance. Your job is to show up at the gates of influence in your assigned sphere. What matters is that you are well known in heaven. When that happens, you will be respected in the gates of influence. The truth is, evil spirits recognize the depth of relationship with our Lord. We all want to be known by evil spirits. Not for the purpose of us to be harassed, but for the intended outcome that when demons hear our voices they are struck with fear, trembling at the sound of Kingdom holiness and authority causing them to obey and leave. I love the fact that darkness knows my name and trembles when I intercede, war, prophesy, and decree.

LEARN TO DISCERN BY OBSERVATION

The truth is, we too can learn to grow in our discernment through questions and observation. I will share a more practical way that has been used for many years. Many have been involved in deliverance ministry and have used a questionnaire to learn what the open doors for demonic influence are in the life of the individual they will be ministering to. Allow me to share some of the following questions in order for us to engage in an exercise together by mapping out a portion of the questions to help identify a specific area. I will provide example answers to each question to lead us to a conclusion at the end of our investigation.

1. Was your relationship with your parents good, bad, or indifferent?

   I had a strong relationship with my mother, but relationship with my father was indifferent. I never felt or experienced a strong emotional connection with him.

2. Were you a planned child or a surprise child?

   Surprise child, and my parents spoke about this often.

3. Were you conceived out of wedlock?

   Yes. And I am the main reason why my parents married. Their marriage was never good, I felt responsible for this.

4. Were you adopted?

   No.

5. If adopted, do you know anything about your natural parents?

   N/A

6. Do you know if your mother suffered any trauma with you during her pregnancy?

   Yes. She was very sick the entire pregnancy.

7. Do you know if you suffered a difficult or complicated birth?

   Yes. I was born through a cesarean section. My mother bled extensively and required a blood transfusion.

8. Were you bonded at birth?

   According to what my parents told me, not right away. Due to her health issues during pregnancy and the complicated birth, I was whisked away to the nursery and did not get personal time with my mother for three days.

9. Were you a breast-fed baby?

   No.

10. Do you have brothers and sisters?

    One brother and one sister.

11. How was your relationship with your siblings growing up?

    Closer to my brother, distant from my sister. She never had time for me. She was very popular. I always struggled to feel accepted by her.

12. Are you a critical person?

    Sometimes I can be very critical. Especially of myself.

13. Do you feel emotionally immature?

    Yes.

14. Highlight what applies to your self-image.

    Low image

    Condemn myself

    Feel worthless

    Punish myself

    Feel insecure

Hate myself
Believe I am a failure
Question identity

15. Was your father passive, strong and manipulative, or neither?

    My father was emotionally absent. No words of affection or affirmation. He provided money for the family but was not engaged emotionally in our lives.

16. Were you close to your father?

    No.

17. Was your mother passive, strong and manipulative, or neither?

    She was strong, but not manipulative.

18. Was yours a happy home during childhood?

    Sometimes yes. Sometimes no.

19. Were you lonely as a teenager?

    Yes. I never felt received by my peers. Did not have a lot of friends.

20. Has lying or stealing been a problem to you?

    No.

21. Have you suffered an injustice in your life?

    Yes. Was greatly bullied in school.

22. Do you have trouble giving or receiving love?

    Yes.

23. Do you find it easy to communicate with persons close to you?

    No. I feel it is hard to trust people so I find it hard to communicate.

24. Do you have or have you had problems with:

    Impatience

    Pride

    Racial prejudice

    Moodiness

    Anger

    Temper

    Rebellion

25. Do you have unforgiveness, resentment, bitterness, or hatred toward anyone?

    I find myself angry with my dad for not giving emotional support. Resentful toward my sister.

    I believe I struggle with unforgiveness to those who bullied me in school.

26. Do you struggle with a cycle of broken friendships?

    Yes.

27. Do you feel no one wants to be your friend so you isolate?

    I'm afraid to trust people, so yes, I isolate.

This is an extensive list of questions. But based off of this gathered data, I would like to pose a question. Are you able to state what this person might be battling in their spiritual walk? If you answered or discerned a spirit of rejection, you are correct. By the observations drawn from these questions it is quite easy to perceive that freedom from the stronghold of rejection is needed. Let's continue by sharing a testimony by my friend Jareb Nott. In this demonstration, a way was paved to achieve keen discernment through an investigation process composed of thought-out questions that led to a great victory.

When used properly, a questionnaire is a very helpful discernment tool when utilized prior to and during deliverance sessions. The questionnaires are designed to be very thorough and help us gain a clear understanding of what strongholds we will likely need to address during the deliverance session.

For example, we often have clients send completed questionnaires that contain contradictory information. One such contradiction that shows up frequently pertains to their involvement in witchcraft activities. Many people do not fully understand what involvement in witchcraft truly means; in their minds, it means specifically that a person belonged to a witch coven or has been in the practice of casting spells, etc. Therefore, their understanding of how to answer questions pertaining to that stronghold is often wrong.

We once had a woman return a completed deliverance questionnaire that highlighted a deep witchcraft stronghold. This woman had previously sought deliverance several years ago from another ministry and received some freedom. But she was reaching out to our ministry now because there were still areas where she was tormented and had not been able to receive freedom in her life. For years, this woman dealt with frequent headaches and constantly battled a fear that she would never be good enough for God to love her or accept her. Her life was full of religious actions designed in her mind to earn favor from God and, in return, freedom and the Father's love that she greatly desired but could never grasp.

In the questionnaire she filled out prior to her session, she clearly stated that she had never been involved in occultism or witchcraft. That, combined with all of her statements pointing toward a religious spirit, could have made it seem like an open and closed case that religious bondage was the only reason why freedom had been out of reach for her for so long. Some deliverance ministers may even be inclined to move on and look for the "greater" stronghold such as a spirit of rejection or fear based on her insecure, self-doubting nature. However, the questionnaire is designed to dig deeper and gain further clarity on these important strongholds.

The very next question on the form asked her if she had ever been involved in specific witchcraft *practices*. This is where things became interesting. She then identified on the questionnaire that she had in the past directly participated in seances, Ouija boards, visited mediums, practiced astral projection, had palm readings, and practiced with spirit guides. The woman then proceeded to add written comments, indicating that their involvement with the Ouija board was an innocent one-time occasion when she was in high school many years ago. She then continued to answer more questions and specifically indicated that her grandparents were involved with Native religions as full-blooded members of the Cherokee nation. This family involvement created an open door for generational bondage and a familiar spirit of witchcraft to freely operate throughout the generational lineage of which she is included.

All of these involvements are clearly interactions with witchcraft. However, because many of these practices are deceivingly advertised as spiritual helps and self-improvement aids, they become falsely detached from what is generally believed to be involvement in witchcraft. This person's beliefs that she was not involved in witchcraft left an open door for the enemy to continue tormenting her even after completing previous deliverance sessions without a questionnaire. In this instance, using the questionnaire we were able to quickly discern that she was bound by the stronghold of divination and the familiar spirit of witchcraft.

During the deliverance session she forgave herself and her family for involvement in witchcraft and divination. I then walked her through a prayer of repentance from her willing involvement in these evil practices. Moving on she then renounced the evil things that she had done and practiced over the years. From there she broke the resulting curses and tormenting spirits that had been brought on her as a result of her willing practice. With these prayers and acknowledgements, finishing the deliverance was simply a matter of me taking the final authority over the trespassing demons of divination and witchcraft and evicting them from her life, her body, and her mind. Finally, we dealt with the familiar spirit of witchcraft in her family lineage and closing the entry points and doors where it entered, and she was miraculously set free. In that moment, we witnessed a physical transformation of this woman's countenance and body posture. At last, she had received the freedom that she had desired for so long but was thought to be out of her grasp. She was miraculously set free from a stronghold of divination and witchcraft that has been deceiving her and binding her for decades.

Today, this woman does not struggle with her identity; she is now gaining a greater understanding of her unique place in the Kingdom as a daughter of the King. The freedom she received has enabled her to see herself as a true daughter, with authority and a place in this world where she is free to use her God-given gifts and abilities to glorify God and bring healing and joy to others around her as she in turn ministers to others in her own spheres of influence.

The questionnaire did not set her free; our ability to use the questionnaire along with the Holy Spirit as a guide is what often leads to greater discernment and freedom for our ministry clients. The questionnaire should not be used as a sole technique when ministering freedom, but paired with guidance from the Holy Spirit it is a powerful tool that can be used in the process of setting captives free.

What a powerful testimony of freedom and victory. So, we clearly see that through natural observation and the process of asking questions, individuals can be radically set free and transformed. Let's now look at how we can observe in the natural and through investigative research we are able to grow in discernment at a regional level.

HOW TO GROW IN DISCERNMENT IN CITIES AND REGIONS

I have taught for many years that knowledge builds power of action. While we have spoken about discernment in the spiritual sense and will continue to discuss even further in this book, let's investigate how we are able to grow in discernment by a series of actions that we will term *spiritual research* or *mapping of regions*. While I will not give a full teaching on this topic, you can read my books *Authority to Tread* and *Glory Warfare* to gain further understanding and insight. But for the sake of learning how to grow in discernment through observations in the natural, I will discuss several key points.

A good place to start is to determine what you are seeing in the natural about the sphere of influence, city, region, or nation of interest. Is there prosperity or poverty? Or is there both? Do you see people walking in hope and joy? Or do they exhibit hope deferred or despair? Is there a high crime and death rate or abundant life? Is the region clean or dirty? Is there active idolatry? Are women and children free or oppressed? Do you see and witness God moving among the people and the churches?

Another area to obtain wisdom and insight is by researching the sphere of influence, city, region, or nation. Truth be told, satan is a strategist. While this thought might make some uncomfortable, the reality is he and his army of darkness are busy implementing their strategies. Therefore, we must learn to be strategists. In order to do so we must learn his evil and demonic schemes so that he might not outwit or outmaneuver us. Effectual and victorious prayer strategies often come from informed deliverance and informed intercession empowering us to pray on site with insight. Think of it this way—when special ops teams go into a battle to discover and to defeat a ruthless and evil tyrant, they do so in an undercover hidden tactic. It occurs under the radar. And more times than not the enemy's stronghold and defense has no clue the special ops team has advanced until the target is under fire and being overtaken in a time of defeat. In order to do this, there are hours of investigation, undercover work, research, studying the movement of the tyrant and his accompanying battalion. This is the type of warfare tactics we are to operate in. So, what are key points we can investigate at a regional level for the purpose of forming an effective and victorious strategy?

1. Who were the original inhabitants of the land and what happened to them? Who or how did they worship?

2. Is there idolatry in the region? If so, who is it that is being worshiped?

3. Is freemasonry at the foundation?

4. Why was the city established? Is there a history of purity or corruption at the foundation? Was the government established on Kingdom principles?

5. What were the principles at the foundation? Were they ungodly or Kingdom in focus? Or a mixture of both?

6. Is there trauma at the foundation of the city?

7. Were there corrupt practices and broken covenants?

8. Were there pacts made with evil?

9. Was there a dedication to the Lord and His purposes?

10. Is there violence, trauma, and bloodshed?

11. Is there rampant sexual perversion?

12. Has the economy and economic structure been established in a Kingdom paradigm or is it built on greed and robbing God's Kingdom plan?

13. What are the prophetic words concerning the region? Have they come to pass? If not, what is the Lord's strategy to see breakthrough come and prophetic destiny released?

14. Have righteous root covenants been established throughout the history of the region?

15. Have there been moves of awakening and transformation?

These are all focuses of study, research, and investigation in order to pray from an informed position. This gathered data is then combined with spiritual insight such as dreams, visions, and prophetic strategies birthed in prayer. This provides a focus that hits the mark in the Spirit and realizes great victories. The following is a powerful testimony at a regional level that effected legislation for the entire nation.

Patsy's Testimony

In 2010, I was on a prayer assignment with Rebecca Greenwood and several other team members in Dallas, Texas. One of the places we researched and felt we needed to pray at was the Cathedral Shrine of the Virgin of Guadalupe. This is the cathedral church of the Roman Catholic diocese of Dallas, Texas. It is the mother church of the 630,000 Roman Catholics in nine-county dioceses of Dallas. It is the second largest cathedral congregation in the nation, second only to St. Patrick's Cathedral in New York City, and it has 25,000 registered families. It is one of seven basilicas/cathedrals/shrines built for devotion to the Virgin of Guadalupe of Mexico.

The mother church in Mexico is the most visited Queen of Heaven shrine in the world. Seven million people from the Americas visit the Virgin of Guadalupe every year. The shrine was built in the rubble of an ancient pagan temple in a village near Mexico City. The belief system was taken from a vision encountered by an Aztec peasant of a young girl he claimed was the Virgin Mary. The lady asked for a church to be built at that site in her honor. When the church was erected, they took the worship of Aztec and Mayan deities and combined their symbols into their new idol, which they named the Virgin or Our Lady of Guadalupe. One of the deities morphed into the idol was Ixchel, the goddess of medicine, childbirth, and war. Although she was the goddess of childbirth, in the ancient worship of this entity they would sacrifice 12-year-old virgins by throwing them into the cenotes to drown. This was done as a sacrifice to appease and empower Ixchel's hold. Therefore, she was also the entity of childbirth and child sacrifice.

Our team visited the cathedral church in downtown Dallas and prayed there. We felt we needed to cut, sever, and destroy the ley lines and power grids connecting the cathedral in Dallas to the mother church in Mexico and every influence it has over God's people. (For further understanding of ley lines and power grids you can find further information in my books *Authority to Tread* and *Glory Warfare*.) The day we visited the cathedral it was crowded, which made it more difficult to find a private area to pray. As we were leaving, I was walking beside Becca and mentioned to her that I didn't feel we completed everything that needed to be done on this assignment. She agreed, and because I'm from Texas she asked me to come back, bring a team, and finish the task. I did not forget, but the timing didn't present itself for a period of time.

On June 24, 2018, I was asked to be on a prayer team to pray against abortion inside the old United States District Court for the Northern District of Texas in Dallas—the location where Roe v. Wade was held. It is not an active courtroom now and special permission is needed to get in. The judge's original bench is still there. Our small team spent about two hours inside that courtroom adding our prayers to the many others who have prayed against abortion.

On July 27, 2019, I was leading an assignment in downtown Dallas for Becca's Strategic Prayer Apostolic Network (SPAN). I knew the timing was right for us to go back to the Cathedral Shrine of the Virgin of Guadalupe and finish the assignment there. During research, I found that the site where the cathedral is located today is not the original location. After completing our prayers at the cathedral, we decided to pray at the original site.

When we walked up to the location my heart started pounding. It was the exact location of the courthouse where Roe v. Wade was held. What a revelation from God! This changed our whole course of prayers from that location as we connected the root of the death spirit of Our Lady of Guadalupe to abortion. On January 3, 2020, we saw on Facebook the following article: "200-plus members of Congress asked the Supreme

Court to 'reconsider' legal abortion rights. The lawmakers, who are mostly Republican men signed an amicus brief urging the court to reconsider Roe v. Wade as well as a 1992 ruling barring laws putting an 'undue burden' on abortion access. The brief comes ahead of arguments in an abortion case that will consider a Louisiana law that was passed in 2014 but never enacted. If enacted, the law would severely restrict abortion access by imposing stricter requirements on doctors providing abortions. Lawmakers who signed the brief argue that Roe v. Wade and the decisions that stemmed from it are too obscure and opaque, leaving judges unable to determine how to apply the rulings. The Supreme Court will hear oral arguments on the Louisiana case."

On March 9, 2020, I was part of a team that once again gained access to the courtroom in Dallas where Roe v. Wade was held. We worshiped and made many decrees and declarations that took on new meaning and power since the revelation of the Queen of Heaven's altar being on that site. The timeframe of this assignment was over a period of ten years, which included several combined initiatives. This is a good example of how important it is to continue to research and discern what the Lord is saying in each assignment, make connections, and continue to push through until you have breakthrough!

NOTE

1.   Joe Navarro, M.A., "Perspective: Detecting Deception," *Law Enforcement Bulletin*, August 1, 2012, https://leb.fbi.gov/articles/perspective/perspective-detecting-deception.

Chapter Six

DISCERNING ANGELS

Are not all angels ministering spirits sent to
serve those who will inherit salvation?
—HEBREWS 1:14 NIV

It was by far the most difficult night of my life. My father, Ronnie Long, had passed away four hours earlier. My mother and I had returned to their home in East Texas, while the rest of the family would make their way the next day. It was an extremely emotional moment to walk back in the home for the first time without my father. Just no words. Now, my dad was a strong believer and Christian; we knew he was with the Lord, but how difficult were those "firsts" without him. We were tired from the previous sleepless week spent in the hospital with my dad and decided that we must try to rest and sleep, considering that the next few days were going to be even busier planning his memorial service. I ensured my mother was settled in her room and asleep before making my way to the guest bedroom.

As I sat on the bed, I admit I was emotionally overwhelmed and numb all at the same time. You see, I had always been a daddy's girl. I loved my father. He was a wonderful, wise, kind, patient, fun, and loving father. I just could not imagine what life was going to be like without his physical presence. As I laid my head on the pillow in an attempt to sleep, I heard a sound and felt a presence. So much so, I sat up in bed and listened intently to what I was hearing. "What is that sound?"

Quickly, I decided to check on my mother. I walked to her room and stood outside her bedroom door. All was quiet. But now it seemed as if the sound was coming from the family room or maybe the dining room. As I entered the dining room I continued into the kitchen as I felt an overwhelming feeling of love and peace drawing me in that direction. Suddenly, I could feel a supernatural presence of peace, joy, and love that enveloped me. At this moment I was clearly engaged in the spirit realm and realized I was hearing and sensing the presence of ministering angels. Suddenly, I heard these words and my father's voice, "I am good, Becca. Be strong. Be courageous. All is well." Then I heard voices speaking in the tongues of angels and felt the holiness of pure emotion of rejoicing surrounding me. Suddenly their voices quickly grew more and more distant. Overcome and overwhelmed, I fell in a heap on the kitchen floor and began to weep tears motivated by awe and gratitude.

How beautiful it was that the Lord sent me this encounter and message from my father along with His ministering angels. I shared this story with my mother the next morning. We both wept tears of joy. This angelic encounter brought us great comfort and peace in a time of the sudden and unexpected loss of my father. These moments genuinely cause the following truth to come to light—that the veil between eternity and the natural realm is truly a thin place.

WORKS OF ANGELS

In the above encounter, I did not see these angels, but I discerned their presence and heard their voices as described by Paul, "The tongues of men and of angels" (1 Cor. 13:1 NASB). The Bible is replete with testimonies of angelic encounters with the saints of God. So let's continue to discover the different areas we see in scripture in which angels work and share insight and testimonies to empower us to discern each of these angelic activities. Keep in mind this is not an exhaustive account concerning these heavenly agents. But I have tried to include the most significant roles that we are all graced to encounter.

Angels Are Messengers

The Greek word for *angels* in the Bible is *aggelos* (Strong's #G32). The Hebrew word for *angels* is *malak* (Strong's #H4397). Both words translate to mean "messenger." In the simplest terms, angels are both God's messengers and God's message. They will always carry His message and fulfill the mission He has sent them to accomplish. Billy Graham shares concerning the role of these divine angels:

> Angels belong to a uniquely different dimension of creation which we, limited to the natural order, can scarcely comprehend. In this angelic domain the limitations are different from those God has imposed on our natural order. He has given angels higher knowledge, power and mobility than us. Have you ever seen or met one of those superior beings called angels? They are God's messengers whose chief business is to carry out His orders in the world. He has given them an ambassadorial charge. He has designed and empowered them as holy deputies to perform works of righteousness. In this way they assist Him as their Creator while He sovereignly controls the universe. He has given them the capacity to bring His holy enterprises into a successful conclusion.[1]

Angels Are Bearers of God

Angels not only bring messages, but they also bring the presence of heaven and eternity. And it appears that within an initial encounter some experience an overwhelming awe and reverence when seeing an angelic being sent from heaven, evidenced by them falling face down in the presence of holiness angels bring. We spoke of this in Chapter Four, when Joshua encountered the commander of the Lord's heavenly army. Their messages are pregnant and pulsate with the presence and holiness of God. Sometimes they don't even have to say anything, but the essence of who they are and whose presence they live in communicates the love, guidance, comfort, holiness, presence, fire, and glory of the Lord.

Angels Bring Answers to Prayer

In Acts 12, we clearly discover that angels assist God in answering prayers. It was during the time when King Herod had incited persecution against the church to such a degree that, "He even had the apostle Jacob, John's brother, beheaded" (Acts 12:2). Upon this horrible act, Herod quickly realized that this action greatly pleased the Jewish leaders and decided to have Peter arrested and thrown into prison during Passover. He was so aggressive to ensure that Peter would not escape, he assigned sixteen soldiers to guard him until he could be brought to public trial. "Immediately after the Passover celebrations were over. The church went into a season of intense intercession, asking God to free him" (Acts 12:4-5). Let's continue to read the story as it is so beautifully told in *The Passion Translation*.

> *The night before Herod planned to bring him to trial, he made sure that Peter was securely bound with two chains. Peter was sound asleep between two soldiers, with additional guards stationed outside his cell door, when all at once an angel of the Lord appeared, filling his prison cell with a brilliant light. The angel struck Peter on the side to awaken him and said, "Hurry up! Let's go!" Instantly the chains fell off his wrists. The angel told him, "Get dressed. Put on your sandals, bring your cloak, and follow me."*

Peter quickly left the cell and followed the angel, even though he thought it was only a dream or a vision, for it seemed unreal—he couldn't believe it was really happening! They walked unseen past the first guard post and then the second before coming to the iron gate that leads to the city—and the gate swung open all by itself right in front of them! They went out into the city and were walking down a narrow street when all of a sudden the angel disappeared. That's when Peter realized that he wasn't having a dream! He said to himself, "This is really happening! The Lord sent his angel to rescue me from the clutches of Herod and from what the Jewish leaders planned to do to me" (Acts 12:6-11).

What a powerful testimony. You see, Peter discerned that he was encountering an angel in spite of the fact that he thought it was in a dream. Isn't it beautiful how the angel brought Peter and the entire praying church into a supernatural encounter in response to intercession! The angel delivered the miraculous answer to prayer.

Angels Provide Protection and Deliverance

God sends angels with special orders to protect you wherever you go, defending you from all harm (Psalm 91:11).

When he came near the den, he called to Daniel in an anguished voice, "Daniel, servant of the living God, has your God, whom you serve continually, been able to rescue you from the lions?"

Daniel answered, "May the king live forever! My God sent his angel, and he shut the mouths of the lions. They have not hurt me, because I was found innocent in his sight. Nor have I ever done any wrong before you, Your Majesty" (Daniel 6:20-22 NIV).

The attacks of satan and his army of darkness, who in their evil schemes desire to harass us incessantly, would often be thwarted if we as believers would grasp the assurance that His mighty angels are always nearby wanting to help. Sadly, many believers have failed to accept this fact so frequently expressed in the Bible. You see, God dispatches His angels to protect us from harm. We should be encouraged and strengthened to know that the angels are watching. They mark our paths. They oversee the events of our lives and protect the interests of our Lord, always working to promote His plans and to bring about His highest destiny for each of us. What good news this is! Our heavenly Father assigns angelic powers to watch over us. I have testimony after testimony that attests to this fact.

It was 2013, I was ministering in the city of Nairobi, Kenya. It was late as we left the church from the meeting that night. The pastor hired a taxi, giving the driver the address of the hotel. We began to make our way down the unkept roads of the city center. This particular day, there was great tension and fighting occurring between the city bus drivers and taxi drivers. The bus drivers felt they were losing too much business to the taxi drivers and were not happy about the situation. While stopped at a street corner, we were suddenly surrounded by buses being driven by unhappy men. They literally encircled our taxi, making it impossible for us to move. Our driver was noticeably nervous.

After a few minutes passed, which produced no foreseeable hope of this scene changing, he suggested we get out and walk the rest of the way. I instantly heard the Lord say, "Do not get out of this taxi in the midst of this angry display." I told him, "No, we are not going to do that. It would endanger us."

He responded, "I am not going to be able to get you out of this situation and to the hotel."

I gently and confidently replied, "But I know someone who will make a way out of this situation. We all must begin to pray and now!" I turned to my friend and traveling companion, Pam, and said, "Pray in tongues out loud now!" So we both began to pray in the Spirit. I then entreated the Lord, "Lord, send an angel to deliver us from this situation."

Suddenly, from nowhere, in the middle of the circle of buses appeared what looked like a kind and wise elderly man. Friends, I am here to tell you that he just appeared behind the taxi and made his way to the window of the driver. He motioned for him to roll down his window. He calmly and confidently stated, "I will get you out of here." He walked to the bus directly behind us. Tapped on the door motioning for the driver to open it. They had what appeared to be a calm and brief exchange in which the bus driver gladly began to pull forward making a slight open space for our taxi driver to maneuver through in order for us to exit the increasingly volatile scene. All the while this elderly man was directing the taxi driver on how far to back up, how sharp to turn the wheel. He did this until we were safely outside the ring of buses.

As I turned to wave and thank the man he had vanished.

The taxi driver quickly quizzed me, "Did you see where that man went? He is gone. Where did he go?"

I joyfully responded, "Friend, the Lord answered our prayer. He sent an angel to deliver us out of this danger."

"You ladies pray different than what I have been taught. You prayed, the Lord sends an angel, and we are delivered out of danger!"

We had a powerful time of witnessing and prayer with our taxi driver before leaving the cab to enter our hotel. You see, angels will come to us in times of need and distress to encourage and release a message, and they are faithful to deliver us out of danger.

Angels Can Appear in Human Form

I believe, whether we realize it or not, that we have all entertained angels who appear in human form. Hebrews 13:2 clearly shares, "Show hospitality to strangers, for they may be angels from God showing up as your guests." Many translations will express it as, "Some have entertained angels unawares." Greg and I have encountered several occasions when we know beyond any doubt that an angel was sent by the Lord, appearing as a human to aid us. The above testimony from Kenya was one of them and the following testimony shared by my friend Dawn Reece is another.

Angels Distribute Supernatural Provision

He lay down and slept under a juniper tree; and behold, there was an angel touching him, and he said to him, "Arise, eat." Then he looked and behold, there was at his head a bread cake baked on hot stones, and a jar of water. So he ate and drank and lay down again. The angel of the Lord came again a second time and touched him and said, "Arise, eat, because the journey is too great for you." So he arose and ate and drank, and went in the strength of that food forty days and forty nights to Horeb, the mountain of God (1 Kings 19:5-8 NASB).

The Lord uses angels to bring supernatural provision as seen in this encounter between the angel and Elijah. He had just defeated and executed the prophets of Baal and also prayed to see the supernatural ending of the drought. As Ahab reported the great exploits to Jezebel, she was angry and sent her servant to tell Elijah she would end his life as he had ended the lives of the prophets of Baal. Therefore, Elijah fled to Beersheba and asked the Lord to take his life. But the Lord had other plans in mind for Elijah and sent the angel of the Lord to nourish him in his time of need. Below is a beautiful testimony of provision and aid in a time of loss and uncertainty in the life of my beautiful friend Dawn Reece.

> I was in a completely overwhelmed time in my life. It seemed like if anything could go wrong it did. I was on my way to the grocery store with my daughter when I heard something loud dragging below my vehicle. When I got to the store, I looked underneath and realized it was the cover plate that had partially broken off and was dragging. And that was the straw that nearly broke me.
>
> I walked into the store at my breaking point and standing in the produce section I lifted my hands to heaven. With tears streaming down my face I cried out to God, "Lord, when I lost my husband You said You would take care of every detail of my life. Well, I need help now and I don't know what to do. *I need You!*" Peace came over me; I lowered my arms and did my grocery shopping.
>
> When we walked out of the store, I remembered my dilemma and looked underneath the vehicle again to see if I could crawl under there and remove it. There happened to be a homeless person with a cardboard sign sitting next to the front entrance. He saw me, jumped up, and asked if he could help. Before I could barely tell him my issue, he crawled underneath my vehicle onto the oil-covered parking lot and removed it for me. I was actually a little horrified because he was wearing off-white linen clothing. I knew his back was going to be covered in that oil.
>
> I thanked him with tears in my eyes and offered him some money. Then Kelsea and I drove off. We hadn't even made it out of the parking lot when we both looked at each other as it suddenly dawned on us what had just happened! What

homeless person wears perfect off-white linen? And has a ruddy, glowing complexion! We both said, "Oh my goodness, *that was an angel!*" We immediately turned around and went back to the store but he was gone. We drove all around and he had completely disappeared!

When I had hit my breaking point and called out to Jesus, He was there. He sent a ministering angel to provide for us and help us out! I know today there are so many of you who are struggling. But the Lord is there, He hears you, and He will most definitely help you! All you have to do is call out His Name!

Angels Are Ministering Spirits, Sent to Minister for Us

And behold, one who resembled the sons of men touched my lips. Then I opened my mouth and spoke and said to him who was standing before me, "O my lord, because of the vision anguish has come upon me, and I have retained no strength. For how can such a [weakened] servant of my lord talk with such [a being] as my lord? For now there remains no strength in me, nor has any breath been left in me." Then the one (Gabriel) whose appearance was like that of a man touched me again, and he strengthened me. He said, "O man, highly regarded and greatly beloved, do not be afraid. Peace be to you; take courage and be strong." Now when he had spoken to me, I was strengthened and said, "Let my lord speak, for you have strengthened me" (Daniel 10:16-19 AMP).

Angels are involved in the ministry of comfort, mercy, and service. As we read above, Gabriel appeared to Daniel to refresh him following his fast and warfare intercession for God's purposes to be released in the earth. The resulting encounter and vision caused great anguish of which Gabriel spoke and released divine peace. Remember, it is not just what they say, but how they say it. They bring the *shalom* presence of the Lord. *Shalom* means peace, but it also means everything the presence of the Lord brings and imparts to us such as welfare, health, prosperity, peace (Strong's #H7965). Just as Daniel needed this encounter and word of strength and peace, I can truthfully say I have experienced an angelic encounter and message of shalom peace as a result of a message written on a scroll sent by a ministering angel.

I was speaking at a conference in 2014. It had been an intense season of ministry. I had been intentionally and seriously seeking the Lord over our calling to nations and was needing clear direction and peace as we continued to move forward. Shawn Bolz was also ministering at the conference. We had not met until he arrived for the evening session he was assigned at the gathering.

As Shawn has done for several years now, he began to minster very deep, profound prophetic words. I was rejoicing as I witnessed many of my friends receive such beautiful, life-giving hope messages from the Father's heart. Soon, Shawn asked if the date August 20 was significant to any of us in the room. Thinking the word was for someone else I scanned the room looking for the raised hand. Shawn once again asked the question. I suddenly realized that date was significant to me. It is the date Greg and I were married. I raised my hand and shared this fact with Shawn. He then began to call out my daughters by name and also their birth dates. He shared beautiful words concerning their destinies. He prophesied about our calling to China bringing great clarity and confirmation.

He then made a statement, "I am really going to step out on a limb right now. As I was flying here today an angel appeared to me with a scroll in his hand with the following words written on it. I have no idea what they mean, but can I read them to you?"

I quickly replied, "Yes!" When he spoke of seeing this angel with the scroll in hand, a holy presence was settling in the room and the anointing was weighing heavy on me. I began trembling in my seat in response to the holy presence now enveloping me.

He spoke the written words, "Goin' to China or maybe Siam, they call me a dreamer; well, maybe I am." With genuine curiosity he asked, "Do those words mean anything to you?"

By this time, I was doubled over in my chair, tears gently streaming down my face. "Yes. Those are the words to a song my father used to sing to my sister and I when we were little girls. It is titled 'Far Away Places.'" I was undone.

Shawn, also emotionally impacted, replied, "Oh, this is such a holy moment."

Even scribing this testimony, I feel the presence, peace, comfort, and holiness I felt that night. An angel of the Lord sent a message of great peace and comfort to me from the eternal realm. I call this experience *a kiss from heaven*. It brought and imparted great peace to keep moving into the nations the Lord was calling me into. Angels can and are used to minister to us when sent by our heavenly Father.

Angels Rejoice When a Sinner's Heart Is Saved

> *That's the way God responds every time one lost sinner repents and turns to him. He says to all his angels, "Let's have a joyous celebration, for that one who was lost I have found!"* (Luke 15:10)

Seeing someone receive the gift of salvation is such a beautiful, supernatural experience. There have been many times when I have led someone to the Lord at the altar. As one who hears in the Spirit, I have heard upon several occasions the rejoicing of the angels as the newly saved soul encounters Jesus and the security of forgiveness and eternity is made manifest. Angels are sent to partner with us in reaping the harvest!

Angels Assist God and Us in Shaping History

We see numerous encounters in the Bible in which angels were sent to release messages, but also to secure victory and to shape history. The truth is our heavenly Father uses angels to work out the destinies of men and nations. He has altered the courses of busy political and social arenas of our society and directed the destinies of men numerous times. We must understand and be aware that angels keep in close and vital contact with all that is unfolding in the earth. Their knowledge of earthly matters exceeds that of men. We must acknowledge their invisible presence and unceasing labors.

We know Gabriel appeared to Mary and shared that she would birth Jesus. An angel came to Joseph telling him to still follow through with his marriage to Mary. He also warned Joseph to take Mary and Jesus and flee to Egypt and also when to return home. We will discuss this further in this chapter, but Michael battled the Prince of Persia so the angel of the Lord could deliver a message of breakthrough to Daniel. There was the encounter when the angel of the Lord stood between Moses and the children of Israel and Pharaoh and his army. The angel did so to stop Pharaoh's intent to recapture the nation of Israel as slaves and to help secure the new era of freedom for Moses and God's chosen people. And again, as seen in Exodus 23:20-24, the Lord sent an angel to guard and lead the way for Moses and the children of Israel.

> *Behold, I am going to send an Angel before you to keep and guard you on the way and to bring you to the place I have prepared. Be on your guard before Him, listen to and obey His voice; do not be rebellious toward Him or provoke Him, for He will not pardon your transgression, since My Name*

(authority) is in Him. But if you will indeed listen to and truly obey His voice and do everything that I say, then I will be an enemy to your enemies and an adversary to your adversaries. When My Angel goes before you and brings you to [the land of] the Amorite, the Hittite, the Perizzite, the Canaanite, the Hivite, and the Jebusite, I will reject them and completely destroy them. You shall not bow down to worship their gods, nor serve them, nor do [anything] in accordance with their practices. You shall completely overthrow them and break down their [sacred] pillars and images [of pagan worship] (AMP).

Here the Lord is directing Moses and revealing clearly that God wants obedience and that the angel was prepared to go with them. It is obvious that the angel knew the plan as the Lord had prepared him. And it is evident that he carried the Lord's authority. He was assigned to bring Moses and the children of Israel into the conquest of the land that the Lord had promised as their inheritance. I appreciate the following teaching from my friend Kevin Zadai in his book *The Agenda of Angels*:

Although that angel was not always visible to the children of Israel, there was a hidden agenda—the angel was assigned to bring them into the land that God had prepared for them. We must always remember that though an angel is not always visible, God asks people to be aware of the angel, to obey his voice, and not to provoke him. Therefore, by this example we know that we are not to provoke angels. God even goes as far to say that we are not to disobey him because he will not pardon such transgressions for God's name was in him. The good thing about the angel in this situation was that God clearly stated that if you obey the angel, the Lord says that He will be an enemy to our enemies as well as an adversary to our adversaries. The angel was going to go before them and cut off their enemies. The Lord has promised that these angels will help to overthrow our enemies and completely break down the secret pillars that uphold our enemies. It is obvious that working with angels is something that really happens for those who choose to walk in the spirit. We must not faint or hold back from God's call and mission. We must be confident that angels are present to help us when we do what God has ordained us to do.[2]

History-Shaping Angels Assigned to Me

I will share further about this prayer assignment in Chapter Eight, but we had just experienced a tangible, amazing breakthrough and victory as a result of a mission revealed in an open vision the Lord caused me to see. Not only did I see the vision, it was as if I was in the vision while it was playing out. To make a long story short, trust me when I say that the prayer assignment the Lord directed us to engage in that evening was historic. As we finished praying and making our way back to the car, the country dirt road we walked down was alive with supernatural spirit realm activity. On the left side of the road there were demons standing side by side facing us in a stance of trying to intimidate. But on the right side of the road, warrior and defender angels were also standing side by side facing toward us and the demons, in a stance of defending and protecting. Why was there so much spiritual activity and a showdown occurring in our midst? Because an exacting blow of defeat was issued to an ancient principality that had gripped that region.

The following morning in the church service at Global Vision Faith Center, we experienced an open heaven and weighty glory. At one moment, the Lord's presence was so holy that we were all prostrate on the floor. I felt and heard the presence of angels. There were four that surrounded me. One in front, one behind, one on the left, and one on the right. In a vision, my eyes were opened in order to see them. The Lord spoke to me, "These angels are now assigned to you and will be with you wherever you go. They are warrior angels, sent on assignment to defend and ward off all attacks of the enemy and to help in your ministry of making history as a prophet and prophetic intercessor to the nations."

Friends, I can honestly say they have been with me since. Although I might not see them all the time, I know they are there. I have heard multiple times from those who see clearly and consistently in the spirit realm that angels are with me on the platform as I minister. And another beautiful experience I have had since that evening is the sound of the worship through these angels in partnership with our worship and intercession as we advance in prophetic and strategic warfare assignments in the nations. Not only do I hear the singing, but the clashing of swords when we pray to break strongholds. This does not occur all the time, but to be truthful it does quite frequently.

Personal Angels

> The angel of the Lord encamps around those who fear Him [with awe-inspired reverence and worship Him with obedience], and He rescues [each of] them (Psalm 34:7 AMP).

The Word of God clearly tells us that our heavenly Father commands angels concerning us. These angels will guard us and encamp around those who fear Him. We have always been very aware of those angels that the Lord has guarding each of us in our family. Allow me to share one of my favorite testimonies of our daughter Kendall when she was the age of four. Some of you will already know this testimony and are very familiar with it. But oh, how awesome and special it is and what a great encouragement it will be to those who have not heard it. Kendall is a seer, and it became evident that this was the case in her life from an incredibly young age. She would speak of activities in the spirit realm that a child her age would have no gauge for or ability to explain unless she was truly discerning and seeing.

Kendall Sees the Angels

Kendall, our oldest daughter, was four years old. I was cooking dinner and suggested that she clean her room. Being a happy and obedient child, she quickly agreed. Within a short amount of time, she returned to the kitchen, stood with her hands on her hips tapping her foot as if she was mad.

"Momma, you want to know what just happened?"

"Sure, baby. What?"

"Momma, you told me to clean my room. Well, there was one of those little bad things. You know, Momma, those bad things in my room."

"Honey, do you mean a demon?" Let me interject before I go further that we did not talk about demons and darkness in our home around our young children, because we did not want to frighten them. But our oldest daughter has always been sensitive to the spirit realm and began seeing in the spirit realm at a very young age.

"Yes, Momma, that bad thing. You know what it said to me?"

Not liking the thought that a demon was in my baby's room, I quickly replied, "Yes, baby. I do want to know what it said to you."

Tapping her foot quicker and harder, "Well, it told me not to clean my room!"

Having my complete attention, I asked her what she did.

Smiling in pleasure she replied, "Well, I stomped on its head and told it no in Jesus' name! And you know what, Momma? It *disdappeared!*" (She could not pronounce "disappeared" correctly. In her four-year-old vocabulary, it was pronounced "disdappeared.") "And you want to know something else, Momma?"

Totally intrigued and wondering what else she would say, "Yes, baby. I do want to know something else."

With total confidence in her wisdom and understanding, she began to teach me. "Momma, we all have angels. You have angel, Daddy has angel, and the babies have angels. And, Momma, the angels help us. They have that pointy, shiny thing, Momma. You know the thing they hold that is shiny."

"Baby, do you mean a sword?"

"Yes, Momma, that! You know what, Momma? They take that sword and do this!" I observed as my four-year-old daughter acted out an angel using a sword as if in a spiritual battle. She then exclaimed, "And Momma, when the angels do that, the demons *disdappear* (disappear)! Momma, you want to know something else?"

Wondering what else would flow out of that baby's mouth, I quickly replied, "Yes, I do!"

"Momma, those demons do not like you and Daddy. No, not at all! You know what they do when you pray in Jesus' name?"

"No, baby. What do they do?"

"Well, Momma, they do this." Enacting her story, my daughter began to aggressively shake her body as if nervous and in a loud voice exclaimed, "*Aaaaagggghhhhhh!* And then they disdappear! Momma, those demons don't like you and Daddy. No, not at all!"

My daughter happily left the kitchen to return to cleaning her room. Stunned and amazed, I called my husband explaining that I just had a spiritual warfare 101 lesson conducted and taught by our four-year-old daughter!

I love to share this testimony due to the beauty it exhibits when there is childlike faith involved. Listen to the level of discernment and faith of a four-year-old. I fully believe many of us were this sensitive when we were younger, but were un-taught the gift of discernment, seeing, and hearing because we were told the things we were seeing and hearing in the spirit were not real. "It was just your imagination." But look at the faith a of four-year-old concerning spiritual authority. If a seer child this age can exhibit this level of confidence in the Lord and His angels, then, oh, friend, how much more should we! Out of the mouth of babes we shall learn.

Warrior Angels

> But the prince of the kingdom of Persia was standing in opposition to me for twenty-one days. Then, behold, Michael, one of the chief [of the celestial] princes, came to help me, for I had been left there with the kings of Persia (Daniel 10:13 AMP).

Here we see that Michael, the archangel, was sent to engage the Prince of Persia, an ancient principality holding Babylon captive and blocking the answer to Daniel's prayer. The Hebrew word for *archangel* is *sar*. It means "representative of the king, commander, military officer, governor, ruler" (Strong's #H8269). Michael is the elite of the elite of the military and commanding angel armies. He is the top commander of the elite forces of heaven. And he is sent to contend with the prince or chief principality positioned in the second heaven over Babylon. Why? He is, as it were, the prime minister in God's administration of the universe and is the *angel administrator* of God for judgment.

You see, angels are the ones who do administrate judgments of the Lord. In this instance, Michael was dispatched in order to ensure breakthrough so that the angel of the Lord was able to deliver the answer to Daniel's prayer. In fact, some Bible students and scholars have speculated that Michael cast lucifer and his fallen angels out of heaven, and Michael enters into conflict with satan, his principalities, and evil angels in our present time to destroy their power and to give us—God's people,

Ekklesia—the expectation of and assurance of our secured ultimate victory. To be honest, I love this! It makes me shout a big hallelujah as I type this on the page. Friends, hear those words again as they are worth repeating. And don't just hear them but receive them. *Michael enters into conflict with satan, his principalities, and evil agents in our present time to destroy their power and to give us—God's people, the Ekkleisa—the expectation of and assurance of our secure ultimate victory.* Thank You, Lord!

Defender Angels

One of my favorite Scriptures of the many that reference God's protector and defender angels is Second Kings 6:15-17:

> *The servant of the man of God got up early and went out, and behold, there was an army with horses and chariots encircling the city. Elisha's servant said to him, "Oh no, my master! What are we to do?" Elisha answered, "Do not be afraid, for those who are with us are more than those who are with them." Then Elisha prayed and said, "Lord, please, open his eyes that he may see." And the Lord opened the servants eyes and he saw; and behold, the mountain was full of horses and chariots of fire surrounding Elisha* (AMP).

What a powerful encounter! The king of Syria had dispatched his army to Dothan, learning the prophet Elisha was there. Upon dressing in the morning, Elisha's servant exclaimed nervously and excitedly that that the countryside was teemed with armies and implements of war prepared for battle. Elisha exhorted him, "Don't be afraid! Those who are with us are more than those who are with them." In other words, our army is bigger than theirs! Elisha then prayed that the Lord would open the eyes of this young man to see the multitudes of protector and defender angels.

His eyes were opened, and he saw the truth of the spiritual forces gathered to defend their safety and to secure victory.

The beauty of this story is that the spiritual reality of God's army became real to Elisha's servant once Elisha asked the Lord to open his eyes. Elisha already had the spiritual sight and wisdom to know. His faith did not need to be adjusted. We clearly see that when the spiritual eyes of understanding and discernment were opened to his servant, his fears of loss vanished.

I want every reader to hear this truth—there are more for us than are against us. Our army is bigger than theirs! Our army is bigger and stronger than any assembled army of darkness. What a powerful Kingdom inheritance and promise for each of us. These defender angels are sent to bring messages, serve as ambassadors, defend, protect, keep, act as watchmen, preserve, and set in order our course of life, journey, pathway, and course of action. Thank You, Lord, that we are never alone.

What Angels Do Not Do and Do Not Want

Let's discuss briefly what angels do not do in order to help us increase in our discernment in supernatural encounters. The Lord's angels never change scripture and their messages will never contradict scripture. Angels do not want to be worshiped. They want all worship, honor, and glory to be to our heavenly Father, the Most High God, and Jesus. The entire book of Revelation was delivered to John by angels. Revelation 1:1 says: *"He* [Jesus] *made it* [the revelation] *known by sending his angel to his servant John"* (NIV). As we read near the end of this encounter, we discover that John was so overcome by what had been delivered to him he fell down at the feet of the angel to worship before him. Let's read the full encounter.

> *I, John, am the one who heard and saw these things, and*
> *when I heard and saw it all, I fell facedown to worship the*

messenger who showed me these things. But he said to me, "Don't do it! I am but a fellow servant with you and your brothers, the prophets, and with those who cling to the words of this book. Worship God!" (Revelation 22:8-9)

This scripture paints a clear picture. Angels do not want to be worshiped. Angels are not to be objects of prayer. They may help in releasing the message, breakthrough, or answer to prayer, but they are not to be prayed to. Angels do not desire to draw attention to themselves. They often do things in secret. They may get our attention, but they do so on behalf of God and the assignment He has prepared for them to accomplish on our behalf. Angels do not violate the free will of humans. God uses angels to guide us, not to control us; to teach us, but not to dictate to us; to protect us, but not to violate our free will. However, it is clear in scripture that when an angel delivers a command or instruction from heaven we are to obey: "You have been given the law by the visitation of angels, but you have not obeyed it" (Acts 7:53). The Greek word for *visitation* in this scripture is *diatage,* which stems from the root word *diatasso.* Together both mean "to command, give an ordinance, or to decree, appoint, ordain" (Strong's #G1296 and #G1299).

THERE ARE MORE FOR US THAN AGAINST US

While we look not at the things which are seen, but at the things which are not seen; for the things which are seen are temporal, but the things which are not seen are eternal (2 Corinthians 4:18 NASB).

I want to reiterate here that the spirit realm is alive and active. I believe this is made so clear through all that we have discussed. The truth is its activity does not depend on our belief in or lack of belief in its existence. It is real and buzzing with activity 24 hours a day, 7 days a week.

The spirit realm is never on vacation. God is and His army of angels are always about His business of His Kingdom. And His business is ruling the entire universe for an eternity.

I agree with the following quote from my friend Eddie Smith, "God is not waiting to rule. He is ruling now. As He listens to the prayers of His people, He continuously decrees and implements His purposes from the throne. The throne of God literally vibrates with divine activity."[3] Therefore, for us to be effective sons and daughters in His Kingdom, we must not ignore the most active part of His creation. Why? Because as scripture tells us concerning our position that we are seated with Him in heavenly places (see Eph. 2:6). If God is concerned about the spirit realm and He resides in the eternal spirit realm, and our position is one of being seated with Him in heavenly places, then it is our responsibility to accept the reality of this vital portion of His Kingdom.

While some of us might not have the experience of seeing in that supernatural realm as of yet, obtaining understanding of this Kingdom truth is imperative. Begin to ask the Lord to open your spiritual sight and eyes of discernment and perception in the reality of the spirit realm. Soon, you will be aware of those heavenly supernatural activities that are occurring on behalf of all sons and daughters of our heavenly Father.

NOTES

1. Billy Graham, *Angels: God's Secret Agents* (Garden City, NY: Doubleday & Company, Inc., 1975), 18.

2. Kevin L. Zadai, *The Agenda of Angels* (Shippensburg, PA: Destiny Image Publishers, 2019), Kindle loc. 21-22.

3. Eddie Smith, *Spiritual Advocates: How to Plead for Justice, Stand in the Gap, and Make a Difference in the World by Praying for Others* (Lake Mary, FL: Charisma House, 2008), 81.

Chapter Seven

DISCERNING THE DEMONIC REALM

Delightfully loved friends, don't trust every
spirit, but carefully examine what they
say to determine if they are of God.
—1 JOHN 4:1

We were on a layover in the city of Houston on the way home following a powerful weekend of teaching on the topic of deliverance. As is normal, the Houston International airport was busy with many travelers on that Sunday afternoon. We went to a restaurant to eat dinner in between flights. Now, for those who are not familiar with a lot of travel, public restaurants in airports do not allow for personal bubble space. Neighboring tables and chairs are usually only inches away. This was the case in the chosen restaurant for that meal.

As we settled in to read the menus, a young man was seated in the booth approximately 12 inches away from me. It quickly became apparent that he was demonized, or as some others would say, demonically oppressed or influenced. How did I know? Because I could feel an agitating vibration coming from him as soon as he was seated next to me. My friend traveling with me that weekend also functions in a high level of discernment. She too is one who feels, sees, and hears. We quickly yet subtlety made eye contact with one another over the top of our menus acknowledging to each other the awareness of the "visitors" who were brought in with this young man.

Soon the waitress returned to order our food. Following her exit, I could sense this young man staring at me. I turned to greet him, "Hello."

He kindly and warmly replied back with a greeting, "Hello. If you don't mind, may I ask you an unusual question?" Curious as to what it would be, I agreed. "Who do you mediate to? I meditate a lot. But you have a warm glow and presence surrounding you. You have a really nice vibration. I would like to know who it is you mediate to."

Obviously, the format in which these questions were presented revealed beyond any doubt that this young man was into some form of new age meditation. And I now also felt with assurance that this was a divine setup for this young man to have been seated next to me. I warmly replied, "It is Jesus of Nazareth. This is who I pray to and who I am in relationship with."

He joyfully responded, "I just returned from Tibet where I was taught to meditate with one of the top Buddhist monks. He taught me how to engage all the chakras and to also call on spirit guides. Jesus appeared to me while I was meditating and He is now one of my spirit guides. Can you tell me if you feel and sense things in the spirit? And if you do can you tell me if I vibrate like you do? Do you feel the warmth of Jesus?"

My heart was quickly moved to compassion for this young man, but I also laughed with joy on the inside because this could not be a more perfect setup from the Lord for the love and presence of God to touch him.

I gently answered, "Wow. You were in Tibet. May I answer your questions honestly?" He nodded his head in agreement. "Yes, I do feel and sense things in the spirit. And I want to be as real with you as I can. The vibration coming from you is not one of peace, warmth, and comfort. It carries with it an aggression and agitation." And then I demonstrated physically the agitation I was feeling in the spirit.

He was genuinely shocked. "How can that be when Jesus is one of my spirit guides?"

"Well, the Bible tells us that satan can and does appear as an angel of light. You see, Buddhism is not a Christian belief. And when you engage in opening up chakras and welcoming spirit guides in new age meditation, oftentimes demons will first appear as an angel of light in order to trap you in their deception. But when you really encounter the true Jesus, He will change your life and will cause you to feel this warmth, peace, love, and supernatural presence."

He responded, "I want what you have. My mother is a Christian and she has been telling me to not get involved in Buddhism and new age meditation. She told me she has been praying for God to send me someone I would listen to. Can you pray for me?"

I gladly obliged and the Lord touched Him with His presence in that booth at the restaurant.

As we made our exit, he joyfully explained, "I am going to go to church with my mom this weekend. Thank you for showing me the love of Jesus. I am going to look at the Bible again and seek the truth found in Jesus."

WHAT ABOUT CHRISTIANS?

I love the above testimony. It is obvious this young man was not a Christian and this encounter set him on the right path toward Jesus. But what about us as Christians? Can we be demonized or demonically oppressed? The answer is yes. While this is not a book on deliverance ministry, it is important to know this truth. Christians are given the right of choice and free will; therefore, yes, we can have anything we welcome into our lives. Trust me, I know. I used to be bound by fear, depression, and anger. I walked three years in rebellious sin while being a Christian. As a result of this time, I walked through a season of overcoming those demonic spirits. To learn more concerning personal deliverance ministry, you can read books I have previously written on the topic—*Breaking the Bonds of Evil, Let Our Children Go,* and *Defeating Strongholds of the Mind.*

DISCERNING DEMONIC STRONGMEN

That being said, I would like to dive into a teaching time of how to discern some of the most common and also not-so-common demons that we deal with. Please keep in mind this is not an exhaustive list. I have narrowed this discussion down to those demonic spirits that I feel are encountered on a more regular basis in our culture, in the Church, and sadly enough the lives of Christians. When we gain understanding on how these spirits operate and are discerned then it empowers us to pray victoriously. The Hebrew word for *spirit* is *ruwach.* It is defined as wind or breath with a resemblance of a spirit, which can be violent. It affects the mind or a region by its expression and its function. It stems from a word that implies that it can be smelled, perceived, touched, seen, and identified (Strong's #H7307). Interestingly enough, as previously shared, these are the ways we are able to function in discernment when we are operating in the gift.

It is important to state before diving into this discussion that spirits of darkness have distinct personalities. For instance, the personality and action of a spirit of fear is fear. A spirit of death involves everything encompassing death. This understanding will be evidenced as we further our discussion and lay out ways these dark spirits are discerned. I will state emphatically before moving on that we do not focus on spirits of darkness on a continual basis. I am writing this portion of this message to help teach discernment revelation in order to empower each of us to an overcoming life and victory. For a complete overview of these strongmen and their activities please see the thorough listing found in Appendix A.

FEAR

For God will never give you the spirit of fear, but the Holy Spirit who gives you mighty power, love, and self-control (2 Timothy 1:7).

As one who used to be bound by a spirit of fear. I can attest to how it operates and many of the lies it speaks to its captives. The Greek word for fear, *deilia,* is defined as "lack of courage or moral strength, to have a fallen heart, or one's heart has disappeared" (Strong's #G1167). This demonic enemy will cause all types of fears and phobias such as fear of heights, dark, closed-in places, spiders, snakes, etc. Fear can cause confusion, mental torment, fear of authority figures, fear of failure, migraines, self-rejection, distrust, worry, anxiety, and panic attacks just to list a few. Furthermore, fear can cause a deep-rooted hardness of heart, which can make one feel as if they're dead inside. This, too, comes from fear. Let's discuss further ways to perceive and discern when fear is in operation by talking about different areas of our senses.

Seeing

Some individuals who have a seeing gift will actually discern fear by seeing it in the spirit, as is the case with all of the strongmen that will be discussed. But there is also the ability to see the presence of fear on someone who is bound by this spirit. The one bound will appear anxious, nervous, uneasy, fearful; suffer from visible panic attacks; their spoken words and resulting actions will be ones of anxiousness, fear, worry. It will be evident that this spirit intends to hinder and paralyze. Noticeable confusion will be seen. Fear in a region will be seen by bars on windows and extreme measures of protection on property. People are afraid and intimidated to be out at night. Individuals are afraid to make eye contact and are visibly fearful to acknowledge those around them. Suspicion of others and paranoia will be visible on many in the region. A large portion of the population will struggle with anxiety disorders, panic attacks, and heart conditions throughout the region.

The writing of this book has occurred during the worldwide shutdown due to COVID-19. We are seeing many of these above-mentioned manifestations on people, our nation, and the nations. This virus has unleashed a spirit of fear affecting the nations of the world. But we as believers do not live in fear. He has given us power, love, and a sound mind.

Hearing

When hearing in the spirit, the words of this demon will be ones of fear, such as:

- "If you do that you will be harmed."
- "No one wants to hear what you have to say."
- "If you get on that plane, it is going to crash."
- "If you leave this house, you will be in danger."
- "The only safe place to be is isolated in your home."
- "You will never have enough money to pay your bills."
- "God cannot protect you from harm."
- "You cannot trust anyone. All people are out to hurt you."
- "You are going to die a young death."
- "If you climb that ladder, you will fall and break your back."
- "The world is a very scary and dangerous place."
- "If you say no to people it will not please them and they won't like you."

- "All people of authority are bad."
- "When you fall asleep, I will be there to torment you in your dreams."

You get the idea. Lies of fear will reverberate out in the atmosphere. Sometimes when I am praying for people or even regions, I will hear fear shriek when I call it by name. It will plead and weep, begging in a fearful manner through the ministry recipient to not be cast out. And when praying for regions, I can hear fear pleading in the spirit realm for me not to break its hold.

Feeling/Sensing

When feeling or sensing this foe, the discerner will feel an atmosphere shift from calm and peace to anxiousness, worry, tension, and fear. And it often can be a sudden shift. There is the feeling of danger or harm coming. When felt in regions, you can sense the anxiousness of the people and a sudden sense of wanting to flee quickly. Sometimes a racing heartbeat and increased adrenalin will occur. Here is where maturing in discernment is so key in order to move in victory. Why? Because oftentimes the one discerning will feel or sense so strongly that they believe they are the one with the fear.

It is my hope as we discuss this openly that all reading will be empowered to grow into maturity to perceive and know when discernment is in operation, not only with this spirit of fear but all of these discussed in this chapter and the following chapter.

FAMILIAR SPIRIT, ALSO KNOWN AS WITCHCRAFT AND DIVINATION

One day, as we were going to the house of prayer, we encountered a young slave girl who had an evil spirit of divination,

the spirit of Python. She had earned great profits for her
owners by being a fortune-teller (Acts 16:16).

Give no regard to mediums and familiar spirits; do not seek
after them, to be defiled by them: I am the Lord your God
(Leviticus 19:31 NKJV).

For rebellion is as the sin of divination, and insubordina-
tion is as iniquity and idolatry (1 Samuel 15:23 NASB).

Witchcraft and divination, also termed a *familiar spirit* in many Bible translations, has greatly infiltrated our society with much of our culture steeped in its influence. Through books, music, media, movies, and practices such as wicca, New Age, yoga, psychics, mediums. To be truthful, the list can go on and on. To give a brief overview, in the above scripture from Acts 16, the Greek word for *divination, putho,* is exactly as translated in the above reference—the spirit of Python (Strong's #G4436). In that time in Greek culture Apollo was the god of prophecy. Python was also another name and symbol assigned to him in their occult belief. In this region, this slave girl was an oracle or fortune teller for Apollo; therefore, she was also known as a pythia.

In the Leviticus 19:31 text, the Hebrew word for *medium* is *yidd'oniy,* which is defined as a conjurer or knowing one (Strong's #H3049). The Hebrew word for *familiar spirit* is *obe,* meaning necromancer, one who speaks to the dead (Strong's #H178). In the First Samuel 15:23 scripture, the Hebrew word for *rebellion* is *mriy,* which means "bitter, rebel, disobedience" (Strong's #H4805). The word for *divination* is *qecem,* which is also defined as oracle and witchcraft (Strong's #H7081). As you can now perceive, a familiar spirit, witchcraft, and divination encompasses more than occult practices. Our rebellion and sin against the Word of God and control over our own life is also witchcraft. Let's continue our discussion of how to discern this spirit.

Seeing

Those who are steeped in witchcraft practices will have a countenance that appears dark, without hope, and sometimes very oppressed. Their dress attire will often reflect their stance into darkness and many times will be seductive in nature with occult symbols boldly shown. Often, there is an intense or piercing darkness in their eyes and a mocking attitude. Those who have embraced rebellion will appear manipulative in their actions, worldly in how they dress. Aggressive actions will be witnessed and there will be a hopelessness yet controlling, defiant look in their gaze. In regions steeped in witchcraft you will see new age shops, occult bookstores, psychics, stores carrying seductive and very worldly products, and a high amount of idol worship. Masonic and Eastern Star lodges will carry a significant presence.

Hearing

What does this spirit sound like? There will be a hissing sound, an evil whisper, and mocking. It speaks lies of temptation to cross into rebellion and evil occult practices. This spirit will often laugh and mock at the righteous and will speak religious and legalistic lies to keep one bound to its web of deceit. It will and can speak as one beyond the grave when it manifests in occult practices such as seances. It will appear in dreams as a lost loved one and speak with a voice that sounds like the one who is being seen or heard.

Feeling/Sensing

Those who are feeling and sensing this spirit will often feel a sudden nausea, have a pressure or headache, or feel as if something is wrapping itself around their mind. When there is strong witchcraft in a region it feels as if the ground is moving under your feet; feelings of dizziness might be experienced. There will be an intense oppression and darkness in the atmosphere. Some will say when they are sensing this spirit it feels as if they are trudging through mud when they move.

HAUGHTY SPIRIT

An arrogant man is inflated with pride—nothing but a snooty scoffer in love with his own opinion. Mr. Mocker is his name! (Proverbs 21:24)

Pride and a haughty spirit are synonymous. This is a spirit that is extremely active and working overtime in our world. The above scripture describes well what pride actually encompasses. The Hebrew words used in the referenced text are *zed* and *yahiyr*. The two coupled together both carry meanings such as haughty, arrogant, proud, high-minded, presumptuous (Strong's #H2086 and #H3093). This spirit causes agitation, anger, entitlement, an elitist mindset, gossip, greed, holier-than-thou attitude, deception, hatred, false humility, judgmentalism, religious spirit, lack of compassion, wrath, rejection of God, self-righteousness, etc.

Seeing

When in operation through a person, they will make mocking sneers and gestures or have a holier-than-thou disposition. This individual will carry themselves with lofty looks and an air of arrogance. Not always, but pride oftentimes can appear as perfectionism in an individual and a region. Now, there is nothing wrong with good stewardship. But when appearances are used to make others feel "less than" and there are scornful, stiff-necked, and stubborn actions involved, then you know pride is at work. If it is in a region or sphere of influence, you will see these types of manifestations on many of those you encounter within that area, along with a higher education focus, humanism, Darwinism, perfectionism, elitism. There is also evidence of racism and prejudice.

Hearing

When hearing this spirit, it will be just as stated in the above scripture—whispers and phrases of scoffing and mocking. It will cause its victims to speak in a controlling, competitive way. It will speak obstinate, rebellious lies, such as:

- "You are so much better than everyone else."
- "Others are less than you."
- "You are so right in your critical and condemning thoughts."
- "You are more spiritual than everyone else. You know more."
- "You don't need God. You can achieve everything on your own."

It sounds out with insolence, intolerance, self-centeredness.

Feeling/Sensing

When felt and sensed in the spirit realm, pride causes agitation. It carries a feeling of anger and aggression. For those close to the Holy Spirit it will feel as if there is a mocking about who you are. There is condemnation that lingers, a sense of having to be perfect and being in a competition. Some who feel pride in a region will feel a stiffness on the back of their neck. It feels as if there is a heavy glass ceiling over the region. Some feel a heaviness on their shoulders and a tightening of their spine and righteous indignation and anger toward this defiant spirit.

LYING SPIRIT

There are six things which the Lord hates, yes, seven which are an abomination to Him: haughty eyes, a lying tongue, and hands that shed innocent blood, a heart that devises

wicked plans, feet that run rapidly to evil, a false witness
who utters lies, and one who spreads strife among brothers
(Proverbs 6:16-19 NASB).

One of the many things my parents, especially my father, did not tolerate was lying. We were taught from a very young age—lying is unacceptable and truth is the only available and correct path to follow. Sadly enough, lying and a lying spirit are hot topics in our society and culture. It seems that when we turn on the news the majority of the time we are viewing and listening to lies from the pit of hell! While to some this might seem to be an exaggeration, the truth is it really isn't. Those who lie and do it on a consistent basis without conscience are indeed bound by this deceptive demonic spirit. In the above scripture there are two Hebrew words used for *lie*. *Sheqer* is defined as deceit and to deal falsely (Strong's #H8267). *Kazab* is defined as falsehood or liar (Strong's #H3577). Lying is the initial open door to walking in rebellion.

Seeing

One might ask, how do I see a lying spirit? Drug use and abuse. This is the strongman behind all addiction. You will witness actions of cheating and deceit, financial problems, confusion over sexual identity. A lying spirit is the strongman behind all sexual confusion, lust, and mental bondage. It acts similar to a Jezebel spirit. Why do I state this? Because a Jezebel spirit partners with a lying spirit. It's also seen in someone who consistently appears a victim. Those who have strong religious actions may be driven by a lying spirit and a spirit of religion. Those who act from a worthless self-image. Hypocritical behavior. Which leads me to share a powerful quote by Jake Kail:

When God opened my eyes to the true nature of hypocrisy it was a game changer. Jesus warned us to be aware of hypocrisy, but we've often not understood what it truly means. The word hypocrite means to be an actor; someone who wears a phony mask to hide evil intentions and evil behavior. In short, the hypocrite is not the righteous person who sins, but the evil person who pretends to be good. Do you realize how common it is for chronic liars, domestic abusers, and sexual predators to blend into our churches undetected? How does this happen? In short, hypocrisy.[1]

I would also like to add a lying spirit partnering with hypocrisy empowers the issue so well described in the above statement. Jake goes on to say, "God is exposing hidden things in this hour. He is shining His light so that justice, healing, and reformation can happen!"[2]

Hearing

Identifying a lying spirit in action is not that difficult. You will hear slander, accusation, and deceit; twisting God's Word; twisting truth on a consistent basis, as is seen in the majority of media outlets at this point in history. Gossip and spoken heresy. Self-inflicted spoken curses. Excessive talking of falsehoods. Vengeful words. A lying spirit will demonically whisper lies concerning identity into the ears of those who will listen. It will forcefully speak lies with aggression to intimidate one to embrace the lie or to act on it. It has the sound of a hissing snake when it speaks out to an individual or in the spiritual atmosphere of a region. We will discuss Leviathan in the next chapter, but it is evident that a lying spirit works hand in hand with Leviathan at a regional, spherical, principality level.

Feeling/Sensing

I don't know how else to say this, but a lying spirit makes you feel as if your skin is crawling. When it is speaking, red flags will be sounding out in your spirit. Thoughts will quickly cross your mind such as, "I don't believe that. That cannot be true." If you hear or sense that in your spirit then pay attention to that prompting and dialogue with the Lord about what you are sensing. Some who feel and sense this demonic spirit in operation will feel a righteous anger begin to rise up. Don't ignore that. Again, engage the Holy Spirit and ask Him to help you know why you are feeling and sensing this.

RELIGIOUS SPIRIT

Jesus spoke up and said, "Watch out for the yeast of the Pharisees and the Sadducees" (Matthew 16:6).

The Pharisees were a part of a strict legalistic religious party in Judaism. The Sadducees were a politically influential Jewish party. These two groups exemplified religious structures and leaders operating under a religious spirit. Jesus warned His followers to stay away from their yeast. The Greek word for *yeast* is *zyme*. It is defined as pretense and hypocritical teaching (Strong's #G2219). A religious spirit is a demonic force that influences people to act pious, self-righteous, or super-spiritual. It avoids true spiritual authority, denies the power and gifts of God, and lives by rules and legalism instead of a personal, on-fire relationship with the Lord. It does things the way they have always been done. It disorients one's perception of who Jesus is, and it stands in the ways of God's efforts to build His glorious church. It resists change and causes critical, judgmental thinking. It often opposes new moves of God in a knee-jerk reaction.

It is imperative to state here that we must remember not to be critical of past moves of God, because they once were the new move of God. If we do become critical then we are discerning and judging from a wrong intent and motive and are ourselves empowering a religious spirit.

Seeing

To me the most obvious sight to witness and to know when a religious spirit is in operation is active idolatrous worship. If idols must be present or prayed to in order for a person to feel close to the Father, Son, or Holy Spirit, this is an indication that a religious spirit has an established stronghold. Idols that represent false religions are a sure sign of a religious spirit over a region. The Word of God is clear concerning the worship of idols. Also, another sight indicator of a religious spirit is zero joy on the worshipers. Worship being done by rote and no personal connection to Jesus does not cultivate a healthy spiritual life.

We all know and understand the truth that salvation and our personal growth are based on a personal relationship with Jesus and growing in depth through reading His Word, worship, prayer, intercession, and discipleship. Please hear my heart. I am a prophet. I believe in shofars, banners, dynamic worship, and dancing. This is awesome. But then there are those who insist on pushing the envelope by plowing through or forcing their form of worship on others who do not have this understanding. And there are those who dress to appear as an angel, to look like Jesus, or to draw attention to themselves and not the Lord. These individuals appear and act in such an out-of-the-norm manner that no one wants to relate to them. Often, these individuals are lone rangers with no friends. These also are consistently seen to be bound to a religious spirit.

Hearing

One who is operating under a religious spirit will always have a holier-than-thou attitude along with pious dialogue. They are above others in their conversation. They are often critical of others' worship if it differs from their idea of worship. Their words will freely express this sentiment. Also, this individual will monopolize prayer meetings and their voice is the one that has to be heard. If they prophesy, they will try to get the mic in their hand and take over the meeting. A religious spirit will whisper lies out in the spiritual atmosphere to the bound individual, such as:

- "You are the only one who knows the truth."

- "You are the one who must be the Holy Spirit to others."

- "No one knows how to prophesy as effectively as you."

- "You must pray longer than everyone else because no one else knows how to pray."

- "You are the only one with the true, pure message of the Lord."

- "You must show up at this church/ministry/prayer meeting and announce to the group they are in error and being judged."

- "Bowing your knee and worshiping that image is the only way to answered prayer and salvation."

Here are key questions to ask if you feel the one you are dealing with might have a religious spirit, along with the answers that will confirm the spirit in operation.

1. "Do you go to a church, home group, Bible study?"

   "No, there is no church or group that is right for me. I don't like them; they don't like me. So I am not connected anywhere."

2. "Who are you in alignment with or have relationship with in the Body of Christ?"

   "No one. I just need God."

3. "Why did you come here today?"

   "God revealed to me that you and your group needed correcting and sent me here."

4. "Interesting. You have never been here before. We have never met. Oh, and excuse me, what is your name?"

"Yes. But I have read articles about you and have heard about this group from the Lord in my prayer time. He told me you are a false prophet and He is going to hold your group's feet in His fire of accountability. And I will not tell you my name."

You get the idea. At this point I am gladly escorting this person out of the meeting or inviting someone on my leadership team to do so. So how do you recognize a religious spirit in the region? Muslim calls to prayer five times a day over a loudspeaker. This would also be an anti-Christ spirit in operation considering that Muslims worship a false and demonic god. Hearing the majority of the churches in that region speak messages against a move of the Holy Spirit. Messages shunning the gifts of the Holy Spirit. Teachings based and steeped in head and book knowledge with no presence of the Lord. Many in a religious region will speak about the Lord daily in their lives on a continual basis, but there is no fruit of salvation. They have a vocabulary that sounds Christian, but a lifestyle of zero relationship with the Lord.

Feeling/Sensing

I will begin with a completely "feeler" statement. Those of you who feel will probably giggle and shout out in agreement. When a religious spirit is in operation and the person bound by it speaks or you hear it in a region, it makes you feel like fingernails are being dragged down a chalkboard. There is a quick sense of agitation and strong and urgent sense of wanting the person speaking or the sound being made to stop. It also carries with it the feeling of being slimed in the spirit. It has a dark and weighty feel, and believers operating in purity and holiness will often feel as if they are being harassed and backed into a corner in order to be shut down. It also carries a sense of grief because the activity of this spirit greatly grieves the heart of the Father, Jesus, and the Holy Spirit. And there is also the righteous indignation or anger that will rise in the feeler or the one sensing when they are made to entertain or tolerate this spirit for long periods of time.

Hear me, leaders—if this is not dealt with and is ignored in a corporate group, then eventually those who are discerning this spirit correctly will leave or no longer attend prayer meetings or gatherings with this individual.

SHADOW OF DEATH

Even though I walk through the valley of the shadow of death, I fear no evil, for You are with me; Your rod and Your staff, they comfort me (Psalm 23:4 NASB).

The Hebrew word for "shadow of death" is *salmawet* (Strong's #H6757). It means gloom, dark shadows, terror of darkness, the place of death. This spirit will rob life in all areas—physical, spiritual, emotional, mental. It is a tormenting spirit whose goal is to cause ultimate death in all the above-mentioned areas. It will cause repeated accidents, trying to rob life. It is the grim reaper.

Seeing

Someone bound by this spirit will repeatedly abandon their family and friends. One bound by this entity will often have dreams of seeing and being attacked by animals, demons, or what looks like the grim reaper. There will be dreams of being chased by dead people, being hit by a vehicle, or falling into a pit and being unable to get out. They may see a tall demon with a dark robe, wearing a hood. It can also appear as a shadowy figure lurking around the atmosphere of a home, building, city, and region.

In regions where there is a stronghold of death, there are patterns of people dying young and untimely deaths will appear across generations. Among those who live in the area of its influence, there will be unexplained cases of incurable diseases. People will have no spiritual hope and life. Often, even within church services there will be no life or movement of the Holy Spirit. The region will report high suicide rates. Not always, but many times where there is a high death/suicide rate, poverty will also be seen. That being said, a spirit of death or shadow of death can easily grip affluent regions as well. Abortion rates will be high and numerous active abortion clinics will be seen. Death will also be empowered or enthroned in a region where ungodly massacres of the innocent have occurred or there have been many battles with a high number of casualties. Murder and homicide will occur regularly.

Hearing

This spirit whispers to those bound by it that he or she will die an untimely death. It will whisper lies of no hope causing great depression. It will whisper lies encouraging its victims to kill themselves. "You should just end your life. There is nothing for you here but misery. When you die you will go to a better place. You will go to paradise. Death is better for you than life." Hear me—the level of torment this demon brings as it partners with heaviness and depression can be unbearable to the one suffering from these tormenting lies if deliverance is not received. Spirits of death cannot be medicated. The medication will cause the person to go into slumber and to have less strength to fight the spiritual battle raging in their minds. When the issues are spiritual only, deliverance and casting out the demon will help this individual. In the region, these same lies will be spoken out in the atmosphere. Prophets and prophetic intercessors will hear these lies reverberating out in the atmosphere in an attempt to steal life. Ministries will have a difficult time surviving in the region. Terms will often be heard, "This place is a graveyard for pastors and Christian leaders."

Feeling/Sensing

Those feeling and sensing death will feel an eerie cold in the atmosphere. Sometimes there will be such a heavy oppression that it feels difficult breathing. Allow me to explain. You can breathe, but in the spirit you feel heaviness as if there is an assignment trying to snuff the life out of people by robbing breath in their lungs. There is a feeling and a sensing of depression. Being in a region with this in the atmosphere will make you feel as if your energy and resolve to accomplish tasks and to walk in joy is being drawn out of you. There will be much sorrow and despair looming in the atmosphere from all the death and suicides that have occurred.

SPIRIT OF HEAVINESS/DEPRESSION

To grant those who mourn in Zion, giving them a garland instead of ashes, the oil of gladness instead of mourning, the mantle of praise instead of a spirit of fainting. So they will be called oaks of righteousness, the planting of the Lord, that He may be glorified (Isaiah 61:3 NASB).

Isaiah does a thorough job in this above scripture speaking of a spirit of heaviness, which I also call depression. The Hebrew word for *mourn* is *abel* (Strong's #H57). It means "lamenting, mourner, and to bewail." He then goes on to share that the Lord will give the oil of gladness. This is what we are to have! The Hebrew word for *ashes* is *eper* and it describes extreme mourning that leads to thoughts of worthlessness, insignificance, and distress (Strong's #H665). This spirit of fainting is where we really begin to understand this demonic foe. The Hebrew word for *fainting* is *keheh,* which also means "colorless, disheartened, heaviness, distress, troubled, despair" (Strong's #H3544). This spirit does all of the above to keep a demonic grip of despair on all of those encountering it.

Seeing

Grief, sadness, torment, depression, anger, fatigue, hopelessness, dread, guilt, rejection, suicide, tiredness—these are just a few manifestations of this spirit. Ones who are gripped with this stronghold will exhibit all of the above symptoms and more. While some might be able to hide it well publicly, they will have patterns of not wanting to be in crowds or a pattern of extreme emotional changes, meaning really high emotional peaks to sudden really low emotional valleys. This individual can for a period be happy around others, but soon you will see repeated patterns of isolation or periods of emotional despair. A region gripped by this stronghold will look depressed with no life. I realize this will sound different, but even the town will appear sad, asleep, dreary, with no life.

Hearing

All demons want to torment, but this one in particular is aggressive in its evil desire to cause anguish. It is busy speaking its lies into the ears, mind, and emotions of the one it has demonically gripped.

- "You are worthless."
- "God will never love you."
- "God can never forgive you."
- "No one loves you."
- "You are a nuisance."
- "You think you can be of any good?"
- "Your life has no meaning."
- "You would be better off dead."

Where it has a regional influence, these lies will be repeated out loud by many. This is a true sign that this is a territorial issue. There have been numerous times I have gone into a region and spoken about this stronghold and when it is time for ministry the entire congregation or conference will come forward. This is seeing a territorial stronghold in action, meaning all or the majority in the area struggle with the same mental or emotional onslaught unleashed in the spirit realm.

Feeling/Sensing

When in proximity to this spirit, it feels as described above—very oppressive and stifling. It makes it hard to feel and experience joy. Some will feel a heaviness on their shoulders as an indicator that it is in operation. There is a feeling of shame and guilt in the atmosphere where it has established a foothold. And it can often be felt and sensed as a restlessness in the spirit causing people to want to wander instead of planting roots.

SPIRIT OF BONDAGE

> *Stand fast therefore in the liberty by which Christ has made us free, and do not be entangled again with a yoke of bondage* (Galatians 5:1 NKJV).

The Greek word for *bondage* is *douleia* and it means slavery (Strong's #G1397). Bondage is a demonic spirit that establishes its hold and grip on an individual to keep them bound as a slave to numerous things. Basically, bondage and any and all forms of addiction go hand in hand. Alcohol, caffeine, drugs, cigarettes, sexual addictions, overeating, anorexia, bulimia, over-spending, shopping, exercise, addictions to medications, hoarding, and compulsive behaviors are just a few examples of demonic bondage. Those who wrestle with this might also experience the following: chronic fatigue syndrome, ADD or ADHD, MPD, fear, anxiety, shame, hopelessness, and self-condemnation. This person will feel lost and greatly battle in the ability to gain freedom. There is much more to the activity of this demon, as you will discover in Appendix A.

Seeing

Someone bound by this spirit will be enthralled in a battle with some sort of addiction that in time will no longer remain hidden but be made evident. This addiction and behavior will overcome the captive so that all will be able to visibly see its destructive hold. Those gripped by this will appear restless, hyperactive, have compulsory behaviors, and suffer with strife. Other visible actions will be a vagabond lifestyle or a tendency to wander with an inability to settle down. Sometimes in the spirit realm this demon will be seen with chains.

If a region is held by this stronghold it will be one with an unusually high percentage of individuals who struggle with all forms of addiction. Activity of addicts will be highly visible in the region. Many will also be bound in poverty. Sex has now become an addiction for many. There will a high number of prostitutes, sex trafficking, sex shops, etc. Within the area there is little visible sign of hope, joy, and Kingdom living and blessing.

Hearing

This demon speaks lies such as the following:

- "You need that drink to cope."
- "You cannot make it without that cigarette."
- "Drugs are your comforter. You don't need God."
- "You are hopelessly poor and can never have wealth."
- "You can never be set free. I will never leave your life."
- "Spending another thousand dollars on that credit card is not a problem. You cannot live without those clothes."
- "Go spend money on that prostitute just one more time."

The problem is that lie will be spoken every day and sometimes multiple times a day. You get the idea. At a regional level it will speak out these same lies to the majority of the population and the lies will be embraced as part of their culture.

Feeling/Sensing

Hopelessness, worthlessness, and a very heavy yoke of oppression will be felt emotionally and physically. While I do not have a section listed on smelling, I will make it a point when discussing this demon to say it does have an odor and it smells like nicotine on steroids—so strong it is almost impossible to ignore.

SPIRIT OF ERROR

We are of God. He who knows God hears us; he who is not of God does not hear us. By this we know the spirit of truth and the spirit of error (1 John 4:6 NKJV).

A spirit of error is not the same as a lying spirit, although they do work together. A spirit of error is often one that grips someone who is in doctrinal error. This individual easily embraces false doctrines and exhibits the tendency to be drawn to occult and new age practices. The Greek word used for *error* is *plane* (Strong's #G4106). It is defined as a straying from orthodoxy, to deceive. It stems from a root word that literally means an imposter, misleader, deceiver.

Seeing

The one who is demonized by this spirit will be very argumentative, always trying to be right, or have a pattern of lying. Their actions will be ones of no submission. And often they have occult and new age books and items. They will wear occult jewelry and dress in attire reflecting their false beliefs. Visibly it is evident that those who are being influenced by this strongman are contentious and highly argumentative about their beliefs. A region gripped by this demon will have an abnormal amount of new age, occult stores and cult activity and gatherings. People will flaunt their false doctrines and the region will appear and seem totally out of place with the normal and accepted way of life. Regions steeped in error and false beliefs will not welcome a lot of outsiders.

Hearing

This spirit will obviously speak lies. It will entice with its doctrines of devils and false doctrines. Falsehoods such as the following are an example of what it speaks out:

- "It is good to embrace this teaching."
- "You are superior to the rest of the world."
- "You are above all others and have attained to a higher spiritual plane."
- "Reject the truth."
- "It is best to speak lies. The truth will get you nowhere."
- "You do not need to be under anyone who has authority over you."
- "This meditation and these spirit guides will lead into true enlightenment."
- "It is good to want to know more about spiritual things and the universe."

There will be a dissonant sound such as a demonic humming that can be heard in the atmosphere.

Feeling/Sensing

Righteous indignation, agitation, and a nauseous feeling are normal when encountering this spirit. A feeling and sensing of things not being right. Usually you will feel, for lack of a better term, your skin wanting to crawl. You will sense hatred from this person, and the witchcraft and occult empowerment will also feel like a strange and intense shaking and vibration in the spirit, much like I described to the young man in the airport, mentioned earlier. You may also feel a tightness around your forehead and chest or a sense of not being able to believe one word being said by the one bound in error. All the while there will be alarms sounding in the spirit and multiple checks, which will cause thoughts like, "That person is speaking false doctrine. That is a lie from the enemy," and, "I want this person to be quiet and not speak another word." It is not the person who causes the irritation; it is the spirit speaking through this individual. Remember, our battle is not against flesh and blood. We love the people and hate the sin. It is important to keep our focus in the right perspective.

SEDUCING SPIRIT

But the [Holy] Spirit explicitly and unmistakably declares that in later times some will turn away from the faith, paying attention instead to deceitful and seductive spirits and doctrines of demons (1 Timothy 4:1 AMP).

When we hear the word *seducing* it is fairly normal for our minds and thoughts to quickly categorize this with perversion. While some of this is true, a seducing spirit is one that entices people into evil actions and ways. The Greek word for *seducing* is *planos*. It is defined as an imposter, misleader, seducer, and deceiver (Strong's #G4108). It is extremely active in the world today through entertainment, which pulls people into a fascination with evil such as vampires, warlocks, witches, werewolves, zombies, ancient principalities, and satan and his army of darkness.

Seeing

It will be seen manifesting through someone who greatly seeks attention and many times it is accomplished through sensual dress and actions. Visible false signs and wonders will operate through this person. Or someone bound by this spirit will regularly be attracted to false prophets, signs, and wonders. Many evil objects and ways will be seen in the individual entertaining this demon. Regions gripped by a seducing spirit will be steeped in the fascination of evil. Many will dress sensually, and their actions and beliefs will be excessive and worldly. False prophets will regularly be drawn, attracted to, and operating in the region.

Hearing

This spirit will be heard through music, movies, and television shows that defy, mock, or reject God. Spheres of influence and individuals operating under the influence of this spirit will have a sound of darkness and evil in what they produce. The following are examples of some of the lies it will speak:

- "You will attract interested parties with sensual and revealing dress attire."
- "These lyrics defy all things pure and good, which is a great accomplishment."
- "Listen to the wisdom that the prophet is revealing. It is wisdom that is above the knowledge contained in all other spiritual beliefs."
- "Christians have inferior understanding. You have attained to a higher level of spiritual enlightenment."

Obviously, a seducing spirit has a very dark and enticing sound. It is not only aggressive, but it has an eerie, haunting, and otherworldly sound in order to entice its victims and lull a region into its demonic grip.

Feeling/Sensing

To a believer is feels unclean, unholy, dirty, and evil. Even when others might be drawn to a certain minister, you will sense or perceive seduction and falsehood. You will feel the pull in the spirit that entices, but everything in you will know that it is false and it is necessary to walk away. There will be no desire to be near the false prophet or healer. There will be a strong sense and knowing that the person, music, object, or action is not of God but is truly evil.

SPIRIT OF INFIRMITY

And behold, there was a woman who had a spirit of infirmity eighteen years, and was bent over and could in no way raise herself up (Luke 13:11 NKJV).

The Greek word used for *infirmity* is *asthenia*. It means "to make feeble, weak, malady, disease, sickness" (Strong's #G769). I will never forget ministering to a pastor who will remain nameless. In two days, he was scheduled to have surgery on the arteries leading to his kidney. He had battled kidney disease for many years, yet he knew it was a spiritual condition. As we prayed, I saw the spirit of infirmity gripping his arteries with its demonic talons in order to bring death. I broke its demonic grip. He went to the hospital the next day and as they ran the final test before surgery it was discovered that there was no blockage and his kidneys were functioning normally. No more disease. Not every illness is caused by a demonic spirit. But in this particular situation it was. It is important to know and discern when this is the case so we can see people healed.

Seeing

As I stated in the above testimony, I could see the demonic grip and hold of the spirit of infirmity gripping the arteries. When ministering you will see in the spirit where the infirmity has attached itself to the physical body. I function in this manner often when praying for healing. When this spirit in active in a person there will be chronic illness, sometimes epilepsy, seizures, physical feebleness, lameness, or mental illness. Regions bound by infirmity will have an unusually high rate of terminal or chronic illness. There can also be a higher death rate per capita as a spirit of infirmity and death will often go hand in hand. There will be a high diagnosis of unusual diseases. The young in this region will be sick with illnesses that are not normal for their age.

Hearing

The most frequent lies of this spirit are the following:

- "God brought this disease on you."
- "It is His will that you are sick."
- "He does not want to heal you."
- "Your mother and grandmother suffered from this illness and you will as well."
- "You can never be healed and whole."
- "You have a right to be mad and to not forgive those who have wronged or hurt you."

Unforgiveness is one of the main open doors to attract a demonic spirit of infirmity. To be truthful, it is a tormenting spirit and will speak out its lies consistently to achieve its plan of robbing and stealing health and life.

Feeling/Sensing

There will be a knowing that the illness being dealt with is not normal and that it is not a physical problem but one caused by this demonic spirit. The heaviness of the torment caused by this spirit will be tangible. You might feel a twinge of pressure on a certain part of your physical body when ministering to someone who needs healing and deliverance in that exact area. A sense of pending death will be felt. A coldness and weighty oppression will be tangible in the atmosphere.

SPIRIT OF JEALOUSY

> *And if a spirit (sense, attitude) of jealousy comes over him and he is jealous and angry at his wife who has defiled herself—or if a spirit of jealousy comes over him and he is jealous of his wife when she has not defiled herself* (Numbers 5:14 AMP).

Jealousy and envy will lead its victim to a path of discontentment, anger, rage, violence, coveting, or bitterness. The Hebrew word for *jealousy* is *qana*. It is defined as being zealous in a bad sense, to envy (Strong's #H7068). It embodies excessive and sometimes extreme competitiveness. Bob Sorge shares a powerful truth concerning jealousy and envy from his book *Envy: The Enemy Within*:

> As the Lord has challenged the envious tendencies of my soul, I have come to realize how pandemic envy truly is and how deadly it is every time it infects the church of Jesus Christ. Envy has the power to sabotage our own personal destiny in God because God cannot honor our efforts when they are subliminally driven by impure motives. As long as envy remains hidden in the crevices of our hearts, our fruitfulness in Christ will inescapably be impeded. But more than that—and here's where I sense an even greater urgency—when we envy one another in the Kingdom of God, we release dynamics that actually bind the progress of the Kingdom in our sphere, or region. Envy has the power to obstruct the release of Kingdom blessing, even in places where massive amounts of intercession for revival

and visitation are ascending to God's throne. In fact, I will argue in this book that envy has been responsible, perhaps more than any other evil or vice, for quenching the fires of revival both in the past and in the present.[3]

Seeing

Jealousy manifests in many unpleasant ways. One who is influenced by this spirit will have anger, envy, strife, competition, backbiting, belittling, bitterness, coarse jesting, enmity, division, mocking, slander, suspicion, gangs, fighting, and stealing. Just as in a person, these demonic manifestations will also be witnessed in a region. When this strongman has gripped a territory there will be much division among the people and also, sadly, within churches. There will be gang activity, prejudice, materialism, and competition to the degree that even grown men and women will be embroiled in quarrels and fights, for example, parents engaging in physical altercations at their child's sporting event. Great hindrances to a move of God and revival will be tangible.

Hearing

You will hear coarse jesting and inappropriate and dishonorable words and actions. *Spiteful* conversations. Outbursts of rage and hatred. In the spirit, lies voiced by jealousy will carry this sound:

- "You are better than everyone."
- "You must win everything at all costs even when it harms someone else. That doesn't matter. All that matters is you winning and being the one most recognized."
- "I hate my neighbors."
- "I hate people who do not have money."
- "I hate people of color."

- "Go ahead and get angry. You have a right to be mad."
- "Violence and anger are good."
- "You need to murder that man."

These statements should help paint the picture. This spirit, as all demonic spirits, is pure evil.

Feeling/Sensing

It is not hard to recognize that the presence of this spirit would cause feelings of uneasiness and vulnerability. There will be a strong feeling or sensing of wickedness. Grief in the spirit will also be felt and sensed because of the extreme competition and hardness of heart. Now, I do not follow through with what I am about to share with you, but when I feel, sense, or witness this spirit manifesting through a person, sometimes there is such a righteous indignation that rises up, I feel as if I want to reach out and smack this individual a good one! I love people and I would not do this. It is a righteous indignation toward the demonic spirit. The region will have a feeling of aggression, hard-heartedness, and extreme competition. There will be a sense of not being welcomed.

SPIRIT OF REJECTION

Rejection is by far the most common spirit I have witnessed in my years of deliverance ministry. Almost everyone I pray for has experienced rejection in one way or another. It can occur anytime from conception into adulthood. Remember that demons live up to their names, possessing those attributes and personalities. When a spirit of rejection is in operation, therefore, it causes the victim to be rejected on a repeated basis. The response that the person fears is the exact assignment and objective of this demonic being. The reality of never being accepted causes these individuals to behave in a manner that hastens the sad and discouraging outcome.

Seeing

This spirit is a major issue in the Body of Christ. In *Evicting Demonic Intruders*, Noel and Phyl Gibson explain the fruit of rejection:

> The roots of rejection produce three different fruit-bearing branches. Firstly, rejected people show a variety of aggressive attitudes. Secondly, they suffer from symptoms of self-rejection which may or may not be seen. Thirdly, motivated by their fear of rejection, they make constant attempts to avoid being rejected again. The following list clearly show the fruit systems:

1. AGGRESSIVE REACTIONS	2. SELF-REJECTION SYMPTOMS	3. MEASURES TO COUNTER FEAR OF SELF-REJECTION
Refusing comfort Rejection of others Harshness, hardness Skepticism, unbelief Aggressive attitudes Swearing, foul language Argumentativeness Stubbornness, defiance **REBELLION** Fighting	Low self-image Inferiorities Insecurity Inadequacy Sadness, grief, sorrow Self-accusation and self-condemnation Inability or refusal to communicate Fear of failure Fear of others' opinions	Striving, achievement, performance, competition Withdrawal, aloneness
		INDEPENDENCE Isolation Self-protectiveness Self-centeredness, selfishness Self-justification Self-righteousness
	OTHER FEARS Anxiety, worry Depression Negative attitudes Pessimism Hopelessness, despair	**SELF-IDOLATRY** Criticism Judgmental attitudes Envy, jealousy
		COVETOUSNESS Self-pity
		PRIDE Ego, haughtiness Arrogance Manipulation Possessiveness Emotional immaturity Perfectionism

Hearing

This spirit is relentless in deceptively speaking out demonic lies to keep its hold.

- "No one likes you."
- "Everyone is against you."

- "You must not ever trust anyone."

- "All people want to hurt you."

- "You are ugly."

- "You are so unworthy."

- "All people conspire against you."

- "Your parents love your brother (or sister) more than you."

- "Your boss dislikes you."

- "All men (or women) will betray you."

- "Your parents did not want you."

- "You are a mistake."

Feeling/Sensing

Rejection is a spirit that self-sabotages. Therefore, when it is in the atmosphere there is a sense of hopelessness. There is an intense selfishness and self-centeredness exuding off the one who is held captive. Fear will also be tangible and a strong feeling of a pull on emotions in order to control or manipulate.

SPIRIT OF PERVERSION/WHOREDOM AND LUST

The Lord has mingled a perverse spirit in her; so they have caused Egypt to err in her every work (Isaiah 19:14 MEV).

The Hebrew word used for *perversion* in this scripture is *av'eh*. It is defined perversity (Strong's #H5773). It also stems from the root word *avah*, which gives further insight. It means "to bow down, make crooked, commit iniquity, pervert, turn, and do wickedly" (Strong's #H5753). Perversion, whoredom, and lust are one and the same. In the New Testament, the word *uncleanness* is also used to describe this entity, meaning that someone is physically or morally impure. Unfortunately, perversion has largely gripped our culture and society and, what is even more sad, many in the church.

Seeing

In writing, it is difficult to know where to begin on laying out the seen activities and partnering spirits that work in conjunction with this evil strongman. As a reminder, the demonic grouping list in Appendix A is very thorough to help in identifying and discerning this spirit.

This spirit is seen in acts of adultery and arrogant actions. Those who are trapped in bisexuality, homosexuality, lesbianism, transvestite actions, and transgender transformations are definitely bound. Prostitution, drunkenness, and actions that exemplify all kinds of lusts such as lust for authority, sexual lust, lust for food, money, position, perverse sexual acts, power, sex, social standing, and the world. Acts of seduction and greed.

When a region is steeped in the demonic grip of this unclean spirit there will be all kinds of sex shops and prostitutes on the street. Pimps walking the streets at night. There will be strip clubs and porn shops. Men and women exhibiting extreme driven actions to achieve power through the means of evil acts.

Hearing

I am hesitant to type the horrible things that this spirit speaks out in the atmosphere or to those held captive by its evil web. Let's just include a few examples, but also not linger here long.

- "Turn on that computer and view that woman on that porn site."
- "Adultery is not wrong, you are just satisfying your human desire."
- "Look at the young boy."

- "You are a woman and you like other women. You were born this way."
- "Go ahead and have sex. If you get pregnant abort it."
- "There is no such thing as God."
- "I am going to get the executive position no matter the cost. I will run over and harm everyone in my way."
- "I must have more money. Money is my god."

What is it that the discerner might hear in the spirit when you are in proximity to perversion? Usually an evil mocking and laughing aimed at you and God. Things such as, "We hate you here," and, "Leave." Sometimes if abuse and abortion is in the region, there will be the sound of weeping in the spirit for those who have been tragically harmed, trafficked, and aborted. The way to describe this is when the Lord spoke to Cain, "I hear your brother's blood crying out from the land." This same phrase will also be heard when a spirit of death is active.

Feeling/Sensing

A dirty, perverse, unclean feeling in the atmosphere. A feeling and sensing of the depravity of the sin. A feeling of wanting to not be around those gripped by it or in the region where it is active. Sensing the extreme greed and worldliness and much grief concerning those trapped in this life of sin. There can often be a feeling and sensing of the tragic abuses that have occurred.

SPIRIT OF SLUMBER/UNBELIEF

God granted them a spirit of deep slumber. He closed their eyes to the truth and prevented their ears from hearing up to this day (Romans 11:8).

The Greek word in this scripture is *katanyxis*. It means "stupor, slumber, deep sleep, sluggish, dullness, lethargy, unable to think" (Strong's #G2659). This spirit will cause people to fall into a deep sleep when trying to cast it out. Many years ago, I served on the altar ministry team at a conference hosted by Peter and Doris Wagner and Global Harvest Ministries. During a break time, I began to pray for a woman who had requested prayer. As soon as I began to minister, she slumped over, leaning her head on my shoulder. She was in a deep sleep and began to snore loudly. The rest of the altar ministry team found it quite humorous and began to laugh at what was unfolding. I pretty much knew instantly what I was dealing with. I called it out by name: "You spirit of slumber and unbelief, I break your hold right now in Jesus' name. Get off of her!"

She instantly awoke and stood straight up while shouting joyfully, "I am free." And she took off running. Yes. She was a runner. She did a joy run around the entire auditorium repeatedly shouting, "I am free! I am free!" This story is humorous in many ways, but it is also a very accurate portrayal of this spirit.

Seeing

Obviously, someone falling asleep while receiving ministry as shared above is a manifestation. Also, those bound by this spirit will fall asleep regularly in church, but not from boredom. This spirit will cause the sleep on the one gripped by it while reading the Word or attending a church service. There will be an inability to stay awake. One bound by this spirit and who is gifted in the seer realm will experience great torment resulting in terror and fear. Actions will exhibit mental slowness, fear, being easily distracted, or confusion. Regions bound by unbelief will oppose truth, meaning they are not able to hear the truth. Churches will be dead—absolutely no life. And the region might have many who suffer mental slowness and sicknesses such as arthritis, chronic fatigue, circulatory problems, eye disorders, hearing disorders.

Hearing

Repeated spoken words of unbelief are the telltale sign that a person is held captive by this spirit. Often there will be statements of blasphemy and obvious confusion in their thinking and words. The following are some of the lies that are spoken by this spirit:

- "Don't listen to the message."
- "You don't need the word of God."
- "You will always be fearful."
- "Deny the Holy Spirit."
- "Deny God. You don't need Him."

Feeling/Sensing

When encountering this spirit, there will be a heaviness and a feeling of sleepiness. Perversion works with this spirit, so the perverting of truth will be tangible in the atmosphere. Sometimes when sensing this spirit there might be a slight sensation of dizziness. At a territorial level, the region will feel asleep and will not be able to hear or respond to the Word of God or His truth or any movement of the Holy Spirit.

DEAF AND DUMB SPIRIT

Now when Jesus saw that the crowd was quickly growing larger, he commanded the demon, saying, "Deaf and mute spirit, I command you to come out of him and never enter him again!" (Mark 9:25)

The Greek word for *deaf* is *kophos* (Strong's #G2974) and for *mute* is *alalos* (Strong's #G216). This spirit is exactly as described—one that hinders and paralyzes the ability to speak and hear. Interestingly, it also will cause things such as drowning accidents, accidents around fire, and repeated accidents.

Seeing

This spirit is discovered when repeated accidents occur, especially those surrounding water and fire. Other manifestations are the inability to speak and hear. Now, this does not apply across the board. If someone is mute or deaf, it is not always caused by a demonic spirit. Those bound by this will visibly exhibit insanity, destructive behaviors, schizophrenia. Some will also suffer from seizures, foaming at the mouth, gnashing of teeth, chronic infections. This spirit can also be the cause of Tourette's, but not all cases of Tourette's are caused by a deaf and dumb spirit.

At a regional level there will be a high percentage of the inhabitants who struggle with insanity or schizophrenia. Many will battle with epilepsy and seizures. A region will appear crippled spiritually. What do I mean? It will be difficult for people to hear and speak out or prophesy.

Hearing

Spoken words of unbelief will be heard as these two spirits often work together. Words of bitterness and unforgiveness. Repeated schizophrenic episodes of great confusion in which the one bound will be convinced they have seen and also heard voices of people who are not real. Of course, I believe that much of the time when this occurs they are seeing and hearing demons. In a region, hearing prophetically will be difficult as this spirit will want to silence or mute the message of truth and the Gospel.

Feeling/Sensing

To the one held captive there will be a sense of death approaching. Those who have the gift of discernment will feel this looming in the atmosphere surrounding the one they are ministering to and also in the region. As described in scripture, it is an aggressive spirit when it manifests. The sense of this aggression will be tangible. Many of the people in the region will struggle with mental issues. The result is a sense of confusion and a difficulty in thinking with clarity. It will feel as if there is a brass ceiling over the region making it hard to receive, hear, or speak fresh revelation imparted through the Word of God or by the Holy Spirit.

IN CLOSING

For some, this might be an overwhelming amount of information to digest. To be honest, it is not fun or enjoyable for me to outline these spirits and how they are perceived. But it is my prayer that this will help explain some of what many have encountered or discerned yet did not have words or vocabulary to adequately express these spiritual realities. I also pray that this has brought an empowerment to deeper understanding, which will lead to maturity.

A word of caution—do not allow this information to make you act overly zealous like a loose cannon toward these dark spirits. Hear me—I have perceived, discerned, and known the activities of these demons for quite some time. The ability to share all this comes from over thirty years of maturing in this gift. Our heavenly Father, Jesus, and the Holy Spirit are my focus and should be the focus of each of us. We do not glorify darkness. Nor should a fascination with darkness be the outcome of what has been taught. No demon, principality, nor scheme of the enemy is more powerful than the Great I Am. My worship and praise is always directed to our Lord, and this information is only tapped into when in a ministry setting or on a regional assignment in which this knowledge builds power for effective and victorious action. It is my hope that this now will empower each of you to the same desired outcome.

NOTES

1. Jake Kail, Facebook post, April 12, 2020, https://www.facebook.com/ JakeKailAuthor/posts/weve-totally-misunderstood-the-concept-of -hypocrisywhen-god-opened-my-eyes-to-th/2965309196862275.
2. Ibid.

3. Bob Sorge, *Envy: The Enemy Within* (Bloomington, MN: Chosen Books, 2012), Kindle loc. 10.

4. Noel and Phyl Gibson, *Evicting Demonic Intruders* (Chichester, UK: New Wine Press, 1993), 200.

| Chapter Eight |

TERRITORIAL DISCERNMENT

We had moved from Texas to Colorado Springs in the year 2000 to work for Peter and Doris Wagner and Chuck Pierce at Global Harvest Ministries. We were confident that this was the new season the Lord had for us. Before our move, several friends had cautioned me concerning the spiritual atmosphere of the city explaining that it was not easy for those gifted in prophecy and intercession. However, in my unprepared thinking I would ponder how this could be true. After all there were over 120 Christian ministries thriving in the city and many key leaders made the city their ministry base.

Once we arrived and settled into our new norm, I soon realized that my friends were speaking truth. It is a beautiful city, but at that time it proved to be difficult to prophetically hear the Lord and to break through into His presence. As a worshiper, prophetic intercessor, and warrior this was not an easy adjustment. I was also born and raised in Texas and had lived in that state my entire life prior to this move. I often tease that you can take the girl out of Texas, but you can't take Texas out of the girl. The atmosphere in Texas and Colorado proved to be vastly different. We were beyond honored to be with Peter, Doris, and Chuck. The job part of our move was wonderful, but I was struggling in the city. I began to inform the Lord that we had misunderstood Him by making this move and asked Him to open doors for us to return to Texas. I prayed this consistently for over five years. Not only was I attempting to sway the Lord to relocate us, but I regularly spoke about the difficulty of the city and with my mouth released negative words and curses out in the atmosphere.

It was 2007. I was speaking at a lady's retreat in Vermont. In prayer the Lord led me to teach about possessing the land. I was already feeling this was a different topic to teach at a women's gathering but strongly felt the Lord leading this direction. That night the glory of the Lord fell in that gathering. Everyone was either kneeling or laying prostrate on the floor. No one, including the worship leader, was standing. She was lying on her back on the platform, playing the guitar. His presence was so holy she did not want to stand.

As I lay prostrate on the floor, I heard Him ask a question: "Becca, you are teaching these women about possessing their land."

I replied, "Yes, Lord, You led me to teach this, right?"

He gently spoke without hesitation, "Yes, I did, but how can you teach these women to possess their land if you despise the Jerusalem where I have placed you?"

Ouch! I will be very transparent. I began to weep, "Lord, please don't ask me to do this." But soon I was completely undone and did exactly what He was asking of me, "Lord, please forgive me for despising where You have placed us and cursing the people and the land. Help me to love my city, the region, and the state with Your heart."

As soon as I prayed that prayer, He took me in a vision. I was soaring with Him over the state of Colorado. He asked me, "Becca, do you see it, do you feel it, do you hear it?"

Why was He asking this? Because in this vision I could see, hear, and feel the winds of revival blowing across the plains of Colorado. I assuredly said, "Yes, I see it, I hear it, I feel it!"

He responded, "Then get up, go back, and be one to help make that happen." Wow. Even typing this I am undone. While I am not certain we will live all of our days in this state, I can guarantee you that I now love the people, city, region, and state with His heart. I no longer curse the city in which I live but speak blessing to the people and land. Friends, if you want to have impact that transforms and brings His glory to the lands and nations He is leading you to, do not despise the Jerusalem where He has placed you, but love the people and the land with His heart. Pray, intercede, and contend from His heart and Kingdom perspective.

THE SPIRITUAL ATMOSPHERE IS HARD

Why was I struggling in the city the Lord had moved us to? Because of the principalities enthroned in the region. They influenced the spiritual atmosphere to cause feelings and thoughts of not belonging, being isolated, and alone. There was a strong spirit of covenant breaking and a true hold of a Jezebel spirit empowered by a religious spirit that worked aggressively against the gift of prophecy. Not only was this over the region but also strongly influencing Christians within the churches of the city. Let me give further examples to illustrate what some of you might have experienced in the territorial discernment realm.

Your marriage is good and strong. The two of you are getting along beautifully. All is well! However, as soon as the plane lands for the beautifully planned and much anticipated vacation there is a tangible agitation the two of you begin to experience. Before you realize it, the two of you are irritated with each other and the bickering and arguing ensues. What changed? What caused this to occur? It is not the two of you, but it is the spiritual atmosphere in the region, which has a history steeped in covenant breaking and a spirit of division. It is causing the tension you are experiencing and pulls you into dishonoring and divisive reactions toward each other. Why? To accomplish bringing division in your covenant relationship.

Or maybe the family is on a road trip. It has been a pleasant and enjoyable time thus far. All are resting peacefully while the driver forges onward making headway toward the desired destination. Suddenly, there is a feeling of an intense evil oppression. You go from a very peaceful sleep to an instant wide-awake moment while strongly sensing deep darkness and evil activity. What is the cause of this? You have entered a region active with occult groups who engage in occult practices. When we lived in the city of Houston and would drive to see my husband's parents in Mississippi, our travel route took us through the state of Louisiana. As soon as the wheels of the car hit the boundary line of New Orleans, I would instantly awaken from a deep sleep to sitting straight up in the passenger seat and on full alert. At that time, the spiritual atmosphere of the city was dark, evil, and suffocating. This, my friends, is territorial discernment in action.

YOU CAN DISCERN AND LIVE ABOVE IT

The word of God tells us that we are seated with Him in heavenly places. Therefore, we do not have to be influenced by the territorial spirits that are enthroned in the second heaven. We can learn to recognize who or what has established its demonic grip and is seated above the region in the heavenlies instigating schemes of evil. What do I mean by this? We can discern and identify who those spirits are and their strategies while not allowing their evil doings to affect or control our spiritual walk. We are of His Kingdom, carrying Kingdom authority. Once the discerned principalities are discovered, we intentionally understand its traps and choose to rise above it. This knowledge builds power for action that will involve strategies to see the demonic grip of these principalities lose their evil sway, influence, and hold. But before discussing these action steps, let's briefly discuss the actions and principles we can implement to live from heaven's perspective and our Kingdom position. The following are proven weapons to aid us in this process. I want to emphasize that when oppression from territorial spirits is attempting to hinder hearing His voice and the Holy Spirit flow, no matter what our feelings are dictating, it is imperative to press through those emotions to encounter Him.

Worship

Worship is a powerful weapon. It empowers us to ascend into His presence above the darkness of oppression, which aligns and connects us once again in a place of remembrance, recognition, and empowerment that we are indeed seated with Him in heavenly places. We then descend refreshed, empowered, renewed from the life-empowering and supernatural glory infused, inspired, and immersed in the awakening that only comes from pure and holy glory encounters with Him. Worship invites us into the eyes and sight of heaven. Therefore, we see the way He sees, hear what He is welcoming us to hear, and walk in supernatural grace and wisdom that is more powerful above all principalities and powers.

His Word

Reading His Word out loud. Speaking His Word out in agreement. Voicing out and magnifying Him. Letting His Word not only empower us but also proclaiming it out and declaring it forth to shift atmospheres. This is key in shifting the feeling caused by regional oppression and causing faith to rise up in order to advance.

Life Giving and Holy Spirit Anointed Alignments and Relationships

Being engaged in vibrant intercessory prayer groups, Bible studies, and churches hungry for the presence and fullness of the Lord is imperative. We will discuss the importance of Ekklesia later in this chapter. I will state here that having and developing a close relationship with those who understand these concepts is vital for growth and support. If you are living in a region and experience the same type of confusion as I did when we first moved to Colorado Springs, begin to pray and ask the Lord for the assignment He has ordained to bring His Kingdom plan into the region. This leads us to the next focus of this chapter.

PRINCIPALITY DEFINED

Your hand-to-hand combat is not with human beings, but with the highest principalities and authorities operating in rebellion under the heavenly realms. For they are a powerful class of demon-gods and evil spirits that hold this dark world in bondage (Ephesians 6:12).

I have mentioned the term *principality* many times. Let's take a moment and define this term in order to ensure we are all in the same vein of understanding. The Greek word for *principality* is *arche*. It means "chief magistrate or ruler who originates from the beginning" (Strong's #G746). The word for *authorities* is *exousia*. It means "superhuman, delegated influence, jurisdiction" (Strong's #G1849). *Kosmokrator* is the Greek word for *demon gods* and it refers to world rulers under satan (Strong's #G2888). This word was often used to refer to a conjuring of pagan deities or supreme powers of darkness mentioned in occult rituals. *Poneria* is the word for evil spirits. It refers to maliciousness, iniquity, vicious, degenerate, sinful, dark spirits who are possessors of this dark world (Strong's #G4189). The scripture makes it clear that our battle is not with each other but should be aimed in the spirit realm and directed toward satan and his hierarchy of rulers and demons.

Other names frequently used for *principality* are *territorial* or *master spirit*. These evil spirits are assigned to geographical territories and social networks. Their assignment is to keep large numbers of humans networked in spiritual captivity—through cities, neighborhoods, regions, nations, people groups, industries, government, businesses, education systems, religious alliances, media, or any other form of social institution. Results of this oppression include but are not limited to the rampant injustice, oppression, misery, hunger, disease, natural disasters, racism, human trafficking, economic greed, wars, and the like now plaguing our world. Some might be wondering where we see these spirits mentioned in the Word of God. Let's investigate several of these entities we read about in scripture and are still dealing with throughout cultures in our world today. And let's look at how to discern if these are in operation.

Before doing so, I want to state that I am giving brief explanations of these principalities. This certainly is not a comprehensive list. But as in Chapter Seven, this will give you a jump start in understanding their functions and activities. Those discussed here will be ones that have been empowered and are active in our culture, society, and nations. And remember, we as believers can identify and discern these entities and absolutely live above their influence.

QUEEN OF HEAVEN

Then all the men who knew that their wives were burning sacrifices to other gods, and all the women who were standing by, a large group, including all the people who were living in Pathros in the land of Egypt, answered Jeremiah, saying, "As for the word (message) that you have spoken to us in the name of the Lord, we are not going to listen to you. But rather we will certainly perform every word of the vows we have made: to burn sacrifices to the queen of heaven (Ishtar) and to pour out drink offerings to her, just as we ourselves and our forefathers, our kings and our princes did in the cities of Judah and in the streets of Jerusalem; for [then] we had plenty of food and were prosperous and saw no misfortune. But since we stopped burning sacrifices to

*the queen of heaven and pouring out drink offerings to her,
we have lacked everything and have been consumed by the
sword and by famine." And said the wives, "When we were
burning sacrifices to the queen of heaven and were pouring
out drink offerings to her, was it without [the knowledge
and approval of] our husbands that we made cakes [in the
shape of a star] to represent her and pour out drink offerings
to her?"* (Jeremiah 44:15-19 AMP)

Who is the Queen of Heaven? The Hebrew word used in the above scripture is *meleket*. It is defined as "a female royal ruler, one who is a governmental head of a kingdom" (Strong's #H4446). It stems from the Hebrew word *malak*, defined to reign and to ascend to the throne (Strong's #H4427). In this scripture, it is specifically referring to a pagan deity who rules in the heavens, meaning the area of the stars, skies, air, as a region above the earth including the horizon. She is an ancient principality also known as the moon goddess that has been worshiped in many forms with many different names, which I term *adaptations* or *manifestations*, some of which I will explain further. Other names for this entity are Ishtar, Astarte, Diana, Artemis, Sophia, Cybele, Minerva, Lilith, Jezebel, Venus, Ashtoreth, Isis, Juno, Medusa, and Santa Muerte.

Peter Wagner states in his book, *Confronting the Queen of Heaven*, "The Queen of Heaven is the demonic principality who is most responsible under Satan for keeping unbelievers in spiritual darkness."[1] Even though that was written by Peter in 1998, I have to honestly admit I still believe this to be true today, in this time and season.

This is a goddess system or structure of worship originating in ancient cultures, most of which engaged in a polytheistic worship structure, meaning they revered and bowed to multiple gods. The worship would often focus on a male god or principality. We will discuss some in this chapter. In some cultures, the male god could be viewed as the moon god, but most often he was portrayed as the sun god. It is important to understand that even in cultures where the sun god was revered, it was the rotation or cycle of the moon that had the "life-giving" significance and superiority. Why? Because it was linked with the cycles of the female body. Therefore, the moon was the source of blood flow and fertility.

It is sometimes found that the male god controls harvest, wealth, and grain while the female god controls fertility, idolatry, and family well-being. In some beliefs, such as the Egyptian deification of Osiris and Isis, she possessed the power through witchcraft to bring resurrection life. Therefore, Osiris, the Egyptian adaptation of the sun god, when killed twice had no power to raise himself from the dead. It was Isis who carried the powers of witchcraft and divination to resurrect Osiris—not once, but twice. The conclusion is that in this structure she is the principality with the ultimate power. The structure of freemasonry positions her with more authority than Osiris, who is known in this secret society as the adaptation of Baal, the sun god.

The Queen of Heaven in her many adaptations and manifestations was also recognized as the goddess of war and who also exerted ultimate control over the agriculture of the world. In these cultures, the belief was that prosperity and blessing were linked with their loyal, abandoned worship and devotion to her. She maintained her grip through the demonic forces linked to her hierarchal structure.

If she was not worshiped and appeased, then people would experience, war, poverty, confusion, and chaos. Barrenness and poverty would be other exacting blows this entity would deliver to those who tried to break free from her evil and demonic control. Through fear, this principality has governed cultures with its many manifestations and adaptations, keeping a strong grasp as a world ruler on wealth structures of influence, religious structures, industries, regions, and nations. We will discuss several of these adaptations. But to fully discuss her many manifestations in an in-depth manner necessary to gain full understanding will require another book.

When this entity has ruled a region there will be blatant visible idolatry where her name, Queen of Heaven, will be proudly displayed. People will be seen bowing to, praying to, and worshiping idols carrying her name or one of her many adaptations. Allow me to clearly state here that worship of an idol is focused on a lesser and dead object. A strong religious spirit will be in operation. Freedom and welcoming of the gift of prophecy or any gifts of the spirit will not be evident. Witchcraft and occult practices will be active. A strong hindrance and evil, divisive schemes to work against true apostolic-prophetic expression of the Church will be a repeated pattern. Let's begin exploring one of the most commonly known demonic entities who is a high-ranking general in the Queen of Heaven structure.

JEZEBEL

Jezebel—the wicked woman from the Word of God we have all grown to dislike. Why? Because this spirit is very alive and active in our culture. The meaning of her name is "where is the prince?" or also "un-husbanded." Isn't it interesting that even the meaning of her name depicts the truly demonic lack of reverence to the Prince of Peace and our heavenly Father who is a covenant-keeping God. Jezebel, or the one un-husbanded, will always aggressively attack covenants made in righteousness. Her name was actually the ritual cry in the worship of Baal. Jezebel's story is told in the Books of Kings. She was a Phoenician princess, the daughter of Ethbaal, king of Tyre. First Kings 16:31 says she was "Sidonian," from Zidon, which is generally a biblical term for Phoenicians. In this city and culture of her upbringing and royal influence, the Queen of Heaven was the eminent and supreme ruler. Therefore, when Jezebel married Ahab, she became the human manifestation and personification of the Queen of Heaven.

Jezebel married King Ahab of the Northern Kingdom of Israel. He was the son of King Omri, who had brought the northern Kingdom of Israel to great power and established Samaria as his capital. This marriage was the culmination of the friendly relations existing between Israel and Phoenicia during Omri's reign, and possibly cemented important political designs. This was the first time that a king of Israel had allied himself by marriage with a heathen princess, and the alliance was disastrous.

Jezebel, like the foreign wives of Solomon, required facilities for carrying on her form of worship. Therefore, Ahab made an altar for Baal in the house of Baal, which he had built in Samaria. She stamped her name on history as the representative of all that is designing, crafty, malicious, revengeful, and cruel. Jezebel went so far as to require that her religion should be the national religion of Israel.

She also destroyed as many prophets of Israel as she could reach and was the first great instigator of persecution against the saints of God. She was guided by no principle, restrained by no fear of either God or man, passionate in her attachment to her heathen worship; she spared no pains to maintain idolatry around her in all its splendor. Four hundred and fifty prophets ministered under her care to Baal, besides four hundred prophets of the groves, Asherah, which ate at her table (see 1 Kings 18:19). The idolatry, too, was of the most debased and sensual kind in which their rituals involved depraved and licentious sexual practices and abominations. Human sacrifice was often made to appease Jezebel's pagan desires.

We are all familiar with her disdain toward Elijah and her plot to destroy and kill him. In First Kings 21, we then learn of another deplorable act she initiated. Ahab desired to have Naboth's vineyard as his own. Naboth refused to sell his inheritance to the king. Ahab was upset and began to pout. Jezebel, through cruel abuse of her power as queen, employed a scheme steeped in lies to secure Naboth's death by stoning. Not only is this an evil abuse of power but it is significant because Naboth's name means "words of prophecy." Her name afterward came to be used as the synonym for a wicked, seductive woman (see Rev. 2:20).

Seeing

Obviously based off of the above description, a Jezebel spirit can be seen operating through someone who dresses in sensual attire or one who is very sold out to all kinds of evil, deception, and control in order to gain and have an exceeding amount of power. There are those operating in this spirit who are seen as very well put together in appearance. One who is in the world driven by this spirit will lie, manipulate, and shake hands with evil, corrupt structures in order to gain wealth and power. This will be seen on a regular basis. Jezebel wants to kill the prophetic voice and rob Kingdom inheritance to make it her own. In the church world there are those who have the demonic stronghold of a Jezebel spirit operating through them. They will infiltrate churches, ministries, prayer groups. Allow me to state this clearly. We do not call a person a Jezebel. That is incorrect terminology. They are being influenced by the demonic spirit of Jezebel. We must know and learn the difference. And this spirit does not only operate through women. It can and does operate through men.

This person engages in quick attempts to get close to leadership. They maneuver to bypass all protocols, but oftentimes with subtle actions. How does this appear in the spirit in regions where Jezebel is seated as a principality? Numerous churches, ministries, prayer groups, and believers will exhibit a strong apprehension toward prophetic intercessors and the gift of prophecy. Churches and ministries in the region will repeatedly shut down the operation of this gift. But to give clear understanding here, I will state this sometimes occurs due to past abuses with the prophetic that cause leaders to be cautious. When speaking regionally, I am speaking of an unusually high opposition to revelatory gifts across the board. There will be consistent, repeated patterns of individuals infiltrating ministries who operate under the influence of a Jezebel spirit. It is an abrasive and controlling figure who works behind the scenes against leaders and all that is godly, all the while stating words, prayers, messages, and prophecy to appear righteous or godly. At the time of the writing of this book we are seeing this spirit manifest strongly and frequently through men and women in the government, media, and positions of power.

I will express this clearly here. Strong, anointed women of God are not operating under a Jezebel spirit. This is an incorrect label that has occurred throughout the Christian Church for too long. Deborah served as a judge for Israel. Esther saved her people and a nation. Lydia led the church movement in Philippi. None of these women were operating under the influence of a Jezebel spirit. They were women whom God anointed to make history in the Kingdom of God.

Hearing

In the corporate expression, those bound by this demon are ones who are against God and prophecy, yet they themselves will prophesy in order to be the only prophetic voice heard. This is done in an attempt to get close to leadership and to outperform the pure prophetic voices and intercessors in this corporate expression. Listening and discerning the words are very important. There will be subtle words or voiced-out intercession that will be slightly off or carry manipulation, a religious tone, and a putting down of others who flow prophetically. Statements like, "Lord, I know that You desire to bring a pure prophetic flow and voice to this Church. Help everyone hear Your voice clearly so the words they deliver will not distract or take us off focus." "We pray for pure prophets who truly have Your heart for this Church and the leaders. God, thank You for bringing me here that I can be that for these leaders and body of believers. It is not the people's agenda, but Your agenda that needs to be accomplished. I bless these leaders." Do you hear the power play in these words? While some of these prayers seem innocent, the words come at the cost of others, but not to the one praying.

If Jezebel is operating across a region, many leaders and believers will voice out that the prophetic direction and guidance of the Lord is not needed with statements such as, "We do not welcome the gift of prophecy." They will use terminology such as, "You will not prophesy here. We do not want to hear what God is saying. You will not speak out or release any words that you are hearing from the Lord." Within the context of manifesting in the world, the one acting out with a Jezebel spirit will speak lies and deception in order to gain power and influence. They will be opinionated, very worldly, seductive, and manipulative without shame. They will stand for everything that is against God, but out of the same mouth will try to sound wholesome, even stooping to read God's Word or to use expressions, words, or phrases that seem pure to spin their web of deception, deceit, and control further.

Feeling/Sensing

For you feelers out there, being in the vicinity of a Jezebel spirit will raise a parade of red flags along with loud alarms roaring out in your spirit. While others will be drawn to this person, you will want nothing to do with the individual in question. There are usually feelings of a righteous indignation, a righteous anger when they speak, pray, or prophesy. It is not unusual to have no desire to interact with this individual. An overwhelming sense of grief will occur because of the level of deception and manipulation being released and the resulting blind receptiveness by those who are not discerning accurately.

For feelers at a regional level, an oppression in the spiritual atmosphere will be tangible, causing hindered freedom to prophesy or to flow freely in prophetic intercession. It will feel like a brass ceiling is over the region. Prophetic gifts will be unwelcome and the atmosphere will be religious and oppressive. Strong, ungodly, feminist ideologies and actions will be consistently witnessed in a structure or region where Jezebel is operating at a principality level.

LILITH

Lilith is cited in Isaiah 34:14: "The wild beasts of the desert shall also meet with the wild beasts of the island, and the satyr shall cry to his fellow; the screech owl also shall rest there, and find for herself a place of rest" (KJV).

The Hebrew word is *lilim* with the English version being *Lilith*, whose name means "the night monster, night hag, or screeching owl" (Strong's #H3917). In 1994, I had a series of dreams in which the Lord opened my spiritual eyes and revealed to me the demonic spiritual entity Lilith. The Lord wanted me to understand how this principality maneuvers. So in my dreams He opened my spiritual eyes, positioning me to spy on her in the spirit realm, yet this entity remained totally unaware. Why was this occurring? Chuck Pierce had given a prophetic word concerning the city of Houston. He saw that the night hag, also a name for Lilith, was singing over the city in an attempt to establish a stronghold. He gave the directive that the intercessors had three weeks to thwart and to stop this demonic assignment. In the dreams the Lord expressly showed me this territorial deity to be one of the principal forces behind death and abortion. After further research, I understood why.

Lilith is an ancient deity that came from Babylonian and Assyrian mythology but was also identified in later Jewish legends as a demon. She is also known as a woman who in rabbinic legend is Adam's first wife. She was supplanted by Eve and then became a demonic spirit. In this legend it is stated that she refused to lie submissively beneath Adam. She fled to the Red Sea. In occult witchcraft and mystic beliefs, it is said she gives birth daily to more than one hundred demons. She is depicted as a nocturnal great-winged goddess with bird-clawed feet. She carries a ring or rod of power, signifying that she is among the first-ranked gods. She is a seductress, replete with destruction, known as the goddess of death or Hades.

I find this portion of her description interesting. In the dream in which the Lord allowed me to see her, she appeared just as described above—a nocturnal, great-winged goddess with bird-clawed feet. She carried a ring or rod of power and was a seductress replete with destruction. In occult witchcraft circles, they believe this dark entity has charge over all newborn infants, and she is worshiped with this understanding. In Jewish mysticism they believe that she is the entity responsible for the unexplained death of newborn babies in defiance to God for her expulsion from the Garden.

Lilith is the entity to which the modern feminist movement gives allegiance. Margaret Sanger, the founder of Planned Parenthood, was engaged in the movement. It is an historically known fact that at the foundation of the abortion industry the purpose was to create a eugenics movement that would kill off the African-American race in our nation. Lilith and racism work together, hand in hand.

Seeing

Abortion clinics will be active in regions where the principality of Lilith has been enthroned. Suicide will be high. Sexual perversion and a seducing spirit will be in operation along with a spirit of death. Spirits of incubus and succubus will appear regularly in dreams. These are demonic spirits that come in dreams in the night hours to harass through sexual encounters. Incubus appears to women and succubus appears to men. Racism will be seen and heard. Repeated movements involving the feminist ideology will be seen as well as a defiant and angry reaction to those who oppose abortion. As stated above, the Lord brought me into a strategic and prophetic time of revelation through a series of dreams in which I spied on the demonic entity Lilith. I would like to share one of those dreams as it brings clear revelation of this entity and her role in relation to the principality Baal.

Greg and I were administrative and prayer pastors on staff at Houston House of Prayer in Houston, Texas. Eddie and Alice Smith were the senior pastors. In the dream, Greg, Alice, and I were driving to attend a church picnic being held on a ranch out in the country. As we arrived, Greg parked the car next to the wood fence where the cattle were kept. There was a large black bull in the pasture. He noticed Alice and I immediately and instantly began charging toward us. He was coming at us in a fast and furious manner with the intent to bring deadly harm. Alice and I in unison stomped our feet and shouted in an authoritative decree, "Stop!" As soon as the rebuke was proclaimed, that black bull went from a full throttle charge to an instant stop. It then stood up on its hind hoofs and took its front right hoof and reached behind its head. It then unzipped a zipper that ran down his front. The black skin dropped to the ground in a heap. It was evident that this was a costume. From inside that unzipped costume as it fell limp and lifeless to the ground, out stepped Lilith fully revealed.

What is the interpretation of this dream? When we deal with the black bull of Baal, we must discern and know that Lilith is the one hidden on the inside. Once the defeat is issued to Baal and he has been rendered powerless, the hidden truth is revealed. It is Lilith inside the bull calling all the shots. Therefore, when dealing with Baal we must always remember only half the assignment has been completed if he is the only entity dealt with. Lilith must not be ignored or forgotten. To see the full breakthrough and victory we must go to the hidden root to ensure Lilith is exposed, defeated, and dethroned. This adaptation of the Queen of Heaven hides inside the essence of Baal. This is a key revelation for all believers and intercessors when dealing with Baal.

Hearing

As I spied on her in my dreams, it is apparent this entity is a seductress. Therefore, a seducing spirit is part of her hierarchy. She also works with death. I share this because in those dreams I could hear their conversations. They will issue threats of death. Allow me to share an encouraging testimony that occurred in 2007.

Believers across the nation began a period of fasting and prayer in the night hours. The idea behind this was to intercede and war when the demonic activity of Lilith is the strongest in order to counter and defeat her strategies. It was an amazing 21-day focus. During this time, I was leaving the prayer time in the early hours of the morning. As I entered my car to drive home, a demonic entity revealed itself in an attempt to intimidate me from moving forward in the assignment the Lord had entrusted to us. It fiercely stated, "If you continue in this assignment, you and your family will die."

Understanding that this demon was coming against me because of what we were doing and the victory we were gaining, I was not intimidated. Instead, I instantly laughed out loud. An authoritative, righteous anger rose up from within me and I quickly bound it. And then I began to joyfully sing out loud songs about the blood of Jesus at the top of my lungs. That demon hated this! Needless to say, my response proved to be a torment to that dark angel. Soon, I heard the Lord: "You have had enough fun. Now command that demon to leave."

In instant obedience I rebuked that demon: "I command you to get out of this car. You will leave and don't you ever come back. You will not touch my husband or my children. If you ever visit me or my family again, you will receive even more torment than you did tonight. Get out in Jesus' name!" It instantly obeyed and it has never visited or harassed me again.

Feeling/Sensing

Based on the description above, it is obvious that there will be great felt grief over the bloodshed and murder of the unborn. A feeling of being unclean will be strong due to the seduction and perversion. Where there is a strong feminist population there will be a sense of not being welcomed for those who are Christian and value the life of the unborn. Strong occult activity will be felt throughout the night hours, specifically between 3:00 A.M. and 6:00 A.M. as this is the time those who worship her gather corporately.

BAAL

Baal is the supreme male divinity of the Phoenician and Canaanite nations. Ashtoreth was their supreme female divinity. She is also another adaptation and manifestation of the Queen of Heaven structure. Baal is also known as the sun god. Baal worship is ancient. This practice prevailed in the time of Moses through the Moabites and Midianites. Unfortunately, it spread to the Israelites. Sadly, in the time of the kings it became the religion of the court and people of the ten tribes. Temples were erected to Baal in Judah where he was worshiped with great ceremony. The worship to this principality was very licentious in nature. Other names for Baal are Bel, Molech, Marduk, and Merodach.

He was the chief god of the pantheon and celebrated in the spring of the year to venerate the awakening and conception of nature. The medieval druids, who saw his name as meaning "the shining one," adopted his worship. In his demonic belief, he earned his ranking position in the Babylonian pantheon by killing the goddess of chaos, Tiamet (see Isa. 46:1; Jer. 50:2; 51:44). By studying the word of God, it is plain he was worshiped under different adaptations and manifestations according to people, cities, and regions.

1. Baal-Berith—the covenant Baal

2. Baal-Zebub—lord of the fly

3. Baal-Hanan—the name of the early kings of Edom

4. Baal-Peor—lord of the opening

5. Baalath-Beer—lord of the well

6. Baal-Gad—lord of fortune

7. Baal-Hamon—lord of the multitude

8. Baal-Hazor—village of Baal

9. Mount Baal-Hermon—lord of Hermon

I believe we get the idea that this territorial spirit was widely worshiped. Other sun god names are Ra, Osiris, Horus, Apollo, Zeus, Hercules, Nike, Helios, Dazhbog, Sunna, Mithras, Shamash.

Seeing

What are its more modern manifestations? Osiris, Horus, and Ra are a part of the sun god structure and make up the demonic deities attached to freemasonry and Eastern Star from ancient Egypt. So where Baal is empowered, lodges and temples will be established in a region. The symbol of Osiris is the obelisk with many being seen throughout our nation and the nations. Baal is also worshiped in the form of a bull or a golden calf. Therefore, he has been given place as the bull outside of Wall Street. Baal and Lilith work together. Therefore, active and thriving abortion clinics will be part of the city landscape.

Hearing

There will a history of repeated covenant breaking. Stories will be shared that this a common reoccurrence in the territory. Words of division, impure conversations of gaining wealth. Strategies to overturn righteous alliances. Media reports swaying public opinion to encourage support of legislation steeped in an anti-Christ agenda.

Feeling/Sensing

Anti-Christ and Baal work closely together. So the things that are felt and sensed when dealing with an anti-Christ spirit will be pretty much the same when Baal is the principality.

LEVIATHAN

Leviathan is the king of pride. He is a coiled animal. The word specifically means "a coiled one given in union by covenant." It is a ruling principality of the serpentine family whose rule and influence is likened to that of a dragon. Also known as a dragon creature of old who was a representation of the devil. He symbolized mystical intelligence and animal force.

The Leviathan of antiquity was an aquatic creature and represented the cruel and absolute forces of nature. He was believed to symbolize that which cannot be subdued. Leviathan is completely associated with chaos. In ancient Babylon, he was seen in the constellation of Dracos and was adopted as the spiritual authority over Babylon. It is also extremely interesting that Leviathan in ancient times was also known as the Lady of the Sea, coinciding with Revelation 17:1. Therefore, Leviathan is actually a converging of the sun god and the moon goddess into one entity—male and female as one.

In Job 41, Leviathan is depicted as a sphere of spiritual power and human experience of pride where he was the ruler of the children of pride. False religion, illusion, delusion, chaos, twisting of words, and confusion are features of this principality's powers. Leviathan was worn on the crown of all the pharaohs of ancient Egypt.

Seeing

This entity is seen and heard daily through many media outlets in this nation. Leviathan is king of lies and deceit empowering an occult veil as its webs of deception are spoken out to seduce people to follow blindly. False religions, delusion, and chaos will be seen. Pride and superiority will be seen throughout the culture. People withdrawing from key relationships. Attempts to rob people of their destiny will be evident. And repeated warfare assignments to halt the apostolic and prophetic churches in the region.

Hearing

Where is Leviathan spinning its web of chaos? The answer is media, corrupt government, and world structures. It can also influence believers. It speaks out blatant lies and falsehoods. Conversations will twist words, resulting in profound confusion. Prideful, arrogant, and boastful conversations are a common occurrence when Leviathan is kingpin over a structure or system. It is heard as the false prophet of this day and partners strongly with an anti-Christ spirit.

Feeling/Sensing

Confusion, chaos, and striving will be felt. An edgy agitation and mocking of Christianity will be sensed in the spiritual atmosphere. It will be difficult to sleep at night. Restlessness resulting in fatigue. Feeling of life and strength being drained out of you. Feeling that no conversation can be trusted and also no relationship is safe and secure. Frustration will occur due to the fact that time continues to get robbed on a regular basis. A whirling of occult activity combined with an overwhelming sense of being deceived.

PYTHON

Python is also a serpent spirit. It is mentioned in Acts 16:16: "One day, as we were going to the house of prayer, we encountered a young slave girl who had an evil spirit of divination, the spirit of Python. She had earned great profits for her owners by being a fortune-teller." In this region, the python spirit was the epithet of Apollo, who was known as the Greek god of prophecy. A chosen individual, often a young virgin, would become the oracle of Apollo. Thus, she would be known as the Python, or *pythia*. As stated above, this spirit was in operation in the city of Philippi. It manifested as a spirit of divination and we still see it active today.

Seeing

This python spirit will manifest in forms of witchcraft, fortune telling, and speaking out false prophecy through occult empowerment. There will be idolatrous allegiance toward an occult spirit or this principality. But it will also try to snuff out the vibrant prayer life in a prayer group, city, or region. There will be psychic businesses and fortune telling activity such as tarot cards, mediums, crystal balls, etc.

Hearing

A strong mocking of the true anointed and called ones of the Lord. A spiritual warfare to prevent corporate times of prophetic prayer. A usurping of spiritual authority through voiced-out challenges with the intentional plan to do so publicly.

Feeing/Sensing

It will attempt to squeeze any fire or life out of the church, ministries, and prayer groups. It will attempt to choke out the vision of destiny, callings, and spiritual awakening. Therefore, a choking or a tightening around the throat will be felt. This entity is also linked with wealth, which will be gained through the hands of divination. So a sense or feeling of a seductive pull to draw people into divination to obtain wealth will loom in the atmosphere.

PRINCE OF PERSIA

But the prince of the Persian kingdom resisted me twen-
ty-one days. Then Michael, one of the chief princes, came
to help me, because I was detained there with the king of
Persia (Daniel 10:13 NIV).

The Hebrew word for *prince* is *s'ar*. It means "a leader, commander, chief, as of troops" (Strong's #H8269). As the word is used in the phrase *prince of Persia*, it is referring to a prince ruling over a kingdom or to a prime minister of the state; but the language also is such that it is applicable to an angelic being that is presiding over a state in order to influence its counsels. When one takes into view all the circumstances referred to in this passage, it becomes evident that this demonic being had some kind of jurisdiction over the kingdom of Persia. It is seen that he had a chieftainship over that kingdom—watching over its interests and directing its affairs.

This demonic entity identified as the prince of Persia resisted Daniel's answer to prayer. As a result, Michael the archangel was sent to overcome this opposition. All of this opposition was an attempt to have Daniel killed. In this evil scheme, the prince of Persia tricked Darius through the same plot he had also used on Nebuchadnezzar by stirring up the governors of the kingdom along with the administrators, counselors, and advisors. It appeared to be a dismal scene for Daniel. This dark prince had done his homework to know what would cause the demise of Daniel. But God rescued Daniel out of the lion's den and once again the power of the prince of Persia was broken for a season. In ancient history, we see this repeated again with Queen Esther. This principality rose up and operated its evil plot through Haman in an attempt to destroy her people, the Jewish race.

What is important to know about this entity in today's world? It remains a chief ruler over the Middle East and beyond. Historically it is a known fact that the ambassador of Persia made an alliance with Nazi officials leading into World War II. Hitler considered the Aryan race, Persians, a superior race, which he wrote about in his publication *Mein Kampf*. When this alliance was formed, Persia officially changed their name to Iran at the leading of the Nazi regime. This pact and alliance made with the Nazi anti-Christ structure is still having an impact today. As clearly stated by my friend Jon Hamill in *White House Watchmen*:

> There is no doubt the Prince of Persia was greatly empowered by Iran's newfound alliance with the Nazis. And it's no coincidence that within only a few years, Hitler's Final Solution sought the eradication of the Jewish people from the entire face of the earth. Beloved, this was the very force Daniel was up against during his 21 days of contending for answered prayer. He did not even know it. And the same holds true today. A clear manifestation of the Prince of Persia's influence over the Iranian government can be seen in its resolute vow, repeated many times, to "wipe Israel off the map." Moreover Israel is considered the "little satan," and America the "great satan."[2]

Seeing

Actions that originate from Iran with the purpose of bringing harm to Israel. Angry protests against Christians and the Jewish nation that originate in the Middle East. Anger, violence, threats of violence. Plots to control and obtain wealth at the cost of other nations. Militant demonstrations.

Hearing

Hate speech filled with anti-Semitism. Phrases such as, "wipe Israel off the map." Speaking out that Israel is the "little satan" and America is the "great satan." Speeches and words of superiority, inciting feelings of hate toward Christian and Jewish nations.

Feeling/Sensing

A knowing in your spirit of a coming crisis. Sensing in intercession that an uprising is being planned. Feeling the warning of the Lord that something is stirring in Iran. The overwhelming feeling of needing to intercede and war to stop this principality from rising up against Israel.

ANTI-CHRIST SPIRIT

Everyone who does not acknowledge that Jesus is from God has the spirit of antichrist, which you heard was coming and is already active in the world (1 John 4:3).

The Greek word for *anti-Christ* is *antichristos*. It means "one who opposes and carries the belief that it surpasses Christ" (Strong's #G500). This is an evil spirit that is completely against our Savior and Lord, Jesus. It is an evil, vicious entity that opposes the blood of Christ, the Bible, the deity of Christ, the humanity of Christ, the fellowship of Christ. It opposes miracles, moves of God, the supernatural work of the Holy Spirit, men of God, ministry, etc. Anti-Christ is lawlessness. Anti-Christ partners with communist governments as usually there is high persecution of people of any type of faith, especially Christians and Jews. An anti-Christ spirit empowers and works with racism. It will cause great chaos, but often will promote peace on its own imposed terms through the confusion and unrest it has created. This is done in order to control and suppress.

Seeing

This spirit will act against the miracles of God and the Word of God. It will disturb the fellowship of believers and harass and persecute the saints. It stirs up strife. It is violent when in action. It will be seen in mocking gestures, anger, and violence. When an individual is gripped by this spirit, you will see the above actions in operation through them. You can see it in movies, television shows, commercials, media, and advertisements that are full of violence and worldliness. In a region where a strong anti-Christ spirit is enthroned over the territory, it will seem that there are many who are steeped in the above-mentioned actions. There will be idolatry, false religions, cults, and occult activity. Christianity will be hidden and persecuted. Many will have been imprisoned and killed for their faith. High activity of intellectualism and worldliness. A great lawlessness toward the Lord and His Word and also outbursts of lawlessness and corruption will be witnessed.

Hearing

Words, along with actions, that attack Christians, Jesus, and the Bible. There will be much dialogue to explain away the miracles of God. Words of hatred will be heard. Mocking attitudes and dialogue will be normal. There will be no hesitation to blaspheme the Holy Spirit. Intense arguments full of defense will regularly ensue. This is when anti-Christ is speaking and manifesting through a person. When heard in the atmosphere of a region, there will be a mocking spirit against the Christian faith. Government and political leaders will not support Christianity or godly values. It will spew venomous threats in the spirit realm sent with the intent to intimidate. It might threaten to kill.

Feeling/Sensing

When sensing this evil entity, you will experience great hatred and resistance. There will be a feeling of violence and disgust toward you. Great darkness and oppression will many times be tangible. A feeling of looming danger and death. A great grief might be felt in your spirit and also a righteous anger because of how this spirit has harmed and oppressed so many. It will feel difficult to stay for extended periods of time. One must be graced to work in this atmosphere. I honor those who are called to such mission fields.

COMMUNISM

We discussed Leviathan, which is also referred to as the dragon, and also an anti-Christ spirit. We will now briefly discuss the definition of communism. I want to make it clear that communism is an anti-Christ system and structure. It is the anti-Christ spirit that drives the communist ideology of extreme control. In order to paint a picture of what is happening across nations at a principality level through the anti-Christ structure of communism I want to give a brief description here. This has been something that our prayer network has been strategizing and praying into for several years.

Communist ideology was founded by Karl Marx. He was a historian, economist, and philosopher whose theories were the foundation of the communist revolutions that erupted all over the world in the 20th century. Marx viewed history as a constant evolution where workers are exploited until they revolt. He was actually building upon the foundation of socialism, but considered communism a higher and purer form of socialism in which all private property would become obsolete, class distinctions would dissolve and goods and services would flow freely according to each one's ability and need. His explanations rang true with the working class of the time who often suffered awful conditions. The communist call was taken up in many countries in the hope of a better life. But to gain further understanding, what were his spiritual beliefs?

[Karl Marx] viewed religion as "the soul of soulless conditions" or the "opium of the people". At the same time, Marx saw religion as a form of protest by the working classes against their poor economic conditions and their alienation. In the Marxist-Leninist interpretation, all modern religions and churches are considered as "organs of bourgeois reaction" used for "the exploitation and the stupefaction of the working class". Due to this, a number of Marxist-Leninist governments in the 20th century, such as the Soviet Union after Vladimir Lenin and the People's Republic of China under Mao Zedong, implemented rules introducing state atheism.[1]

At its peak, over a third of the world's population lived under some form of a communist regime. Although many of these caused more misery than they prevented, Lenin and Stalin were ones who took his model and turned it into brutal control. Then we see others throughout history, such as Hitler who took communism into his evil structure of Nazism and Franco in Spain instituting fascism. Then there is North Korea, who instigated its demonically controlled regime of communism in 1948 led by Kim Il Sung. And we also see China through a revolution in the early 1900s moved from an imperial leadership into communism, with the militaristic arm of the communist party of China referred to as *the red dragon*. Hear my heart. When I am speaking of these structures, I am speaking principalities and the anti-Christ sprit that is driving them. I love the people of all the above-mentioned nations. I have visited all of them many times except for North Korea.

These specific communist structures still active today are controlling and do not allow freedom of religion. All religions and beliefs are highly controlled and, in many situations, there is great persecution to any who profess faith in God, especially Christians and Jews. It is imperative to have our eyes open to this system and to have discerning eyes to see what these structures attempt to accomplish in their nation and the nations of the world. I have met and prayed with many believers who have been tortured, persecuted, and imprisoned for their faith at the hands of communist regimes. If the communist party is not the focus of worship then there will be punishment. This is demonic and stands against all that we stand for in our Christian faith. Therefore, we must have the discernment to see this red dragon spirit of communism, as it is known in China, for what it truly is and also obtain supernatural insight and wisdom of how to pray.

Seeing

As one who has traveled extensively to nations, I will first state on the positive what is seen under an anti-Christ, communist regime—an on-fire, sold-out Church who is willing to follow the Lord no matter what the cost or price. They are so grateful for their faith they live a surrendered and abandoned life that is holy, pure, and beautiful. Often, I feel unqualified to teach these amazing believers as they have paid a price for their faith that I myself have not.

On the other hand, there is visible fear seen on all the inhabitants, except for the Christians. They appear bound, with no hope. Often they will not make eye contact with outsiders for fear of punishment. Usually the people of the land are not prosperous except for a small percentage of the very wealthy. Pictures, posters, or billboards of the ruler will be seen throughout the culture as he becomes the idol toward whom all worship is directed. It is forced idolatry to that leader, but nonetheless it is seen and evident. In some of these nations there will be other entities or ideologies worshiped in culture such as Daoism, Confucianism, dragon spirits, zodiacs, etc. There is control on all avenues of communication.

Hearing

Fear and control over the people. Consistent propaganda in the news. Threats to people who do not obey the strict rules and guidelines of the culture. Lies about free nations, especially directed toward their leaders. Mocking of freedom. Mocking and hatred toward God.

Feeling/Sensing

When in these nations, my heart so connects with the people. I will feel and sense an overwhelming love for the citizens of the land. In the demonic realm there will be an oppression that often feels like you can cut it with a knife. A heavy weight in the atmosphere. A feeling or sense of always being watched and listened to, which is often true because hotel rooms are bugged. Therefore, a sense of extreme caution is tangible. The same feelings and senses that occur with an anti-Christ spirit and a spirit of witchcraft due to the extreme rebellion and enmity toward God that welcomed this principality at a government level and forced it on the people.

ISLAM/ALLAH

Allah is the deity that is worshiped in Islam. *Islam* defined in Arabic means "submission to God." It is an attitude of manliness describing someone who was heroic and brave in battle. It carries a secular concept with the attitude of defiance of death and heroism. There are five pillars of the Islamic faith:

1. Their confession of faith, which is that there is no God but Allah.

2. Prayer in which they bow to the east (Mecca) five times a day.

3. Ramadan—this is their month of fasting, which is considered high holy days. The fasts are different every year based on the lunar calendar, which comes from the ancient worship of the Queen of Heaven in Mecca before Muhammed encountered the demonic revelation to birth Islam.

4. Giving money to the poor and the Islamic state or mosque. This is a mandatory requirement. It explains why we see mosques going up all around the world.

5. The pilgrimage to Mecca, which is their divine shrine located in Saudi Arabia. At least one time in his life a Muslim is to make a pilgrimage here.

Allah, the god of the Koran, is not the God of the Bible. The encyclopedia of Islam states that the Arabs in ancient culture knew Allah as one of the Meccan deities, of which there were 360. What is necessary to highlight here is the Ka'aba, the black stone worshiped at Mecca. This word is translated "black cube stone." It is the Arabic word for an ancient principality of the Queen of Heaven structure called Cybele. Therefore, when Muslims bow to the east, to Mecca, five times a day they are actually bowing to Cybele, the Queen of Heaven. Islam is a demonic network of principalities that reaches across the world. The top spirits operating in Islam weaving their web of deceit are anti-Christ, witchcraft, fear, and lies. These are the spirits that are seen, heard, and felt in a region where Islam has its hold.

Seeing

Mosques being built throughout the region. Erected billboards and signs promoting Ramadan. Muslims engaging in their call to prayer in public places such as schools, airports, hospital chapels, local businesses. An increase in private businesses owned by Muslims. Oppression of women. Acts of anger and violence, such as jihad. Hopelessness and loss of joy begin to take hold in the region.

Hearing

The obvious to state here will be the Muslim call to prayer. In the spirit realm, you will hear those things we spoke about in Chapter Seven when hearing spirits of witchcraft, fear, and lies and the anti-Christ spirit. There will be taunting and intimidating threats voiced out in the spirit realm by these spirits.

Feeling/Sensing

Heavy oppression, fear, intimidation, and danger are common to feel or sense when Islam has its demonic hold in a region. A sense of not being free to trust and a loss of security and safety. Spiritual death with no hope. A strong religious atmosphere. A feeling of being "less than" because of the Islamic belief that all who do not bow the knee to Allah are infidels.

MAMMON

No one can serve two masters; for either he will hate the one and love the other, or he will be devoted to the one and despise the other. You cannot serve God and mammon [money, possessions, fame, status, or whatever is valued more than the Lord] (Matthew 6:24 AMP).

The Greek word for Mammon is *mamona*. It is defined as worldly riches and wealth (Strong's #G3126). Wealth and money in and of itself is not evil. God can and does grant us wealth for His Kingdom blessing and purposes. In this text Jesus is speaking with a strong and intense negative connotation, signifying that someone has made friends with wealth through unrighteous means. Mammon, greed, and avarice go hand and hand. In ancient times, some associated Mammon with Plutus, the Greco-Roman god of wealth.

This demonic spirit is greatly evident throughout culture and the world today with leaders who go to any means to obtain wealth and power. Mammon is strongly connected with all of the above-mentioned principalities. It operates in and through freemasonry, the wealth of

Islam, and all the excessive wealth poured into the worship of the Queen of Heaven in its many adaptations throughout the nations of the world.

Mammon is the principality that empowers corrupt world brokers who consider themselves the elite—those who desire to use their wealth to control governments, legislation, and judicial systems. They partner in the abortion industry with Planned Parenthood. They shake hands in under-the-table deals and bribes. They obtain great wealth through pornography and sex trafficking. Mammon has become their god.

Seeing

This evil spirit inspires actions of envy, greed, and lust so powerful that even good men can be driven to corruption. Its grip leads to obsessive behavior. Once one falls under its spell, they struggle to focus on anything other than the treasure that tempted them to enslavement. There is such a seducing pull that people will do almost anything to get their hands on this treasure. Once enslaved by Mammon, people's energy will be controlled by it. The most surefire way of recognizing Mammon is by watching out for brazen displays of wealth. Such a person will always find a way to flaunt his wealth, whether it is covering himself in precious jewelry, shaking bags of money under your nose, or inviting you to visit him in his treasure-filled lair.

Hearing

People enslaved to this entity will speak about gaining more and more extravagant wealth:

- "I will gain that wealth and power at any cost."
- "I am willing to enter into that corrupt business if the outcome is more money."
- "I want to be the wealthiest person alive."
- "I will accept your bribe."

- "I will donate a million dollars to your campaign if you will do what I say."

- "My wealth has been gained through the murder of unborn children."

- "Pornography and sex trafficking have made me a millionaire."

Feeling/Sensing

Pure greed, evil, and corruption are felt when in the presence of someone partnering with Mammon or in a sphere of influence or region steeped in its web of greed. The sense of corruption, perversion, lust, deceit, and pride will emanate in the spiritual environment. Often witchcraft is discerned due to the blatant rebellion and idolatry of sin, greed, and wealth used for evil and corrupt purposes.

RACISM

From one man, Adam, he made every man and woman and every race of humanity, and he spread us over all the earth. He sets the boundaries of people and nations, determining their appointed times in history (Acts 17:26).

I believe we all agree that our heavenly Father makes no mistakes. He made every man and woman and every race of humanity. What a beautiful tapestry of mankind. God in His perfect vision and Father's heart of love made every race of humanity in His image. Every man and woman, every race of humanity made from one man, Adam, in the image of God. Who is man to determine one is above the other? To do so is to say we are above God and His perfect design for every race and nation.

Every race and all humanity are beautiful in the sight of our heavenly Father. Yet we continue to see prejudice and racism manifest in horrible, violent, and murderous ways, as if one race of people is better than another race. I write this chapter at the time of the devastating and horrific murder of George Floyd. It was an evil act with no visible compassion or humanity by those officers who pinned him down while he died. I want to stop and state right here that I know there are many officers of the law who would never entertain or engage in such an ungodly act. Why is it so difficult for each race to walk in the love of the Lord toward each other? I believe it is because of the sinful heart of man, but I also believe it is an evil principality that stretches across the nations of the world, and it is called racism.

Racism is defined as a belief or doctrine that inherent differences among the various human racial groups determine cultural or individual achievement, usually involving the idea that one's own race is superior and has the right to dominate others or that a particular racial group is inferior to others. A policy or government fostering such a doctrine is discrimination.

Racism has been operating for thousands of years. The children of Israel were enslaved by Egypt. The Jews were treated poorly and discriminated against by the Romans; the Gentiles were considered dogs by the Jews. The Jewish race has suffered and endured horrific acts at the hands of the Nazis and also religious structures steeped in anti-Semitism. Native Americans, African Americans, Asian-Pacific Americans, Latin Americans, and Hispanics have all endured racism and discrimination in our nation. To me it is beyond heartbreaking. John states in First John 2:11, "But whoever hates a fellow believer lives in the darkness—stumbling around in the dark with no clue where he is going, for he is blinded by the darkness." The Greek word for *hate* is *miseo*. It is defined as to hate and detest (Strong's #G3404). It is time to remove the blinders. This evil principality must be dealt with in the hearts of men and the nations of the world. It is my prayer that this truth fully awakens in hearts in this new era and great healing sweeps across lands gripped by racism.

Seeing

I believe I have already given a pretty clear picture of what is seen when this principality is ruling. Acts of violence, anger, hatred, death, murder, and abuse are all ways this entity manifests. Discriminatory actions motivated by lack of human compassion. Organizations whose foundation are racism such as the KKK, gangs and cartels will be active. One side of a town or city is thriving, yet the side of town where the "minorities" live is steeped in poverty, drug use, and gangs. Due to the anger that is involved in racism, at times outbreaks of lawlessness will occur.

Hearing

Verbal abuse, slander, and demeaning name calling. Thoughts and spoken words such as, "I am better than black people," and "I dislike Asians. Why are they in our nation?" Verbal slurs against those from Mexico and Latin American nations. Basically, hate words and demeaning words spoken out against races and ethnicities that find themselves in the minority. This must stop!

Feeling/Sensing

Animosity, bitterness, and anger will all be felt. Grief experienced by the Holy Spirit will be palpable. The pain of great division and the resulting despair, rejection, hatred, pride, rage. A feeling of not being safe and great vulnerability due to looming danger.

BELIAL

Proclaim a fast, and set Naboth on high among the people, and set two men, sons of Belial, before him, to bear witness against him, saying, "You blasphemed God and the king." And then carry him out and stone him, so that he will die (1 Kings 21:9-10 MEV).

The sons of Belial are mentioned throughout the Old Testament. They were considered scoundrels and operated in deceit, accusation, and evil acts. Belial is defined as "wickedness, what does not conform to a right standard, of no worth, evil person, troublemaker, vile thing" (Strong's #H1100). Obviously, this spirit partnered with Jezebel in her evil plot to kill Naboth and carried it through without hesitation. Just to give two more examples, it also stood against David and his kingdom and stirred up strife and dissension between Israel and the tribe of Benjamin. This spirit is a destiny and inheritance robber and will promote lawlessness through its demonic agenda.

Seeing

Under the evil influence of this spirit, those who are actively engaged with someone operating under the influence of a Jezebel spirit will speak accusations and lies against believers and leaders who are positioned in spheres of influence. These repeated patterns are intentional, to wear them out from being able to accomplish all they are called to do. Divisive actions will be witnessed. Stealing from the Lord, as this spirit was also evident and operating through Eli's sons when they stole from the offering given by worshipers to the Lord.

Hearing

Repeated accusations, divisive words, and manipulative conversations. Those who hear in the spirit realm perceive these accusatory lies. This spirit will attempt to whisper its lies to those who are not aware that this is an evil spirit in operation. This is done in order to cause people to believe in and accept the accusation.

Feeling/Sensing

This spirit will cause a feeling of being worn out. There will be a sense of stress and strife that will attempt to rob all strength and joy. It will cause a sense of confusion in an atmosphere where these schemes have been perpetuated.

ABSALOM

Absalom was the third son of David. The full account of the conspiracy that Absalom devised to usurp his father, David, to gain the throne in Hebron can be found in Second Samuel 15–18. Here is a brief excerpt from the Word:

> *Then Absalom sent secret messengers throughout the tribes of Israel to say, "As soon as you hear the sound of the trumpets, then say, 'Absalom is king in Hebron.'" Two hundred men from Jerusalem had accompanied Absalom. They had been invited as guests and went quite innocently, knowing nothing about the matter. While Absalom was offering sacrifices, he also sent for Ahithophel the Gilonite, David's counselor, to come from Giloh, his hometown. And so the conspiracy gained strength, and Absalom's following kept on increasing* (2 Samuel 15:10-12 NIV).

When we read the entire encounter, it is clear that he was a usurper of authority and would go to any means to ensure he was the one who ruled. He established a plan to take the throne from his father, caused the children of Israel's loyalty to sway toward him, and slept with his father's concubine in order to ensure an heir to the throne once his coup was successful and he was positioned as the king. He even had a monument erected in his name:

> *During his lifetime Absalom had taken a pillar and erected it in the King's Valley as a monument to himself, for he thought, "I have no son to carry on the memory of my*

*name." He named the pillar after himself, and it is called
Absalom's Monument to this day* (2 Samuel 18:18 NIV).

Interestingly enough, his name means "my father is peace" (Strong's
#H7965). He did not live up to the prophetic meaning of his name by
lining up with the plans of his biological father David, nor his Father in
heaven. But due to his appearance and charm he was able to win many
over to his side to partner with him in his rebellious conspiracy. This
same spirit that gripped Absalom is still active in culture today and is
known as an Absalom spirit.

Seeing

When this spirit is in operation the vessel or vessels being used will
seem likable and charming. They will be able to win the affections of
people by saying and doing the right things to win allegiances. Vessels
positioning themselves in secret meetings or calling secret meetings to
plan a usurping of the one in authority. Acts of perversion and seduction.

Hearing

Discussions of magnifying the importance of this usurping vessel
will occur. Statements will be made to draw attention to the importance of the one desiring to gain the position of authority. Subtle divisive
remarks will be heard toward the one in authority. This individual's
ability to charm others into the planned conspiracy will be done with
seemingly "wise" words.

Feeling/Sensing

For feelers there will be strong cautions and red flags and a sense of
not being able to trust the one influenced by this spirit. Deception, rebellion, and seduction are commonly felt. Maybe even a strong urge to want
to confront the one who operates in this usurping of authority. Perversion

or twisting of the truth will be felt as this individual will use any means to secure a position of authority, even if it means acts of perversion.

WHAT TO DO WITH DISCERNMENT AT A PRINCIPALITY LEVEL

As previously stated, when discerning spirits at a regional level, knowledge builds power for action. Your first act is to take what you are discerning to the Lord and seek Him concerning the strategy. As a reminder as we advance, this is a brief discussion of how to engage. There is extensive training on these topics in my books *Authority to Tread, Glory Warfare,* and our online training course, Regional Transformation Spiritual Warfare School.

Is This Your Assignment?

Being in your assignment begets authority for victory. What do I mean? My assignment might not be your assignment and your assignment might not be my assignment. If we step into an assignment that is not our portion, the intended victorious results will not manifest. We will be worn out and tired because of time spent warring in the flesh instead of the Spirit.

Strategy for Intercession

When He reveals a strategic assignment for a region, He will also give you the strategy. As a word of wisdom and caution, do not go to battle without His divine tactic and plan. Do not war from the flesh or emotional zeal.

EKKLESIA IN THE REGION

Now when Jesus went into the region of Caesarea Philippi, He asked His disciples, Who do people say that the Son of Man is? And they answered, Some say John the Baptist;

others say Elijah; and others Jeremiah or one of the proph-
ets. He said to them, But who do you [yourselves] say that
I am? Simon Peter replied, You are the Christ, the Son of
the living God. Then Jesus answered him, Blessed (happy,
fortunate, and to be envied) are you, Simon Bar-Jonah. For
flesh and blood [men] have not revealed this to you, but My
Father Who is in heaven (Matthew 16:13-17 AMPC).

Here we witness the history-making exchange between Jesus and Peter. As Peter boldly proclaimed the true identity of Jesus, Jesus then made a paradigm-shifting proclamation of His own to Simon Peter: "And I tell you, you are Peter [Greek, *Petros*—a large piece of rock], and on this rock [Greek, *petra*—a huge rock like Gibraltar] I will build My church" (Matt. 16:18). Simon Peter, the first to make this Kingdom declaration, was the first to receive the promise that God would use him like a substantial piece of rock to build upon. Jesus stated that joining Peter would be other believers who would also proclaim this truth and represent the Kingdom of God. Together this body would make up a great rock, like Gibraltar—*petra*. And on this rock He would build His Church, the *Ekklesia*.

The word *church* in the above scripture does not portray what Jesus was powerfully stating. The literal meaning is "called-out ones or assembly." The word *Ekklesia* is used 114 times in the New Testament, and in 90 of these references a local church assembly is in view. However, in this first use of *Ekklesia* it seems likely that Jesus had a more significant and larger picture in mind. He was not just building a local assembly but a worldwide body of believers composed of all who make the same confession of faith that Peter made.

The word and concept of *Ekklesia* was not new to the disciples. It carried significant cultural emphasis. In this time of history, this word was applied to the popular assembly of Greek or Roman citizens who helped to govern a city or district, as referred to in Acts 19:32,39,41. The Greek translation of the Old Testament used *Ekklesia* to describe the congregation of Israel when it was corporately gathered when Moses presented the Law in order for all of Israel to perform and carry out the Law as a people and a culture.

In Greek and Roman society, the Ekklesia consisted of ones who functioned in their cities as a senate or legislative governors in the land. They were known as a military task force of the culture they represented. Their function carried with it the ideology to disciple people, cities, and nations to cause things to appear as Greek or Roman. To understand our keys of authority to bind and loose, we must realize the history-making message Jesus was relaying at this crucial moment. We are his Ekklesia carrying His Kingdom authority. Not only does Jesus have all authority, He also bestows all authority.

BUILT ON THE FOUNDATION OF
APOSTLES AND PROPHETS

To be effective as Ekklesia it is important to build on the foundation of apostles and prophets. In Ephesians 2:20, Paul shares:

> *You are rising like the perfectly fitted stones of the temple; and your lives are being built up together upon the ideal foundation laid by the apostles and prophets, and best of all, you are connected to the Head Cornerstone of the building, the Anointed One, Jesus Christ himself!*

Apostles are ones who are sent forth with a mission, a message as Kingdom ambassadors. They are thinking forward in how to advance and they are not in the least bit afraid to take on the giants in the land. As already discussed in Chapter Three, prophets have the gifting to hear, discern, and perceive the strategy of the Lord. These two gifts in operation and agreement together become a powerful foundation on which to engage in territorial assignments for awakening and transformation. When we go into regions, we work with apostles and prophets of those lands to ensure we are partnering with those whom the Lord has positioned for victory in the region.

WATCHMAN ON THE WALL

In biblical days, a watchman was one who stood on the walls of Jerusalem or in the watchtowers to observe whatever was coming toward the city. The Hebrew word for *watchman* is *sopeh*. It is translated "lookout, guard, sentinel, sentry, armor, protection, security, shield, keeper, or turnkey of one's territory" (Strong's #H6822). Anything that this person saw approaching, either good or bad, would be announced. Naturally it was vital that he warn of coming danger. He had to remain on the alert for any hostile advances against the city—particularly at night. The night watches were the most likely times of attack.

We are also watchmen in our territories. We must be on alert and see what is approaching in our personal lives and our territories before it arrives at the gate of entrance. Standing on the wall for us is a spiritual stance; it is the Holy Spirit who reveals the spiritual activity around us.

In 2007, I was leading a prayer meeting. As we were praying, the Lord revealed to me a vision of the Church. I saw an army standing in rows of perfectly formed lines. The soldiers were clothed in armor and standing at ease. They were just standing still. They were in line formation but were not moving and were not on the alert. It was as if the soldiers in this army were positioned in formation because they knew they were supposed to be there, but they were passive in their stance and not fulfilling their duty.

Suddenly I heard a heavenly command: *Attention!* As the command was released every soldier in that formation came sharply to attention.

The command awoke and aroused the army. It seemed to awaken their spirits to become alert and ready for their orders and assignments. I heard the Lord say, "*It is time to be alert, to awaken from your position of stillness and come to attention before the King. It is time to stand in authority, hear, and receive your assignments and to advance.*" You see, the army was standing in line and file and rank, but every soldier was standing in position asleep. It was not an awakened army.

As the Lord was speaking this vision, one of the men praying with us began to read these words from the book of Ezekiel:

> *The word of the Lord came to me: "Son of man, speak to your people and say to them: 'When I bring the sword against a land, and the people of the land choose one of their men and make him their watchman, and he sees the sword coming against the land and blows the trumpet to warn the people, then if anyone hears the trumpet but does not heed the warning and the sword comes and takes their life, their blood will be on their own head. Since they heard the sound of the trumpet but did not heed the warning, their blood will be on their own head. If they had heeded the warning, they would have saved themselves. But if the watchman sees the sword coming and does not blow the trumpet to warn the people and the sword comes and takes someone's life, that person's life will be taken because of their sin, but I will hold the watchman accountable for their blood.'*
>
> *"Son of man, I have made you a watchman for the people of Israel; so hear the word I speak and give them warning from me. When I say to the wicked, 'You wicked person, you will surely die,' and you do not speak out to dissuade them from their ways, that wicked person will die for their sin, and I will hold you accountable for their blood. But if you*

do warn the wicked person to turn from their ways and they do not do so, they will die for their sin, though you yourself will be saved.

"Son of man, say to the Israelites, 'This is what you are saying: "Our offenses and sins weigh us down, and we are wasting away because of them. How then can we live?"' Say to them, 'As surely as I live, declares the Sovereign Lord, I take no pleasure in the death of the wicked, but rather that they turn from their ways and live. Turn! Turn from your evil ways! Why will you die, people of Israel?'" (Ezekiel 33:1-11 NIV)

In November of 2017, I began to hear and see this same army again. This time the Lord revealed that it is a new season, therefore I was seeing in a new way. The army is standing in file and rank, fully awakened, marching in place, in step and in unity in a strong military cadence. In the vision, the army is awaiting the announcement of their Commander-in-Chief to advance. The longer the army marches in place, the stronger the sound of the cadence and step of the march becomes. It is increasing in intentional focus and authority—that place of tension for the release from their Commander to advance. Suddenly, the sound of the Commander's voice echoes a decree in the atmosphere, "Advance and possess!" This united, anointed, and prepared army begins to advance with the fullness of Kingdom expression into victory in a battle.

I believe we are in this season now. A season of awakening and advancement to usher forth victorious transformation. The Lord has given to each of us a responsibility to watch, a directive to stand on the wall to see what is approaching, to announce it and to blow the trumpet. As we stand in a place of prayer, watching on the wall, discerning and hearing the voice of the Lord, we can announce and release His directions and commands. We can reveal the presence of the enemy and welcome the presence of the Lord. When we are rightly positioned in our territory or sphere of influence, we can discern how to effectively establish and build a place of habitation of the Lord—the spiritual atmosphere for harvest, awakening, and Kingdom transformation.

GATEKEEPERS FOR THE CITY

As the watchman stands on the wall and sees who is approaching, he reports to the gatekeeper: "Then the watchman saw another runner, and he called down to the gatekeeper, 'Look, another man running alone!'" (2 Sam. 18:26 NIV). The gatekeeper is the one who tends and guards the gate. He has the authority to control access through the city walls. If he does not open the gate, then entrance to the city is not allowed. If he opens the gate, entrance is permitted. In Bible days, gatekeepers were Levites, Temple officers. They were guardians both of the city and of private houses. In one of Jesus' parables, He described the porter or gatekeeper as someone who was also responsible to watch: "The Son of Man is as a man taking a far journey, who left his house, and gave authority to his servants, and to every man his work, and commanded the porter to watch" (Mark 13:34 KJV).

Engaging Principalities Is a Function of the Ekklesia

Hear this important message—dealing with territorial spirits over a structure, system, city, or region is an Ekklesia act. There are no lone rangers when contending at this level. To be Ekklesia at a regional transformation level requires an assembly, a legislative body. Just as one soldier would not go into a physical battle on his own against the army of his enemy, we too must go into battle as an Ekklesia. We are to function as His legislative battalion armed for victory.

Wisdom and Insight to Maintain and Build

Once victory has been realized, it is imperative to also have the discernment of the Lord to build in place of what has been evicted. The same principles apply in regional victories that also apply in personal deliverance. There must be a filling back up in the land and region when the strongman has been removed. Therefore, seeking the Lord in His strategy to build is as important in discerning and taking action to see these principalities lose their demonic grip.

As a national and international traveling minister, I seek the Lord in order to discern the regions I have been invited into—first to hear His word and His agenda for what I will be speaking into. But also, I seek Him to discern what the spiritual climate of the region is. What is the spiritual condition of the region? Are there principalities or issues that have harmed the people and defiled the land that might be holding back a move of God? It is common for the Lord to reveal these to me. It is also a regular occurrence for me to feel, see, hear, or sense the strongman affecting a region. The following is a powerful testimony that clearly encompasses all of the principles we have discussed in this chapter.

Transformation in Philadelphia, Mississippi: A Discerned Time to War

In 2008, I was invited by Ruth Ann McDonald to teach on intercession. Upon my arrival, Ruth Ann shared the history of their small town, Philadelphia, Mississippi. Three civil rights workers—James Chaney, Andrew Goodman, and Michael Schwerner—had been hatefully murdered by the White Knights of the Ku Klux Klan on June 21, 1964. Justice was never duly served. Division, racism, and trauma had gripped the region. Ruth Ann and her small, powerful band of prayer warriors felt it was time for healing and breakthrough. On the same day of the week for two years, she and her prayer team stood on the murder site and prayed that Edgar Ray Killen, a Ku Klux Klan member and orchestrator of the murders, would be brought to justice. A series of events transpired causing the investigation to be reopened. On the 40th anniversary of the murders, a cry of justice rose from the citizens of Mississippi. Edgar Ray Killen was arrested and indicted on January 6, 2005. On June 21, 2005, the 41st anniversary of the murders, the 80-year-old Killen was found guilty of manslaughter and is currently serving three consecutive 20-year prison terms. It's amazing what can be accomplished through a few humble and obedient prayer warriors!

Ruth Ann voiced her appeal, "Teach us how we were able to see justice served. We need to understand strategic warfare more." Thus began the journey of me instructing and partnering with them in strategic warfare intercession.

Prior to my return in 2009, we continued to strategize and pray. From 2008-2009, much of the prayer was focused on the upcoming mayoral elections. On July 3, 2009, this town that had been steeped in racism experienced an amazing historic event. The first African American mayor was elected.

Ruth Ann also began sharing about the Choctaw Nation and the strategic calling they carry to bring breakthrough and transformation. She felt strongly that I must meet a young Choctaw man whom we will call John. Due to his marked sensitivity to the spirit realm, he had been chosen as a shaman. However, as the final rituals of his shaman training approached, Jesus appeared to him in a succession of three dreams that resulted in his salvation.

While ministering again in 2009, the Lord gave me a clear open vision. I saw two Choctaw men in a cave and the demonic principality of the Queen of Heaven descending between the two men. This demonic encounter resulted in division. At that point, I knew little about the history of the Choctaw. Per my request and the nudging of the Lord, we met with John. He confirmed what I was seeing and explained that in the Choctaw creation story they believe they were birthed out of the mouth of the cave in this vision. The head/source of the Pearl River is also situated at the mouth of this cave, which in turn runs into the Mississippi River.

He explained there were two brothers who had an intense disagreement in the cave that was caused by this Queen of Heaven demonic being/principality. One brother left and took members of the tribe with him. This group became the Chickasaw. This gained my attention. Greg, my husband, is Chickasaw. I quickly understood that the Lord was entrusting us with a prayer strategy to deal with the root issue of racism and a covenant-breaking spirit.

When God is orchestrating a kairos Kingdom moment, He will ensure that all the necessary people are present to bring the transformational breakthrough. There were key intercessors and leaders attending the teaching that day. Representatives from the Choctaw and Chickasaw. An intercessor who had married into the family of one of the Klansmen involved in the killings of the civil rights workers. An African American pastor and those whose family members had been highly involved in freemasonry and the Ku Klux Klan. Every representative necessary to bring identificational repentance and healing to the racial covenant-breaking wounds of the region was at hand.

We strategized and drove to the cave. One key factor to include is that we ensured we had the welcome from the Choctaw to pray on their land. When we arrived, it was night time. We were in the country surrounded by trees. Our cell phones had zero service. This was a problem. Greg was to join us by phone so he and John could initiate a time of identificational repentance. Having nothing to lose, I decided to dial our home number. Greg answered with a completely clear connection, "Hi, are you there and ready to pray?" We shrieked in amazement.

It was time for Greg and John to repent and establish covenant. Greg told us to go to the entrance of the cave. I hesitated and explained it was dark outside, that a pavilion had been built above the mouth of the cave and crawling under the pavilion was necessary to reach the entrance. He responded with a clear conviction, "Becca, you must get to the mouth of that cave!" So, we got on our hands and knees and crawled to the entrance. Greg instructed us to put land in our hands, to pour anointing oil on top of the dirt, and to hold hands as an act of agreement. They repented, Choctaw to Chickasaw and Chickasaw to Choctaw, and established a new covenant as brothers with the land. I announced to that Queen of Heaven demonic territorial spirit that it was bound and its influence was coming to an end. All division, racism, and covenant-breaking was ended. We prophetically called in the true apostles/prophets of the Choctaw and Chickasaw to arise and decreed that a move of God would be realized among the Choctaw in Philadelphia and Mississippi. We sounded the shofar and shouted a shout of breakthrough. Instantly, the call was dropped and I was unable to reach Greg again until we were two miles away from the cave.

John was greatly impacted and, upon returning home, shared with his aunt and mother all that occurred. The next morning, his aunt came to the church. I did not know who she was but felt a strong prompting of the Lord to give her a prophetic word. The Lord spoke the word "Chief." I was nervous to share this with her. Questions raced through my mind: "Do the Choctaw allow women to run for chief? Will she be open to hearing and receiving this prophetic word?"

I Introduced myself to her and received permission to share the prophetic word I was hearing. "I know we do not know one another. But as I am praying for you, I keep hearing the word *chief*. Are you thinking about running for chief? If so, I feel the Lord is saying you are to do this."

She replied, "Your word is the confirmation I have been waiting for. My nephew is John and he came home last night explaining the miraculous time of prayer at the cave. The Lord told me that you are the prophet I have been waiting for to confirm I am to run and this is the reason I came today. If you released the prophetic word to run for chief then I am to do it. So, yes, I am to run." As a promise, I told her Greg and I would return the week of the elections.

Over the next two years, she and her campaign team worked tirelessly. She was running against a corrupt leader. Not only was there trouble through his decision-making process, but financially as a people they were struggling. Many were losing hope. To make matters more difficult, drought had greatly affected the region. She strongly desired better for their people. So, on little money and a lot of faith in God, partnered with a strong belief in the power of prayer, they began the two-year campaign.

Greg and I kept our word and returned the week of the election. She stopped her campaign for one evening and served us dinner. She invited me to speak to her entire campaign team. The Lord led me to prophesy that she would win. That the journey to victory would seem impossible, but she would win the election and it would be the Choctaw moment in history.

Earlier that week, Ruth Ann was in the store and had an encounter with a shaman. He stated, "Whoever has the most power will win the election." Based on this encounter, we understood through clear guidance of the Lord that the elections would require further informed strategic warfare prayer to ensure our friend's victory.

The key location of this focused prayer was a burial mound. The day we prayed, it was over 100 degrees, miserably hot with no wind. As we worshiped, Sheila, Ruth Ann's worship leader, said, "It feels as if life is flowing through my feet." I told her to take her shoes off and to release life where there had been death and occult practices. When she did this prophetic act, a strong breeze blew across the fields and over the top of the mound. That breeze soon grew into an overpowering, intense wind, making it difficult to stand. We all went to our knees to keep balanced. The temperature dropped drastically. Just as He had directed me to do at the cave two years prior, the Lord had me bind the Queen of Heaven principality. When I made this warfare decree, a whirlwind came across the field and began circling the mound. Lightning began to flash. We were without words as it became visibly apparent that we had effectively broken the power of this spirit. We made our way to the car elated and awed by the moment we were witnessing. A deluge of rain began to fall. The drought has been broken since this time; the Mississippi River in many places has reached an all-time high in elevation.

On election night, June 14, 2011, a young Choctaw woman shared, "I had a vision of a white horse running across the Choctaw land. Redemption is about to happen." The results of the polls that night positioned our friend and the former chief to enter into a runoff election. A month later she won the runoff, but the corrupt chief refused to leave office. They went into a third election. Again, she won by more votes, and on September 6, 2011 the former chief accepted his loss, announcing her as the first woman chief. During this three-month timeframe, we continued to pray. Illegal money handling between Mercury Gaming and Titan Corporation had been exposed. Forty FBI agents converged on the nearby casino and took all the hard drives and computers from the accounting offices. Since this time, Mercury Gaming and Titan Corporation were also caught in illegal money handling in the state of Oklahoma and have been indicted.

October 4, 2011 was her historic inauguration day. The theme of her speech became the prophetic word spoken that night at the campaign headquarters: "Our Moment in History." There is great power and authority in an apostolic prophetic declaration from the highest governmental leader of a people group and nation. I believe we are seeing the fruit of this in Mississippi.

The Lord has led me to prophesy over this chief several times. One word was that she would become a key voice of Native Americans in Washington D.C. She has made several trips to our nation's capital and carries great favor. Another word was that the Lord is entrusting her with seven keys to bring further wealth and prosperity to the Choctaw, Philadelphia, and Mississippi. She and her key staff and advisors pray through these spoken prophetic words, hear God's strategy, and do what He directs.

Chief completed her first term and was re-elected for her second term in 2015. Here are a few things that have transpired under her leadership.

1. Bald eagles have now returned to Mississippi!

2. Business has greatly increased. Chief has requested that the CEO of marketing pull back from some of the marketing until they can hire more employees to keep up with the booming business in Native American-run hotels, resorts, concerts.

3. They have built a hospital, which is ranked as one of the top hospitals in that region. This has provided jobs and better healthcare.

4. They have built a new preschool providing more jobs and better education.

5. They are working on a transportation system from Jackson to Philadelphia that will financially benefit the state.

6. They are in the planning stages of tapping into the land and implementing an organic farm to provide healthy food and further employment.

7. From March 1, 2012 to March 1, 2013 the revenue in the Choctaw owned businesses increased $3.7 million dollars and continues to increase.

8. They are now ranked the number-two employer in the state of Mississippi. At this time, they employ over 6,000 people.

9. In May of 2013, the chief was awarded the Woman of the Year award in the political/state and government category by the Mississippi Commission on the Status of Women. She was chosen over two state lawmakers, the senate secretary, and an eight-term mayor.

10. In February 2012, Forbes Magazine wrote an article focusing on Chief. Below is an excerpt:

Under the astute leadership of Chief, the tribe continues to thrive and become a magnet for new industry and investors. An innovative, forward-thinking approach to business has always been the tribe's practice. To further its economic success, the tribe is moving from traditional manufacturing into high technology pursuits. The tribe's outstanding progress in economic, educational and community development over the past 30 years not only attracts positive attention at home, but also at the state, regional, national and international levels.

By bringing people together and promoting unity, Chief is successfully leading the tribe out of the shadows of the national economic recession. She has been recognized as a visionary and consensus builder in Indian country and was selected by the White House to introduce U.S. President Barack Obama at the 3rd Annual White House Tribal

Nations Conference, further demonstrating the respect she has earned from Indian and non-Indian leaders alike.[4]

Friends, when we enter into the God-ordained *kairos* strategic moment, that Issachar anointing for our regions, we can and do see supernatural, miraculous breakthrough. Not let's advance further to gain further understanding of how to discern the times and seasons we are in.

NOTES

1. C. Peter Wagner, *Confronting the Queen of Heaven* (Colorado Springs, CO: Wagner Publications, 1998), 17.

2. Jon Hamill, *White House Watchmen* (Shippensburg, PA: Destiny Image Publishers Inc., 2020), 79.

3. "Marxism and Religion," Wikipedia, https://en.wikipedia.org/wiki/Marxism_and_religion.

4. "Mississippi Band of Choctaw Indians Tribal Chief Phyliss J. Anderson," *Forbes Magazine*, February, 27, 2012.

Chapter Nine

DISCERNING TIMES AND SEASONS

*There is a season (a time appointed) for everything and
a time for every delight and event or purpose under
heaven— a time to be born and a time to die; a time to
plant and a time to uproot what is planted. A time to
kill and a time to heal; a time to tear down and a time
to build up. A time to weep and a time to laugh; a time
to mourn and a time to dance. A time to throw away
stones and a time to gather stones; a time to embrace and
a time to refrain from embracing. A time to search and a
time to give up as lost; a time to keep and a time to throw
away. A time to tear apart and a time to sew together;
a time to keep silent and a time to speak. A time to love
and time to hate; a time for war and a time for peace.*
—ECCLESIASTES 3:1-8 AMP

What a powerful statement! "There is a season (a time appointed) for everything and a time for every delight and event or purpose under heaven." The significance of the biblical concept of time is the way in which it unmistakably and divinely presents God at work in guiding the course of history according to His saving plan. The Hebrew words used in the above scripture are *zeman* and *et*. *Zeman* is defined as an appointed, set time. When a time is appointed, it means it is an officially set time (Strong's #H2165). *Et* is defined as an occasion and point in time for an event to occur (Strong's #H6256).

Each of these words and the words we will discuss further in this chapter clearly show that He is Lord over time. It is important to know that time is not passive or unpredictable but, according to the Word, under God's personal direction and control. Time began at creation and becomes the agency through which God continues to unveil His divine purpose. God is sovereign over time. He established the cycle of days and seasons by which time is known and reckoned: "And God said, 'Let there be lights in the vault of the sky to separate the day from the night, and let them serve as signs to mark sacred times, and days and years'" (Gen. 1:14 NIV).

God in His sovereignty is not limited by time. You see, He is in all time at the same time. "One thousand years pass before your eyes like yesterday that quickly faded away, like a night's sleep soon forgotten" (Psalm 90:4) The following is a great description of time written by Chuck Pierce:

> God is not *in time* as we are in time. Our Father has access to every moment in our lives from beginning to end as though they were the present. By the Holy Spirit, we can actually access those times in our pasts when we felt abandoned, abused, betrayed, fearful, happy, fulfilled, or any other emotion or condition. Not only can the believer be forgiven for the past, but he or she can see back in time with God, see Him as "a very present help" in the past, and redeem those past times that the enemy wanted to use for evil.
>
> Imagine for a moment that all of eternity is represented by a large piece of paper. This is where God is unlimited by

time and space. Now draw a line on that piece of paper, representing time. Make sure that line has a beginning and an end. This line begins when God instituted time at Creation, and it will end when God says, "Time's up!" Man lives on the line while God can step in and out of time according to His purposes and plans. God sees all of time at once and doesn't have to wait for anything to happen; all is present for Him. This is a simplified explanation of a complex idea, but it works.

Now pretend that you can pick the line up and use it to make a circle. That better represents how the Lord sees time. Time is generational. Time is cyclical.[1]

It should bring us great comfort to understand that time as we know it in no sense diminishes His person or work—our eternal God does not grow tired or weary and His purposes prevail.

Furthermore, God imminently expresses concern for His creation. He reveals Himself in history according to the times and dates set by His own authority and will bring about in His own time the consummation of world history in Jesus' return. As we read in the Word, He is "the First and Last," "the Beginning and End," "the one who is, was, and is to come," "King of the Ages." The New Testament also presents Jesus as Lord over time. With the Father, He existed prior to the beginning of time, created all things, and sustains all things. He is neither limited by time nor adversely affected by it: "Jesus Christ is the same yesterday and today and forever" (Heb. 13:8 NIV). He too is properly called "the Alpha and Omega, the First and Last, the Beginning and End."

HE DETERMINED OUR APPOINTED TIME IN HISTORY

Let's now begin to apply time and its significance to each of us and how we are all called to partner with Him in the strategic and divine plan of

His unfolding of timeline. He has determined in advance the times set for all peoples and nations as stated in Acts 17:26-28:

> From one man, Adam, he made every man and woman and every race of humanity, and he spread us over all the earth. He sets the boundaries of people and nations, determining their appointed times in history. He has done this so that every person would long for God, feel their way to him, and find him—for he is the God who is easy to discover! It is through him that we live and function and have our identity; just as your own poets have said, "Our lineage comes from him."

So think about this. Our heavenly Father has always known the day, time, and appointed season in which you and I were destined to be alive. We all have a set time in His divine plan of history.

As we grasp this supernatural and awe-inspiring truth, we also must learn to think and discern time based on the fact so well stated and shared in the quote from Chuck Pierce: "Time is generational. It is cyclical." What does this mean? It is God's designed plan for the blessing of one generation to be passed to the next generation. What was established in the generations before provides an already established path for the now generation to step into and to build upon. There is momentum that continues to increase generation to generation in order that the Lord's Kingdom plan of awakening and transformation will be realized in cities, regions, spheres of influence, and nations. So not only do we discern the time we are in for our personal lives, but we are to build upon previous generations while also providing the way for the generations to come.

WE ARE TO DISCERN SIGNS AND TIMES

> But He replied to them, "When it is evening, you say, 'It will be fair weather, for the sky is red.' And in the morning, 'There

will be a storm today, for the sky is red and threatening.' Do you know how to discern the appearance of the sky, but cannot discern the signs of the times?" (Matthew 16:2-3 NASB)

Here we see Jesus rebuking the Pharisees and Sadducees because they insisted that He give them a sign that He was the Messiah. The truth is they were not able to see from spiritual sight the true identity of Jesus and the significant time they were witnessing unfold. How sad this is! If they had chosen to see with the eyes of the Father or with His spiritual understanding, they would have perceived, known, and received. Praise God there was a remnant who were able to discern and step into the promise of the salvation, redemption, and privilege of the calling to continue to spread the Gospel and to make history for His Kingdom and His name's sake throughout the nations of the world.

While all of us reading this book are not denying who Jesus is, we must continually stay in a place of hearing Him concerning the times and seasons we are in personally and corporately. The following are some of the questions to engage in with Him and to discern along our path:

- Is this a season that He is leading us in a new way?
- Is this a season when He is wanting to make new connections?
- Is this a time He is leading you to gain deeper understanding through mentoring and discipleship?
- What season are we in corporately?
- What are we seeing unfold in this time?
- What is occurring in the nations according to His written Word and spoken prophetic direction?

I personally believe and discern, as do many other prophetic voices, that we are alive in the most historic time of Christianity in the history of the world. However, this does not mean everything will be a tiptoe through the tulips type of reality. With harvest and awakening and a new era comes new warfare to engage in. To gain further understanding of how to discern and maneuver in our walk, let's investigate the key "time" words from the New Testament.

Chronos

Jesus taught the people this story: "Once there was a man who planted a vineyard, then leased it out to tenants and left to go abroad and was away for a long time" (Luke 20:9). *After the four men spent some time there, the church sent them off in peace to return to the apostles in Jerusalem* (Acts 15:33).

Here we see two examples in scripture in which the Greek word *chronos* is used for time. It is defined as an indefinite unit of time or period of time. In essence, this word refers to time in general. Therefore, it is the time we spend most of our life operating in. Time to get up, time to eat, time to go to work, time to come home, time for vacation, time for rest. You get the idea. It is our understanding of time and how it operates in our day-to-day lives. We all live in this place. But I also believe and know that the Lord has ordained that each of us will have moments and a key role to play in what is termed *kairos* time.

Kairos

From one man, Adam, he made every man and woman and every race of humanity, and he spread us over all the earth. He sets the boundaries of people and nations, determining their appointed times in history (Acts 17:26).

This scripture shares the fact that the Lord has destined each of us to be alive right now and also caused generational blessing and building.

I want to emphatically state that we are not born by happenstance. Each of our lives has been appointed in a *kairos* time. You see, the Greek word used for *time* in this scripture is *kairos*. It is defined as "occasion, period of time, era, opportunity, and to make good use of an opportunity" (Strong's #G2540). Interestingly, Brian Simmons shares in his brief footnote concerning this verse in *The Passion Translation* that in the Aramaic there is an added nuance to this scripture: "He commands the separation of the seasons and sets the lifespan of every person." *Kairos* is a word that depicts a strategic time to be alive, a strategic time to do something, and a strategic time for an event to unfold and God to move. I have witnessed repeatedly in my walk with the Lord that obedience opens doors to epic *kairos* moments. Many testimonies have been shared that model this truth and one powerful example will be stated at the closing of this chapter.

Hora and Ede

> *To live like this is all the more urgent, for time is running out and you know it is a strategic hour in human history. It is time for us to wake up! For our full salvation is nearer now than when we first believed* (Romans 13:11).

In this above scripture we have three Greek time words in action. *Kairon* is the Greek word for strategic hour and, yes, it is same as *kairos*. Paul then tells us it is time to wake up. The Greek word for *time* is this statement is *hora*. It means the time, occasion, and hour for something to occur. He then explains our salvation is nearer now. The Greek word for *now* is *ede*. It is defined as the day, the time is already here. Or to explain more clearly, it means that time is now. Therefore, *kairos, hora,* and *ede* time are greatly connected and converged together for epic, strategic, history-making encounters and events to occur.

We see this throughout scripture. Just to give a few examples—the birth of Moses, the exodus of the children of Israel out of Egypt. Jesus being born at the strategic fullness of time. He died on the cross as the Passover lamb on Passover. He rose from the grave and ascended into heaven. The strategic time, 50 days following Passover, when the Holy Spirit came as the mighty rushing wind into the Upper Room at Pentecost—which had also been known and celebrated in Jewish culture as the feast of weeks, the feast of harvest, which is important to understand and remember when we discuss the Issachar anointing.

We also see those who missed divine, strategic, *kairos* moments, such as the spies sent by Moses and Aaron to spy out the promised land. Ten of the spies returned terrified of the giants while Joshua and Caleb were not afraid. The fear of those ten spies delayed the possessing of the promised land for forty years—a generation of time. This is so important for us to learn and glean from and to not repeat the same mistake. We should not allow our fear or complacency to delay a move of God for an entire generation. Actually, to be honest, the awakening we all are crying out for is not a moment we are waiting to see suddenly appear out of nowhere. The Lord is waiting on us to say a resounding yes and to come into a place of surrender, welcoming the fire and glory of the Holy Spirit and entering into the awakening that is at hand now. I shared abut a spirit of delay in my book *Glory Warfare,* but let's discuss this here again to ensure we are not bound or operating in agreement or alignment with the spirit of delay.

SPIRIT OF DELAY

What is a spirit of delay? It is a spirit that is unleashed to keep us out of God's time. It will bring circumstances and distractions. It will hinder, put off to a later time, postpone. It will impede the process of moving forward and advancing. As a result, weariness and feelings of being overwhelmed will begin to take hold in order to rob strength or the desire to move forward. If these demonic schemes succeed, then unbelief takes hold. Lies will begin to invade our thoughts and emotions, such as: "His promises will not come to pass. God cannot use you. He is not for you." The truth is, everything in this earth is not in submission to the Lord as of yet. We must allow the warrior within us to rise up and bring correction to that which has not aligned with God and His purposes. When the enemy and his army of darkness are delaying our Kingdom promises, we must speak out loud and demand these evil spirits stop.

We recently hosted a conference in 2017 titled "Engage." My dear friend and mentor in my life, Cindy Jacobs, was a keynote speaker and released an anointed prophetic message on the spirit of delay. She emphatically decreed out loud in a warfare stance over the corporate group, "BASTA!" (The Spanish word for *enough*!) Hear me—if delay is coming against you, there must be a warrior's cry that rises up and that decrees, "Basta! Enough!" When a demonic force is at play and holding back destiny and promises, begging God is not going to bring the breakthrough. We must break those demonic assignments and bind all schemes of the enemy that are hindering, delaying, and obstructing and command them to go! The following is a declaration to declare out loud: "Get out of my life! I break your demonic grip off of my family, my life, my destiny. Your assignment is cancelled, null, and void! Go now in Jesus' name!"

ISSACHAR ANOINTING

These are the numbers of the [armed] units equipped for war who came to David at Hebron to turn [over] the kingdom of Saul to him, in accordance with the word of the Lord. Those of the tribe of Judah...of the tribe of Simeon...of the tribe of Levi...Jehoiada was the leader of [the house of] Aaron... and Zadok, a courageous young man, and twenty-two captains from his father's house. Of the tribe of Benjamin, the relatives of [King] Saul...for until now the majority of them had kept their allegiance to the house of Saul. Of the tribe of Ephraim...courageous men, famous in their fathers' houses. Of the half-tribe of Manasseh...who were designated by name to come and make David king. Of the tribe of Issachar, men who understood the times, with knowledge of what Israel should do, two hundred chiefs; and all their relatives were at their command; of the tribe of Zebulun... Of the tribe of Naphtali...Of the tribe of Dan...Of the tribe of Asher...From the other side [east] of the Jordan River, of [the tribes of] Reuben and Gad and the half-tribe of Manasseh...All these, being men of war arrayed in battle formation, came to Hebron with a perfect (committed) heart to make David king over all Israel; and all the rest of Israel were also of one mind to make David king. They were there with David for three days, eating and drinking, for their relatives had prepared for them. Also those who were [living] near them [from] as far as [the tribes of] Issachar, Zebulun, and Naphtali, brought food on donkeys, camels, mules, and oxen, abundant supplies of flour, cakes of figs and raisins, wine, [olive] oil, oxen, and sheep, for there was joy in Israel (1 Chronicles 12:23-40 AMP).

What an amazing battalion who assembled in Hebron arrayed in battle formation with a perfect, committed heart to ensure David would become king over all of Israel. It is a beautiful depiction and picture of the tribes uniting together in God's Kingdom plan and purpose, which I feel is also a prophetic picture of the season we are in at this time. Just as the tribes aligned for the future king and the nation of Israel, each bringing their own strength to ensure the victory, I believe in our nation and the nations we are in a time of alliances and alignments that will require this type of joining together and unity behind God's appointed leaders to usher in the fullness of the great awakening that so many have been prophesying.

At this point, for the sake of our discussion, we will speak specifically about the story of Issachar and his descendants known as the sons of Issachar. Why? Because it is imperative to have this understanding due to the season we find ourselves positioned in at this time of history. God has been and is continuing to raise up a remnant with an Issachar anointing who are able to discern the times and to lead in the way to go.

WHO WAS ISSACHAR?

Who was Issachar? He was the ninth son born to Jacob and the fifth son of Leah. We are all familiar with the story of Jacob, Rachel, and Leah. If some reading are not familiar with this history, I will give a brief overview. The entire story can be found in Genesis 29–31. Jacob loved Rachel and wanted to marry her. Her father Laban agreed. But Laban lied to and tricked Jacob by sending Leah, Rachel's older sister, to be the first wife of Jacob. However, this truth was hidden and not revealed until her head covering was removed following the marriage ceremony. All the while, during the marriage union, Jacob thought that he was marrying the woman he truly loved. Needless to say, Jacob was not happy when the identity of his bride was revealed. He confronted Laban, who then educated Jacob that in their culture, they did not marry the younger daughter until the older daughter was married. He again promised Rachel to Jacob in marriage, if he would agree to fulfill his week of consummation with Leah. Jacob agreed and then soon married the one he truly loved and originally intended to marry, Rachel. But in order to receive the blessing of Laban to marry her, Jacob had to promise another seven years of labor under Laban's direction.

Leah was able to conceive but was not loved by Jacob. Rachel was the one loved by Jacob but could not give him children. Both sisters were married to the same man and competing and striving for love and affection. After Leah gave birth to Judah, she was no longer able to conceive and gave her maid, Zilpah, to Jacob to bear children in her place. Zilpah bore two sons. Rachel, unable to conceive, in turn gave Jacob her maid, Bilhah, who conceived two children. The painful competition continued to escalate between Rachel and Leah. As a result, Rueben, Leah's son, went out into the fields and found mandrakes, which served as symbols of love and fertility in this ancient culture. He brought them to his mother. Rachel desired those mandrakes because they were a sign of blessing and fertility and she longed to bear children for Jacob. She asked Leah for the mandrakes. Leah gave Rachel the mandrakes as a payment in exchange for a night with Jacob in order to conceive again. Leah sacrificed the mandrakes and Rachel sacrificed a night with her husband, believing that sacrifice and these mandrakes would be the way to be able to conceive.

As Leah shared with Jacob that she had bought a night with him in exchange for mandrakes, Jacob complied. Issachar was conceived at an interesting time. It was the time of the wheat harvest, which also coincides with the day of Pentecost. He was birthed nine months later. Leah gave him the name *Issachar* because of the meaning, "he will bring a reward." Issachar was the reward of that night spent in intimacy with Jacob. And as Leah stated, "God has given me my compensation because I have given my maid to my husband." Leah and Rachel both truly had to persevere through much emotional pain being married to Jacob. Both sacrificed in an attempt to obtain love, favor, and generational blessing.

We read in Genesis 49:14-15 that Jacob, in his act of the father's blessing, blessed Issachar by saying that he was a man of strength who would not pull back from hard work to establish provision and a safe place to rest. Let's now look at the promise and inheritance that was bestowed on the sons of Issachar as one of the twelve tribes of Israel and the many areas in which they discerned and led through the times and seasons.

PROPHETIC INSIGHT THAT LEADS TO VICTORY

As stated above in First Chronicles 12:32, "Of the tribe of Issachar, men who understood the times, with knowledge of what Israel should do, two hundred chiefs; and all their relatives were at their command" (AMP). The men of Issachar were the fewest of all, only 200, but were as valuable to the interests of David as those who arrived in the greatest numbers. The sons of Issachar could accomplish with 200 what took other tribes very large numbers to achieve. They were men of great skill above any of their neighbors as they were men who had understanding of the times. The Hebrew word for *understanding* is *yada*. It means "to advise, answer, appoint, discern, perceive, know, comprehend, to have understanding, to be wise, have skill, and to be cunning" (Strong's #H3045). They exemplified ones who embodied keen discernment and prophetic insight to lead an entire nation and its divinely called leader into its new season and era of victory.

Wisdom for the Harvest

They understood the natural times by *discerning the face of the sky*. What does this mean? They studied the movements of the stars and planets and understood chronological time. They were weather-wise, could advise in the proper times for plowing, sowing and reaping. In other words, the processes to go through to reap a harvest!

Alignments to Assemble and Release Abundance

Through the aligning of the stars they knew when to call the nation to assemble for the ceremonial times, the times appointed for the Jewish feasts. "They will call the peoples to the mountain; there they will offer sacrifices of righteousness, for they will draw out the abundance of the seas and the treasures hid in the sand" (Deut. 33:19 MEV). This is a powerful example of bringing an entire nation together to worship in a solemn assembly as the Ekklesia in the appointed times and season. As a result, favor concerning provision and supply was realized.

Discernment in Advancing Peoples and Nations

The sons of Issachar excelled in knowledge and wisdom of the laws of God. As Israel moved through the wilderness, God chose the sons of Issachar as one of the three tribes to lead the way when the nation advanced. Judah, the ones of worship and war, went first. Then Issachar, the wise and discerning ones, would go second. Zebulun, the financiers and ones of supply, would go third. Issachar had the ability to maneuver in discernment strategies to make a way for provision and supply.

Discernment to Support God's Appointed Leaders

Issachar understood public affairs and political times, the disposition of the nation, and the tendencies of unfolding events. In other words, the tribe had keen insight and made a good use of it. They knew *what Israel should do*. From their wisdom and experience they learned both their own responsibilities and the duty and interest of others. In this critical time spoken of in First Chronicles, they knew Israel was to make David the king. It was not only beneficial but necessary as the state of events and the appointing of the Lord called for it.

In Judges 5:15, we read of "the princes of Issachar" (NIV). As this part of their story testifies, they were with Deborah and Barak and went to battle under her leadership. Although at this time in history women did have some rights in Israel, it was still unusual for a woman to sit in authority over the nation. The sons of Issachar could discern the times and season and they knew God's hand was on her and it was her time to lead.

Anointed and Appointed to Lead

In Judges 10:1-2, we read of one of their own who rose to leadership as a judge: "Tola the son of Puah, the son of Dodo, a man of Issachar, arose to save Israel...He judged Israel for twenty-three years" (MEV). They knew when a leader was falling and a leader was rising. They could discern if they were to lead or who the next leader was to be and then lead by example in following him or her.

APPLYING AND ACTIVATING THE ISSACHAR ANOINTING

The sons of Issachar had something special. Their ability to discern the times and seasons was an incredible advantage. It gave them inside knowledge and understanding of God's activities. They were not taken by surprise when transition and change occurred. They had influence as a result of their unique ability to discern times and seasons. They knew what Israel should do and when it should be done. They walked in wisdom and favor, and the nation followed their example.

So how does this apply to you and I? As stated above, we are in season and time when the Lord has been and is continuing to raise up an army of the sons of Issachar—ones who will *surrender* at the altar of intercession to discern, hear, and prophesy. We will discuss surrender further in the final chapter, but I will briefly give the definition here. It means to cease resistance, yield, give way, unconditional surrender and abandonment. You see, if we are going to walk as a son of Issachar, there must be discernment when the new is upon us and a place of deep obedience and surrender to the new. Just as Leah and Rachel had to sacrifice in order to achieve the blessing for their generations, there will be a price for this anointing.

The truth and good news is, you and I can have the anointing of the sons of Issachar. We can have the same ability to discern the times and seasons. We can begin by asking the Lord for a fresh fire and anointing of His Spirit. Just as Issachar was conceived at the feast of harvest, the time of Pentecost, seek the Lord for a new awakening of His fire and glory. We will continue to speak even further about encountering the Holy Spirit in the closing chapter of this book. Understand that He is no respecter of persons as stated by Peter in Acts 10:34, "Now I know for certain that God doesn't show favoritism with people but treats everyone on the same basis." I fully believe God does not have favorites, but He does have His intimates. And He desires a personal, intimate relationship with each of us. Through Jesus, our heavenly Father has also bestowed on us the blessings He released to Abraham and the children of Israel, and He has blessed all of us with everything that pertains to life and godliness. Therefore, as heirs of God and co-heirs with Christ, it is our Kingdom inheritance to walk as sons of Issachar.

If you desire to be awakened to this anointing and appointing of discernment and wisdom, ask Him. We have not because we ask not. And when you ask, expect Him to answer. Pay close attention to the following:

- When you feel like something new is about to happen
- When you feel reluctant to make a certain decision because you feel like it isn't quite time
- When you feel like you should not take on anything new because it feels as if a door is about to open
- When God leads you to stand for something or someone who is biblically supported but is not popular
- When God starts to give you influence and people follow your example
- When you begin to get strategies to advance in a new endeavor
- When people begin to ask you for more insight

- When the Lord is calling you into a season of fasting and intercession
- Increased prophetic insight from the Lord
- Leading of the Lord to prophesy
- Strategies for victories within your sphere of influence
- An understanding of how to create supply and provision
- Having the boldness to back God's chosen, anointed, and appointed leaders—yes, even governmental leaders
- Having a Kingdom mindset over a religious mindset

TESTIMONY OF DISCERNING THE TIMING OF THE LORD THAT CHANGES OUR LIVES AND THE DESTINY OF A NATION

The Lord impressed upon us to go to Wales to spend time in the Bible college that was founded by Rees Howells. You see, I was reading a book about him in the early '90s when the Lord called me as an intercessor and prophet to the nations. Not only were we to spend time there, but we were to pray in the chapel and the Blue Room where all the years of history-making, Holy Spirit-empowered intercession had occurred. When I was called to intercession for the nations, the Lord said to go back to the place of the anointing that had been so mightily used by Him. Go back to that place, because there was more that He wanted us to receive in that mantle of intercession. It felt as if a holy, glorious impartation would occur, one that would take us beyond, causing us to go higher and deeper in the impartation of our calling.

Greg and I went together in January of 2018. We spent three days in the chapel praying, interceding, and dedicating our lives and our ministry to the Lord. It was a moment between the two of us and the Lord when He spoke so clearly to us personally and for the ministry we lead. It was a glorious, holy, sacred time of surrendered consecration. He ignited our passion for the nations again and sealed it in beautiful glory encounters with Him.

Then in March we took a small group of prayer leaders in our prayer network. We were welcomed and given two full days in the chapel, were involved in an intercessory prayer time for the nations in the Blue Room, and visited Pisgah Chapel and Moriah Chapel where the Welsh Revival occurred through Evan Roberts. I have to admit what transpired for us in those four days in Wales was beyond words. But I am going to share some of the things that I feel will spur each of you to hunger for more of Him and impart faith to enter into a fresh encounter of His fire and glory as this is the time and season we are in—encounters that awaken us for glory and transformation.

I am going to attempt to describe an anointing that we encountered in our prayer times. I do not share this to make it sound as if we are special because of what transpired, but to encourage each of you to move into an abiding, surrendered place that causes you to rise up to purpose, destiny, and victory. His magnificent glory came into our prayer times. It was tangible and holy, a glorious heavenly presence so real that it causes you to want to surrender all you are, to lay down all that you have, and to consecrate everything to Him. A presence where groans begin to rise in the room: "Lord, I want more of You. I need more of You. I surrender all to You. Jesus, we want more of You."

As we entered this place of consecrated surrender, He met with us. There was an expansion in the Spirit that occurred for each person in that divine encounter moment. We caught the glory wave of intercession within the history and the sound of those walls from years of nation-shifting intercession. We could hear in the spirit the decades of intercession that shaped the history of the world. The glory wave of the Holy Spirit swept us up into the atmosphere of heaven. But the beauty was as we were swept up into the atmosphere of heaven, the atmosphere of the glory and heaven met us in that prayer chapel. We were in a womb of intercession that had captured and carried within its memory all of the intercession across the generations. It was a time of synergy, a converging point. We were one with Him and eternity in that prayer room. And as we pressed into a place of complete adoration and abandonment to Him, He expanded us to think far beyond ourselves, sweeping us into a passion for the nations that was beautiful, glorious, full of immense holiness and joy. The nations became the cry of our hearts. It was as if our intercession was a bowl being tipped out for the nations. I am undone all over again typing this. Six of us laid prostrate on the floor holding hands in a circle and covenanting with God for the nations. The lead intercessor of the Bible college had joined us in the chapel and at one point she began to pray, sing, and prophesy. Here is one word she delivered in this holy moment:

> This is special, oh, this is special! I see a window of heaven open and oil just pouring down—there is a pouring forth into this time right now. And I just see a portal and it's open right now in the center of this room. And it's pouring forth oil and the wine. He's pouring it in the center of this room right now. And it is just moving, coming toward us! It's spreading over the whole room. Oh, the oil and the wine. By faith we stand in it. By faith we lay (prostrate) in it. Oh, Holy Spirit, You make all this possible. Oh, Lord, for the healing of the nations. We are at the dawn of an awakening. We are at the dawn of a breaking, a breaking of the Spirit of the Lord. The latter rain. The latter rain. Take your places now. Take your places. You are vessels of honor,

vessels filled with My power and My spirit. Stand before Me, consecrated. There are amazing things I will do. We are at the dawn of an awakening and the dawn of a breaking. Be ready, be expectant!

As we pressed in deeper, we encountered a beautiful moment that transformed all of our lives. It seemed as if the veil between heaven and earth opened and we began to have encounters in the great cloud of witnesses. It was such a holy, holy moment. Weeping broke out across the room. I was totally undone as I saw Jesus, my spiritual father C. Peter Wagner, and Rees Howells. I heard the following words just as if Peter would have spoken them to me when he was alive: "Good job, darlin'. You came to Wales to finish receiving the anointing and mantle for the nations. I'm proud of you. I love you." No words. Just tears of brokenness, awe, reverence, and joy all at the same time.

As we all came out of our encounters, we made our way back to our rooms. We were all speechless at what had transpired. A student from the Bible college saw an object on the floor of the chapel in which all of this had occurred. She picked it up to see that it was a key. A double-sided key with a crown and the word *master* on each side. To ensure we were not in the flesh, everyone on that campus was asked if they had seen that key, owned that key, or knew where it came from. No one had seen it, nor did it belong to anyone. One of the gentlemen who had worked on the campus explained to us what a master key does. It is a key that goes into a lock that has been locked up and cannot be opened. It realigns, resets, and opens that which has been locked up.

If you recall, we discussed the Ekklesia in Chapter Eight. One key point we need to make here is the authority that has been bestowed on each of us as His Ekklesia. When Jesus made the statement, "I will give you the keys of the Kingdom," it carried great spiritual significance. In ancient Jewish culture, to be given a key to someone's home or business did not carry the implication of house sitting. It actually meant that you were being entrusted with the full authority, as if you were the master of the house yourself. So now, in this deep time of surrender, intercession, and making covenant with the Lord for the nations, as a sign from heaven a master key was entrusted to us. We all fully believe that this is a sign and a wonder of the time the Body of Christ is in—awakening to our call as the Ekklesia to see the greatest awakening, movement of transformation, and harvest of souls in the history of the church.

We soon realized after this occurred that we were in that chapel on the 82nd anniversary of when the Lord spoke to Rees Howells to contend against the anti-Christ principalities in operation through Adolf Hitler and the Nazi structure. He also was praying concerning Stalin, Mussolini, and Franco, as the four dictators had made an alliance as communist and fascist leaders. Now we know what occurred with all of these leaders. Hitler, Stalin, and Mussolini died quickly once Rees and his prayer army began to contend against that anti-Christ principality. However, Franco of Spain lived a long life of 82 years, dying on November 20, 1975. He even went to the extreme of overseeing the construction of the mausoleum he demanded to be erected in his honor. It was a death shrine as he had the remains of 33,000 dead bodies buried in the walls as a death memorial to himself—the bodies of those who had died at his hand or under his leadership. He then dictated that his body be buried in the floor of the altar. For 44 years after his passing, ancient Gregorian ceremonies were held over his grave, per his instructions. For years, the people in the nation of Spain had wanted that shrine to the dead dictator shut down. He was a ruthless dictator who had struck fear in his people.

Before this trip to Wales was planned, the Lord had already directed several of us to go to that mausoleum in Spain directly following our time in the Bible college. I have been traveling in and out of Spain since

2003. It is a nation I am called to. Cindy Jacobs challenged me repeatedly over several years to pray to see that anti-Christ structure that perpetuated the worship of a dead dictator dethroned and the mausoleum shut down. We felt the timing was right to go, following our time in Wales. And boy did we discern the times correctly!

On the day that we prayed, we witnessed the worship in the mausoleum over his dead bones and with our own eyes watched that anti-Christ principality rise up out of his grave. The Lord led us to go to the steel gates at the entrance where he had been brought in 44 years earlier to be buried. In the natural, those particular gates were shut that day. But at the leading of the Lord, we engaged in a prophetic act with a key brought by a team member. A prophetic declaration was made that the gate opening up the worship and glorifying of the dead dictator was shut, the worship of Franco would stop, and the mausoleum would be closed. We as a team all heard simultaneously the sound of large, steel, heavy gates slamming in the spirit. The impact of that sound was such that it caused the ground to shake and tremble under our feet. All of us heard it and felt it and shrieked with joy. We knew something had just transpired in the spirit.

I was invited to return and to minister in the nation 18 months later. Upon our arrival, our dear friends and hosts, Jose and Elba Lopez, said they had a great surprise. During that 18-month period, a series of miraculous events had transpired. Legal documents had been pushed through every level of government in Spain and also the government of the Vatican. Why the Vatican? Because they owned the mausoleum; Spain did not. After 44 years of the nation of Spain tirelessly working to see this place of worship shut down, the legal documents were signed and on October 24, 2019, we watched with the entire nation of Spain and the nations of the world as the remains of General Francisco Franco were exhumed and carried through the exact steel gates where we performed the prophetic act 18 months earlier. The coffin was lifted in a helicopter and taken to the cemetery to be buried next to his wife. The gates to the mausoleum were shut, never to be opened again. The Prime Minister of Spain came on national television and made the governmental decree that the remains of a dictator would no longer be glorified in the nation of Spain! Wow! Woohoo! Go, God! We were undone and wept tears of joy as we witnessed this miracle of healing of a nation unfold before our eyes.

DISCERNING THE CALL

This is the historic time we are in. This testimony is a "sons of Issachar" calling and anointing. The Lord desires to use each of us to be history makers even in the midst of the crisis and darkness we see unfolding in the nations in this time. You are also called to be His anointed one moving in a *kairos* time, producing the miracle of the now, *hora,* time and executing transformation and the healing of spheres of influence and the nations with the anointing of the sons of Issachar.

NOTE

1.   Chuck Pierce, *Redeeming the Time* (Biblical Studies Press, 2005), 24-25.

Chapter 10

DISCERNING MOVES OF THE HOLY SPIRIT

Now, may the grace and joyous favor of the Lord
Jesus Christ, the unambiguous love of God, and
the precious communion that we share in the
Holy Spirit be yours continually. Amen!
—2 CORINTHIANS 13:14

When you look at me and my physical body, you see me. Everyone knows I am Becca from my appearance. But the real me is my spirit and soul. This body will pass away and die, but it is who I am as a person—my mind, will, emotions, feelings, personality—that will live for an eternity. What makes me is not my physical body but what comes from the inside out. You see, it is the Holy Spirit alive in me and flowing out of me and through me that is what makes me fully who I am.

Just as you and I are people with personalities, so is the Holy Spirit. He is part of the Holy Trinity. Holy Spirit is not an "it." He is the Spirit of God, the breath of life of God. Religious tradition void of the acceptance and activity of the Holy Spirit has caused many to think that we have to wait to be in heaven to encounter His presence. But the Holy Spirit is a gift from heaven sent to us by our heavenly Father as shared by Luke in Acts 1:4-5:

Jesus instructed them, "Don't leave Jerusalem, but wait here until you receive the gift I told you about, the gift the Father has promised. For John baptized you in water, but in a few days from now you will be baptized in the Holy Spirit!"

The Greek word for *gift* is *epangelian*. It means promise (Strong's #G1860). It signifies that He is a precious and great promise. It is a pledge and a divine assurance of a message.

Friends, the Holy Spirit is a person. And just like you and I, He can feel, perceive, and respond. He can be grieved. He has the ability to love and the ability to hate. He speaks, and He has His own will. But exactly who is He? The Holy Spirit is the Spirit of God the Father and the Spirit of God the Son. He is the power of the Godhead. What is His job? The task of the Spirit is to bring into being the commandment of the Father and the implementation of the Son. To understand what the Holy Spirit does, we need to understand the work of the Father and the Son. Our heavenly Father is the one who speaks out and gives the command. He has always been the One who speaks, "Let there be." From the beginning, it has been Him who issues the directives. On the other hand, it is God the Son who performs the command and what has been spoken by the Father. When God the Father said, "Let there be light," God the Son came and performed it. Then, God the Holy Spirit brought the light.

FELLOWSHIP WITH HIM

The Holy Spirit is the very essence of the Spirit of the Father and the Spirit of Jesus with us. Therefore, it is imperative for us to have a relationship with Him, to discern when He is moving, and to not ignore or shun Him and the moves of His Spirit. I am married to my husband and do not shun him or ignore him. Why? Because my marriage will not succeed if I totally ignore who my husband is as a person and refuse to relate to him. Therefore, we must relate to the Holy Spirit as a person and form a relationship with Him if we want to grow into the fullness of all the Lord has destined for us. Just as Paul so clearly states in Second Corinthians 13:14, we are to have "precious communion" with the Holy Spirit. And it is not just communion but a precious close association, fellowship, relationship, and partnership. I so love that I know and fellowship with the Holy Spirit. We can truly know Him and He becomes our very close friend.

HOLY SPIRIT EMPOWERED

Jesus also spoke of what Holy Spirit brings and makes available to us: "But I promise you this—the Holy Spirit will come upon you and you will be filled with power. And you will be my messengers to Jerusalem, throughout Judea, the distant provinces—even to the remotest places on earth!" (Acts 1:8). The Greek word for *power* is *dunamis*. It means "ability, power, mighty deed, ruler, supernatural power" (Strong's #G1411). For a long time, it seems that we have made the power of the Holy Spirit and the gift of tongues the main focus of being filled or baptized in Holy Spirit. I absolutely agree with and operate in speaking in tongues. But there is so much more available to us, as we clearly see when we study more of the fullness of what occurred in the Upper Room at Pentecost: "Suddenly a sound like a mighty rushing wind came from heaven, and it filled the whole house where they were sitting" (Acts 2:2 MEV). For some reason, in my own thinking I always knew this event was significant, but I never fully understood or grasped how incredibly supernatural this historic encounter was until four years ago in an all-night intercession time. In the early morning hours, the Lord led me to study the full meaning of the words from Acts 2:1-4 and to do so from the Bible software I use when studying and preparing teachings. Suffice it to say that this event in the Upper Room was not casual. Receiving the gift of tongues is awesome and I am so blessed to have a prayer language, but this was only a portion of what transpired for the 120 disciples and what is made available to each of us.

When studying the translation of the words *mighty rushing wind*, a clear and descriptive picture of what happened is established. This wind was mighty, and it carried a force, impact, and burden. As it rushed in, it went to the very deepest part of a man or woman that is able to respond to God. They were suddenly, instantly filled with the very breath and life of God Himself—the Holy Spirit. When they were filled, their minds, thoughts, emotions, and beliefs in spirit-realm encounters were instantaneously transformed into a new paradigm and a Kingdom of God way of thinking. It was a sudden and drastic change that filled each of them with boldness, joy, and fire, and tongues of fire were distributed on each of them. I truly appreciate how this is stated in *The Passion Translation*: "Then all at once a pillar of fire appeared before their eyes. It separated into tongues of fire that engulfed each one of them" (Acts 2:3). The fire of the Holy Spirit anointed and empowered each of them and they were set aflame, a burning torch.

Let's depict this with an even clearer picture. Instead of looking at the burning bush as Moses did in the Old Testament, they became the burning bush—the burning ones commissioned by God Himself to go out and boldly proclaim the Gospel, to see a harvest come forth, and to literally carry an empowerment to dramatically turn the world upside down for the Kingdom of God. The Holy Spirit is this wind— the very breath of God, the fire carrying the glory and His *ruach*, His breath of life that comes into the deepest part of a man or woman who can respond to Him. Just as the 120 were filled, we too are completely filled, transformed from the inside out, and emboldened with His fire and glory to move and advance His Kingdom in this lost world.

HE EMPOWERS OUR INTERCESSION

And in a similar way, the Holy Spirit takes hold of us in our human frailty to empower us in our weakness. For example, at times we don't even know how to pray, or know the best things to ask for. But the Holy Spirit rises up within us to super-intercede on our behalf, pleading to God with emotional sighs too deep for words. God, the searcher of the heart, knows fully our longings, yet he also understands the desires of the Spirit, because the Holy Spirit passionately pleads before God for us, his holy ones, in perfect harmony with God's plan and our destiny (Romans 8:26-27).

As an intercessor, I love this promise. We are in a relationship with the Holy Spirit, so we don't make requests; we come and say, "What is on Your heart today? Holy Spirit, help me to pray." It is my prayer that each of you are receiving an impartation of this truth as you read. He is here to have relationship with us, and He aids us even when we do not know what to pray. When we are baptized, immersed, and cultivate a fellowship and abiding relationship with Him, there is a power and authority given to see breakthrough come. He fills us with His fire and presence. He ushers us into the throne room to encounter Jesus and His glory. In this place, we are awakened to the reality that we are vitally united to Jesus and our heavenly Father and empowered and anointed for great Kingdom exploits. Our spiritual eyes and ears are open to see, hear, and discern as Jesus speaks and leads. We are filled with the might and power of Jesus—a light that causes darkness to be expelled. Boldness, power, and authority are realized to engage in Kingdom assignments to see victory.

Some of you reading might be praying faithfully but not seeing results or breakthrough in your intercession. I want to speak encouragement that if you have not received the infilling of the Holy Spirit, invite Him into your life. Welcome Him to baptize you in His glorious presence. As you cultivate a relationship with Him, His power and authority for victory will be ignited and made known in your intercession.

HE TEACHES US THE WORD

He is the teacher of the Word.

> *For we did not receive the spirit of this world system but the Spirit of God, so that we might come to understand and experience all that grace has lavished upon us. And we articulate these realities with the words imparted to us by the Spirit and not with the words taught by human wisdom. We join together Spirit-revealed truths with Spirit-revealed words* (1 Corinthians 2:12-14).

As I read the Word of God, I pray, "Holy Spirit, cause the Word to come alive to me. Teach me Your Word. I invite Your *ruach* to awaken Your *rhema* word in me." And as this request is made and also granted, holy, key, and strategic revelation is awakened by Him and through Him.

HE WANTS US TO PERSONALLY ENCOUNTER HIM

We are all familiar with the temple of the Lord so vividly described in the Old Testament—the outer court, the inner chamber, the Holy of Holies that housed the Ark of the Covenant, the very presence of God. The blueprint of the temple was a picture that the God we worship is a Trinity, three persons in one—Father, Son, and Holy Spirit. The Word of God tells us we are made in His image and likeness, and we are three-part beings made up of the body, soul, and spirit. Just as the temple was modeled on God's design of a three-person Trinity—Father, Son, and Holy Spirit—the divine forming and makeup of each of us is that, we too, are the temple—body, soul, and spirit. When Jesus came, He made the way for each of us to be anointed and appointed in the throne room of His presence.

When Jesus died on the cross, the veil was rent in two. The Holy Spirit is the heavenly host within the inner chambers of the Holy of Holies. He prepares and serves our spiritual food. He lifts us up into the presence of Jesus, into His throne room to encounter Him in His glory. The fire, glory, and presence that was depicted in the temple in the Old Testament within the Holy of Holies is now within each of us. As ones who are a new creation in Christ filled with the Holy Spirit, we become the carriers of His fire and glory—the living temples of the Lord. Jill Austin shares with great clarity the significance of intimacy with the Holy Spirit:

> He opens powerful doorways of understanding; the Word of God goes from *logos* to *rhema*. He awakens our hearts and we begin to long for deeper places. How can we move through the wildernesses of the earth with any kind of forerunner anointing unless we have that intimate relationship with the Holy Spirit? He wants us to get revelation about where we are going—and revelation of who Jesus is. That is His job. He wants the Bride to love the Son intimately. We are often taught in churches that John the Baptist is the best man for the Bridegroom, but, no, it is the Holy Spirit. He wants to make the Bridegroom's joy complete.
>
> Some of us have never really known the Holy Spirit as a Person, as the best friend of the Bridegroom. If we do not know Him in this way, then unless we are in a season of renewal or attending meetings where the fire is released, we feel alone and abandoned. That is because we do not

understand the bridal partnership: The best man is bringing us to the Bridegroom King.[1]

Friends, this is the dimension in which everything in our Christian walk is to be birthed. So how do we begin to experience, activate, and walk out this commissioning?

ABIDE IN HIM

Dwell in Me, and I will dwell in you. [Live in Me and I will live in you.] Just as no branch can bear fruit of itself without abiding in (being vitally united to) the vine, neither can you bear fruit unless you abide in Me (John 15:4 AMPC).

We already discussed this place of abiding in Chapter Four. But this principle is so necessary for maturity and purity and cultivating a deep sensitivity to the Holy Spirit that I will state it here again. We must be intentional in pursuing an on-fire, abiding, surrendered relationship with Him. What is it I have learned and been awakened to from this relationship with Him? Discerning His presence, moves of His Spirit, discerning when to war and when not to war. How to pray, how not to pray. When He is pleased, when He is not pleased. When to prophesy and when not to prophesy. How to see from His heavenly Kingdom perspective and to not be trapped by my own limited thinking and understanding. And sometimes His presence comes in ways that we don't know how to handle, but even in these moments He moves so faithfully. Why does He do this? Because it keeps us totally dependent on Him and ever increasing and expanding in our experiences and encounters with Him. These times stretch us into higher heights and deeper depths. There truly is a dance we can discern and learn in the Spirit that is beyond our own human reasoning and that brings us into the supernatural truths of the Spirit realm where signs, wonders, and miracles occur.

KNOWING HIS PRESENCE

Greg and I were given a copy of the book *Good Morning, Holy Spirit*. We read the book and it radically changed our lives. I welcomed the Holy Spirit to fill and baptize me, and He did so in such a life-altering, beautiful way. I began spending long hours in prayer, intercession, and worship before the Lord. I had a hunger to know Him. The reality was the Lord had me on a journey that would supernaturally teach me that we can experience His presence. I learned it was not just the sweetness and nearness of His presence He was leading me into, but He was inviting me into His tangible, manifest, and glorious throne room presence.

We were preparing to move to Houston. We arrived in town on a house-hunting trip and met up with a close family friend, Alice Smith, who was also a successful real estate agent at the time. She told us that she had arranged for us to attend a large meeting that night in the Summit, a convention center that holds thousands of people. Benny Hinn would be speaking. We were excited as he was the author of the book that had been the springboard for miraculously changing my life.

Alice prepared us as we drove to the event, as we had never attended a gathering like this. She spoke of how powerful the service the night before had been. She said it was time to lay down all skepticism and to trust God. She did this to prepare our hearts because we were so new to this new Spirit-filled and empowered walk. By the time we arrived, we were both eager for the service to begin.

As the worship leader and choir led us in the songs of adoration to the Lord, the presence that had become so sweet and real to me some twelve weeks before began to flood the convention center. It was a strong and precious presence. What an anointed time of exalting the Lord! Benny gave a powerful message and many people came forward for prayer and were healed.

As he was closing the service, he said that he felt the Lord leading him to pray an "impartation" to those who wanted more of God's presence. He gave this instruction: "Those of you who want this, put your hands up and get ready to receive." Without hesitation I threw my hands up to receive from the Lord. As soon as I did, I began to tremble at the touch of the Holy Spirit.

Alice noticed what was happening and quickly came to my side. "Becca," she asked, "do you need a healing?"

I said no.

"Well," she said, "this is obviously the Lord so we are going to go with it." There were no arguments from me.

Benny extended his hands toward the audience to impart the anointing and exclaimed three times, "Take it, take it, take it!" Well, all I can say is, every time he spoke those words it felt as if a bolt of lightning shot through my body. We were a great distance from the platform—up in the nosebleed section—but I might as well have been on the stage. By the third declaration, I fell backward onto the floor and was instantly swept away in the Spirit.

I no longer knew anything of my physical surroundings. I was clueless that I was on the floor, and if I had known I would not have cared. In the Spirit I had been taken to the throne room of God and was lying face down at the feet of Jesus and our Father. The presence was glorious, awesome, so holy and majestic. The tangible glory presence of the Holy Spirit engulfed me. I could see the feet of Father God and Jesus, but their presence was so holy I stayed on my face and dared not move.

It is difficult to put into words what I felt or the fullness of what I was encountering. It was everything I could ever desire. I wept, sobbed, and rejoiced as I lay at Jesus' feet and began to say, "Lord, this is all I have ever wanted in my life. You are awesome, powerful, wonderful, and holy. Lord, let me stay here with You. Don't send me back."

Jesus replied, *Becca, you must go back. You have a husband and daughter and you will have more children. You have a call on your life that I destined for you. I brought you here into My throne room to call you to Me and for you to understand the reality and revelation of who I am. I want you to experience the throne room. It is from this place where all you do for Me will be birthed. Now go fulfill your call.*

God wants this for each of you reading and participating in this study. It is my heart to write this journey in such a way that each of you can encounter Jesus, our heavenly Father, and Holy Spirit and maneuver from these times spent with the lover of your soul, brother, teacher, all-consuming fire, and friend.

DISCERNING MOVES OF HIS GLORY

As air is the atmosphere of the earth, glory is the atmosphere of Heaven. It lifts us up above the earthly, into the very presence of God.[2]

Glory. We have heard statements such as, "He is glorious!" "Lord, bring Your glory." "What a powerful service; the glory was strong." I myself have even made these comments. Allow me to pose a question. What does this word actually mean? The Hebrew word for *glory* is *kabod*. It is splendor, honor, wealth, manifestation of power, glorious presence, reward, glory in the inner person, ruler, men of high rank, one who governs (Strong's #H3519). As stated in Isaiah 4:5, "Then the Lord will create upon every dwelling place of Mount Zion, and upon her assemblies, a cloud and smoke by day and the shining of a flaming fire by night. For over all the glory shall be a covering" (MEV). In this context it becomes a covering, which is a defense, canopy, shelter from the elements, and bridal chamber. It also comes as the shekinah glory, which is the manifest weight and heaviness of the Lord. We must not mention the glory without speaking of the time when the glory fell so strongly in the temple that the priests could not stand nor perform their duties.

> *The priests then left the Holy Place. All the priests there were consecrated, regardless of rank or assignment; and all the Levites who were musicians were there—Asaph, Heman, Jeduthun, and their families, dressed in their worship robes; the choir and orchestra assembled on the east side of the Altar and were joined by 120 priests blowing trumpets. The choir and trumpets made one voice of praise and thanks to God—orchestra and choir in perfect harmony singing and playing praise to God:*
>
> *Yes! God is good!*
>
> *His loyal love goes on forever!*
>
> *Then a billowing cloud filled The Temple of God. The priests couldn't even carry out their duties because of the cloud—the glory of God!—that filled The Temple of God* (2 Chronicles 5:13-14 MSG).

It is the beautiful reality that the Lord has designed for us to encounter. I will always remember the first time I saw an overwhelming presence of the Lord's glory, a glory cloud that literally descended upon and enveloped hundreds of people in a very dramatic way. It was in the early '90s. The church we were attending was on the verge of an all-out revival. Oftentimes, services would continue until two to three in the afternoon. No one allowed weekend plans to interfere with attending a Sunday evening service because missing a service most assuredly meant missing a move of God. As we gathered corporately, the Lord was faithful to move in tangible and glorious ways.

One particular evening, I was singing on the worship team. That night when we arrived for practice prior to the service, the weight of His presence entered into the sanctuary. Rehearsal never ended. In a place of surrender we continued to exalt Him. As members arrived and entered the room, they instantly responded to His presence and quietly made their way to a seat or the altar. No one had to explain His glory was there. All who entered immediately knew. We had entered the glory realm, the realm of eternity. The realm of the revelation of the presence of God. At one point as we continued in abandoned worship, the weight was heavy and unearthly, beyond human words of expression. I opened my eyes to see. As I looked out over the crowd, I watched as a thick cloud supernaturally descended on hundreds of people. No eyes were opened. Each person was lost in the moment with the Lord. Suddenly, without anyone in the congregation aware of what the others were doing, each person in that sanctuary in full abandonment raised their hands simultaneously, threw their heads back, opened their eyes, and began to shout, "Jesus! Jesus! Jesus!" People fell out in the presence, weeping, and joy broke out across the auditorium. Jesus had entered that room that night. Lives were radically transformed. Many were set free and several saved.

I was recently in a meeting at the House Modesto in Modesto, California. It is an awesome, on-fire church led by pastors Glen and Deborah Berteau. They genuinely welcome moves of the Holy Spirit and have seen thousands of souls come into the Kingdom. It is actually one of my favorite places in which I have ministered. Pastor Glen challenged me, "Becca, teach my people how to walk in their full authority. I want them to understand and know the price of being awakened in the authority that has been given to them." I accepted his request and ministered very transparently in the final afternoon session on the journey the Lord brought me through to awaken the authority He has made available to us.

I must admit, I was in awe and undone by what transpired. The more I spoke, the heavier the tangible, manifest glory descended into that sanctuary. I looked out and saw fog that appeared to be increasing in thickness and weight. I thought to myself, "Did they have fog machines turned on? I don't remember them being on." But as I continued, it was evident it was the glory presence of the Holy Spirit as many of the leaders were weeping and kneeling on the floor under the weight of this presence. Many lives were changed and transformed that day in the weight of His glory. I am still receiving messages of testimony from that time.

DISCERNING HOW HE DESIRES TO MOVE

The Holy Spirit desires to meet with us personally and corporately as shared in the above testimonies. When He comes into a meeting, I have learned it is key to listen intently and closely in order to discern the direction He is intending to lead the meeting. And it is imperative to lay aside what we had previously planned.

> When the Holy Spirit comes into a meeting, He comes with purposes and plans; He has an assignment from the Father. It is not a trivial thing that the Holy Spirit shows up. When He arrives He breaks in with the purposes of heaven for our destinies. He awakens our hearts to Jesus' love for us.
>
> These are radical encounters! Yet, do you know what sometimes happens? The Holy Spirit comes and we do not even talk to Him. We ignore Him because we are too busy with our agendas. Do we say, "Holy Spirit, what do You have?" Or do we say, "Excuse me, but we have ten worship songs on our list and this is not the time for healing. Do You mind following the program?" We grieve Him and shut

Him down. We want Him only when it is convenient and makes us look anointed.

Even when we do move beyond our own agendas and say we want the gifts He brings, do we want those *things* or do we want *Him?* Granted, we are to use the gifts; people need to be set free and healed. But He is more than the gifts. He is a Person. He is our friend. If we have *Him*, He is going to come in and shake the Church. He is going to shake everything in our lives, too. He will bring a refiner's fire because His job is to nurture and to heal and to get the Bride ready. So He comes in and deals with the dross—the bitterness and pain and resentment in our lives.[3]

So how do we discover what to do when He begins to move? Dialogue with Him. Welcome Him to have His way. And as He begins to speak, follow His lead. There are times He will want a corporate move of intercession. There are times He will desire to bring deliverance. There are times He will want to bring healing. There are times to be militant and war and decree. There are times He will want to release a purifying fire or a Holy Love. There are times for an outpouring of His glory. There will be times of great joy. Don't rush what is occurring; give room for this time of encounter.

I was ministering in Scotland at the Glasgow Prophetic Centre led by dear friends David and Emma Stark. We had just completed a powerful prophetic conference they host annually and were in their Sunday morning service. Worship was glory-anointed, and Emma got up to share and to welcome me to speak. She attempted to share but was literally on fire in the anointing of the Holy Spirit. She was shaking and unable to stand still. All knew He was moving and she was encountering His glory and anointing. But I did not comprehend the degree of it until she asked me to try to help.

As I made my way to the platform, that same presence fell on me. My feet felt as if they were on fire and I began to shake. I desperately tried several times to speak and to talk, but I was not able to form the words and to complete a sentence. We finally said, "Holy Spirit, we submit to You. Have Your way!" We both then proceeded to lay hands on everyone in that meeting. People attending in person and online had radical glory encounters with the Lord. Many were delivered. Many were healed. Some were swept into personal encounters with the Lord in heaven. There was not one person in that gathering who did not experience a dramatic supernatural encounter with the Lord. Lives were empowered and transformed that day. This type of move is not something that we can orchestrate or work up in our flesh. When a room of over a 150 people all have a tangible encounter, this is a move of God.

DISCERN THE ANOINTING

This is also a term that we use quite frequently as believers. But what does it actually mean? Simply put, the anointing is the power of the Holy Spirit. You see, as a spiritual people the supernatural should seem natural to us. I so appreciate the phrase Sid Roth has coined: "naturally supernatural." I smile every time I hear him say this. It is the truth spoken so simply—the supernatural is to be natural to each of us. Allow me to give a brief explanation. When we experience the anointing, it causes movement in the spirit and use of our gifts to function and work easily. A person filled with the Holy Spirit is able to do extraordinary things, but to that person it seems quite natural and easy. What do I mean by this? When the anointing is present and working, it is as natural to flow in a gift as it is to speak to a friend. It becomes an expected outflow.

I travel and minister in different churches, cities, regions, and nations on a regular basis. I can pray and feel the tangible presence of God on the message He has led me in preparing. When I speak it in one location, there is a definite ease, presence, and authority. Then other times I will try to speak that same message in another location and there is absolutely no presence on it and the teaching is a labor and difficult. I believe the reason is I can't turn it on or off at will. Yes, the Holy Spirit is with us, but there are times His presence and power are tangibly stronger, allowing gifts to flow with ease.

The apostle John states in First John 2:20 and 27: "But the Holy One has anointed you and you all know the truth...His anointing teaches you all that you need to know, for it will lead you into truth, not a counterfeit. So just as the anointing has taught you, remain in him." The Greek word for *anointing* is *chrisma*. It means "smearing, like smearing of oil, a special endowment" (Strong's #G5545) It is derived from the Greek word *chiro,* which means "to rub with oil, to consecrate to an office or religious service" (Strong's #G5548). Therefore, it is the special endowment of His oil, the oil of the Holy Spirit, which when in operation causes an ease in functioning in a gift or in unison with Him. It is as if we are at home, functioning easily with no pressure, nothing to prove. I can honestly say that when I am functioning in the glory or anointing, I leave from that time of ministry so in awe and humbled by the moving of His Spirit.

Discerning the Anointing in a Corporate Gathering

I was ministering in Cleveland, Ohio and teaching from my book *Glory Warfare.* Our dear friends, Mike and April Farris, were hosting the gathering. We were having a powerful time. We returned from lunch planning to enter into a time of teaching followed by an afternoon break before the final evening session. A long-time friend, Anthony Turner, led us in glory-anointed prophetic worship. I walked to the platform to teach. Instantly, I felt a weighty anointing. I strongly discerned Him leading me to redirect all that was transpiring. Instead of sticking with the laid-out plan, we chose to follow His leading. A revival fire, holiness, and glory move broke out in that gathering. We continued to press into the Lord, and within a few minutes the entire gathering was prostrate at the altar where they stayed for hours. The afternoon soon grew into the evening time. The service lasted five hours with no one wanting to leave.

The next morning as people arrived for the Sunday service, the presence of the Lord was tangible. People responded to the glory, kneeling at the altar in deep surrender before the worship began. By the end of that morning service the entire congregation had again rushed the altar. His presence, glory, and fire are still moving as they gather, and many lives have been radically transformed and Kingdom destinies birthed. It is imperative to discern when a true move of His increased, tangible, shekinah glory is breaking open and to follow the cloud. When He shows up, He is to be given the seat of honor and no man-made agenda is to take His place.

Discerning the Anointing in Everyday Life

There are also times in my everyday life while speaking with someone that I suddenly sense the tangible presence of the Lord to prophesy to one I am encountering. This can occur while I am out and about running errands, enjoying a leisurely time out with family and friends, and while flying on airplanes.

Let's make it even more practical. You might be a schoolteacher functioning in the classroom. It's been a routine, normal day, and the anointing is suddenly tangible. Allow me to share an example of what occurred when I was a substitute teacher many years ago in a small town in Texas, which unfortunately at that time was still functioning in racism and prejudice.

I was subbing for a week in a high school math class. Jeremy was an African-American teenager, and I could see and discern that he felt he had no hope, that he would never be good enough. I discerned prophetically that his family had a long history of financial struggles, so he believed he would as well. And with racism being so prevalent in this town, he now had a new teacher for the week who happened to be a white woman. Jeremy refused to do the math assignments in class and at home. On the second day in the classroom, I felt the anointing of the Holy Spirit to reach out to him.

"Jeremy, you need to do your work. Please pick up your pencil and try."

Not willing to look at me as I spoke to him, Jeremy crossed his arms and looked away. I could see and feel in the spirit the years of hurt, struggle, and the resulting defiance as he spoke. My heart was pierced with the heart of the Father for him.

"Mrs. Greenwood, I don't need to do this work. It is not going to help me in life. I do not want to do this work."

"Jeremy, I need you to pick up your pencil and do your work. Please do what I am asking you to do," I replied calmly and patiently.

"Mrs. Greenwood, I am not going to do this work."

My heart ached as I continued to replay that scene later that day. How could I get through to this young man? That night I went to prayer and Holy Spirit spoke to me: "Becca, I have brought you to this classroom for Jeremy. He is your assignment for this week. There are deep issues in his heart and emotions that need healing." The Lord revealed to me the strategy of how to help Jeremy. I waited for His prompting and anointing while in the classroom for the right time to engage His plan.

It was two days later, as the bell rang; Jeremy came in the door of the classroom at the precise moment that would not make him late. After a week of seeing this behavior, it became evident this was a well-rehearsed routine.

I explained the math assignment for the day. Within a few minutes, Jeremy laid his head on the desk to take a nap while the rest of the students did their work. I felt the anointing of the Lord nudging and saying, "Now."

"Jeremy, you need to pick up your pencil and do your work."

Jeremy responded in the same manner he had the day before. "Mrs. Greenwood, I told you yesterday, I am not going to do this work. I do not need this math. I am not going to use it and I am not going to do it."

I leaned over his desk trying to catch his eyes. In a soft, calm voice I reached out to him. "Jeremy, look at me please. Can you look at me? I would like to talk to you about something."

Curious, he turned his eyes toward mine. "Jeremy, I realize you have lived in an area where you and your family have been shunned and treated poorly because of the color of your skin. Is this true?"

Surprised by my words, he cautiously and quietly answered, "Yes ma'am."

"Well, Jeremy, I recognize that how you and your family have been treated is not right. As a matter of fact, my ancestors were some of the founding fathers of this small town. I don't know for certain, but I realize that it is possible some of my ancestors in my family line might have been among those who said and did hurtful things to you and your family. If they were some of those involved in these words and actions, I want to say that how they treated you is wrong. And I want to ask you to forgive us."

At that moment he shockingly replied, "This sounds like church."

"Yes, Jeremy, it does. I also, as a white woman, want to say that when I look at you, I do not see you based on others' wrong assumptions because of the color of your skin. I see a handsome, bright young man who has unlimited potential to break out of the cycle your family has been in and to do something great with your life. Don't let the past and the wrong actions of the white race and the people of this town control your future. Please forgive us."

Fighting back the tears, he emotionally and quietly said, "Yes ma'am."

"Jeremy, do you live with your mother?"

"No ma'am. I live with my grandmother."

As we had been speaking, I had already seen this prophetically. I continued to ask questions based off of this revelation. "Does she pray for you?"

"Yes ma'am, she does. Every night she kneels by her bed and prays for me."

"Jeremy, I know your grandmother wants you to do your work. I know she wants the best for you. I do too. I prayed for you last night. I believe in you. For your grandmother and me, can you please pick up your pencil and do your work? Are you able to choose to make today a new day in your life?"

A tear gently rolled down his cheek as he slowly pulled himself up in his desk from his slouched position, reached for his pencil, and pulled the sheet of paper toward him. As he began to solve the first math problem, he answered in a soft whisper, "Yes ma'am, I can."

The classroom was so quiet you could have heard a pin drop. I gratefully and lovingly placed my hand on his shoulder and said, "Thank you, Jeremy." As I made my way back to the desk, I was rejoicing on the inside and so moved by the Holy Spirit that I could hardly contain my emotions and tears.

During the following days Jeremy came to class early and would excitedly exclaim, "Mrs. Greenwood, are we going to learn something new today? I am going to do my work!"

The remainder of the school year, Jeremy always tried to find the classroom I was subbing in. One day he asked me, "Mrs. Greenwood, I have friends who want me to hang out with them tonight. They are going to be up to no good."

"Jeremy, are you needing assistance from an adult to help you tell them you can't go?"

"Yes ma'am."

"Jeremy, you go tell your friends that Mrs. Greenwood said that it is not a good idea for you to hang out tonight, and if they have a problem with that, they can come and see me."

I smiled as Jeremy walked out of the classroom confidently exclaiming, "Hey guys, Mrs. Greenwood said it is not a good idea for me to go tonight and if you have a problem with that you can talk with her about it!"

I realize this is a more practical example of anointing, but I felt the Lord leading me to share this particular testimony. Why? Because everyone reading this might not be a platform minister. This example is how discernment, anointing, a prophetic gift, and an obedient act can change and empower a life outside the walls of the church.

Discerning the Anointing in the Family/Home

We have intentionally made our home a place in which the presence and peace of the Lord is tangible. I also have a room that is set a part as my prayer room. It is my favorite room in our home because this is where I spend hours in worship, intercession, writing books, and studying to prepare new teachings. This location is also beyond special to me because my daughters can feel His presence when I am in intercession and worship. There are many times when I have been in abandoned worship and intercession and I hear a gentle knock on the door and the voice of one of my daughters asking if they can join me. This happens with our youngest daughter, Katie, quite often. As I welcome her into the room, she sincerely inquires, "Mom, can I come in and join you? Can I be in God's presence with you? Mom, can you pray for me?" These moments are so beautiful to me. I love that even in the middle of the night my daughters discern the presence and anointing and are drawn to and desire to be with Him. Our homes are to be a habitation for Him.

Discerning the Anointing in Spheres of Influence

Many, including me, have been hearing prophetically that this next move of God will greatly involve church outside the walls in what we have come to call the seven mountains of influence—church, family, government, education, arts and entertainment, media, and business. The marketplace will play a key role in this new era. The following is a great testimony from my friend Jareb Nott.

> Ministry in the marketplace is something that because of its nature is executed differently than other spheres of influence. Ministry in a corporate setting is typically covert and mostly unseen because of the conflicts it presents corporately.
>
> One area of marketplace ministry that should never be executed covertly is that of relationships. People are people, and people just need Jesus, especially at the office. The truth is that people are not lining up anymore to go to church as was the case during the Brownsville revival in Pensacola Florida in 1995. Instead, people are in the office gathering around the proverbial water cooler or coffee maker.
>
> Back in 2010 I began an office relationship with an individual I'll call Mark for anonymity. This individual was attracted to me because of a reputation that I carried within the office. I was referred to as "Pastor Jareb." I earned this title because of my openness to pray for people and share Jesus with anyone who inquired. Over the next two years Mark would visit my office and he would share his story with me. We discussed stories of loss and how he struggled with his relationship with his family. Frequently he would ask what the Bible said about certain issues he was facing, and I would guide him through the appropriate scriptures.

I became a spiritual mentor in his life, with the goal to guide him closer to Jesus. I never preached at him and I always let the word of God speak for itself. For two years I wondered if I was getting through. Finally, one morning in 2012 things came to a head for Mark. I was running about an hour late for work due to an appointment. Mark had arrived at my office early hoping to talk to me about an urgent issue. My coworker was there and explained that Mark was resolved to meet with me that day. Mark had waited in my office for two hours until I arrived.

When I arrived, I barely had a moment to set my bag down and make sense of what was happening. Mark grabbed me and began to tell me that his world had fallen apart. Divorce was a certainty, and his relationships with his children and the loss of his home were all at risk. He was broken in that moment, and in his speech, he told me, "I have nowhere else to go for help." My heart broke for him as he wept in front of me and explained his story of hopelessness. I began to weep with him! Eventually, Mark looked at me with tears streaming down his face and said, "I don't know what to do but I can't keep this up and I need you to help me."

I looked at Mark and said, "I know what you need, we've been talking about it for two years and it's what led you to me in this moment." Looking into his eyes I said, "Mark, you need Jesus!" At those words Mark grabbed both of my hands and immediately fell to his knees. Squeezing both of my hands and weeping uncontrollably, he said, "I have to know Jesus, what do I need to do? Who can I talk to? Do I need a priest? Can you do this?" I said, "Mark, Jesus is here, now, and all you need to do is talk to Him! I will help you find the words." Over the next 20 minutes I had the pleasure of introducing Mark to Jesus and welcoming him into the Kingdom.

When Mark entered my office, he was bound with anxiety, worry, stress, and feelings of hopelessness. When he left my office that morning, he was a free man who discovered hope, and faith, and a Jesus who loves him through all his shortcomings. Today Mark is a happy, Jesus-loving man who has a renewed relationship with his children and has turned his life around for the Lord.

Ministry within our spheres of influence should not be stressful or laborious. Rather, it should be relational and life-giving to the people around us.

Discerning Past the Viewed Anointing

Bringing the context back to inside the walls of the church, Paul states in First Corinthians 5:6, "Don't you understand that even a small compromise with sin permeates the entire fellowship, just as a little leaven permeates a batch of dough?" Is it possible for there to be a powerful move of God? One in which signs, wonders, and healing are overflowing, yet the one being used is flowing out of a compromised life of impurity? The answer is yes, this does happen. If you recall the testimony in Chapter Two, Greg and I had been attending a church and I discerned that a door had been opened to sin. Before the sin was exposed, it appeared God was still moving in tangible ways. It was at first confusing, because God seemed to be blessing those in attendance. It is important for us to mature in order to discern the moves of the Holy Spirit along with sound scriptural doctrine from those moves that prove to be unhealthy, impure, and unbiblical.

Discerning a Move of Signs, Wonders, Miracles, Healings

As in these testimonies, we can know, perceive, and move in the direction He desires to go. In some services, we stay right on schedule with what we prayed into and planned prior to gathering and meeting. However, there are those times He comes to set captives free, to move in signs, wonders, miracles, and healing. For me, when a healing anointing is present, I will begin to feel prompts from the Holy Spirit in my physical body. Sometimes my ears will begin to feel an intense warmth or heat. I might begin to feel pressure in my shoulder, legs, or hips. My heart might begin to flutter. Or suddenly I am hearing or receiving impressions of names of those the Lord wants to bring healing to.

I was ministering at a women's gathering in Colorado. While speaking I felt a tangible heat or warmth on my body. I knew this wasn't from being overly warm on the platform. The warmth of the Holy Spirit feels noticeably different from the normal feeling of becoming too hot. It is warmth that is spiritual, not uncomfortable. I quickly began to pay attention. As I did, I heard the name *Linda*. I asked if there was a Linda present in the meeting. She quickly raised her hand, "Yes! I am Linda."

When she spoke her name to me, my heart began to flutter and the warmth moved to my chest area where the heart is located. I asked her, "Linda, do you need healing from a heart condition?"

She began to weep. "Yes, I was born with a congenital heart defect. I am scheduled for open heart surgery in two days. The doctors have told me if I do not have the surgery, I will soon have a heart attack and die. So I am no longer able to postpone the operation." I asked if I could lay hands on her and pray for healing, to which she exclaimed a joyful, "Of course! Please pray for me!" I laid hands on her and commanded all abnormalities in her heart and the arteries to be healed in Jesus' name. She began to laugh joyously as the irregular heartbeat and flutter that comes with this heart defect stopped. She felt strongly that she was healed. She went to the hospital the next morning, and that heart condition she was born with was completely gone. She had been healed!

THE COST OF THE ANOINTING

All things precious and valuable cost something. And who or what is more precious or valuable than our heavenly Father, Jesus, and Holy Spirit? I so love the old hymn, "I Surrender All."

> *All to Jesus I surrender,*
> *All to Him I freely give,*
> *I will ever love and trust Him,*
> *In His presence daily live,*
> *I surrender all, I surrender all,*
> *All to Thee my blessed Savior, I surrender all.*
>
> *All to Jesus I surrender,*
> *At Thy feet I humbly bow,*
> *Worldly pleasures all forsaken,*
> *Take me, Jesus, take me now,*
> *I surrender all, I surrender all,*
> *All to Thee my blessed Savior, I surrender all.*
>
> *All to Jesus I surrender,*
> *Lord, I give myself to Thee,*
> *Fill me with Thy love and power,*
> *Let Thy blessing fall on me,*
> *I surrender all, I surrender all,*
> *All to Thee my blessed Savior, I surrender all.*[4]

Surrender in not a negative action. It is a beautiful yielding to Him. *Surender* is defined as "to cease resistance, yield, give way, and abandoned surrender." The more we surrender, the more of Him we receive. Why is this necessary to function in discerning the spirit realm? Because it is in the intimacy of surrender where we receive more of Him and we know His ways. Allow Him to awaken your soul, and don't allow your hunger and passion to diminish or fall into slumber. Stay in the place of awakening. Allow His presence to increase in you to the place of anointing and from the place of anointing to abiding in His glory. Guard that which has been entrusted to you as precious. Listen to the powerful words spoken from an anointed woman of God, Kathryn Kuhlman:

> The anointing...It costs much, but it is worth the cost. It costs everything. If you really want to know the price...You really want to know the price, I will tell you. It will cost you everything. Kathryn Kuhlman died a long time ago. I know the day, I know the hour. I can go to the spot...where Kathryn Kuhlman died. But you see for me it was easy. Because I had nothing. One day I just looked up and said wonderful Jesus. I have nothing. I have nothing to give you but my love. That's all that I can give you is my love. And I give you my body as a living sacrifice. If you can take nothing and use it. Then here's nothing. Take it. It isn't silver vessels that He is asking for. It isn't golden vessels that He needs. He just needs yielded vessels.[5]

DISCERN THE ANOINTING FOR REGIONAL AWAKENING

Yielding is such a beautiful and necessary posture to walk with Him to begin to discern Holy Spirit moments and moves personally, as a family, in our spheres of influence, and corporately that lead to a deep awakening. It is also imperative to discern when the Holy Spirit is moving to reveal or bring a region into a new awareness of *kairos* moments to open the door of awakening.

I was ministering again in Cleveland, Ohio. We were teaching Unit 3 of our Regional Transformation Spiritual Warfare School. It was the day we pray together as a class and seek the Lord over the prayer assignment and journey we will engage in as a group in order to bring impartation and activation of what has been taught in this sixty-hour course on how to victoriously usher in regional transformation.

As we began to worship and to seek the Lord together, Holy Spirit moved into the room with a tangible anointing. Friends, I am a history buff and very familiar with the history of our nation. And those whom I was with in Ohio know the history of their state as they have been praying across their region for many years. Through words of knowledge that were revealed in intercession, the Lord took us on a spiritual journey of prophetic revelation and research. One of the key revelations released while in intercession was the phrase "hidden gem." The prayer warrior who spoke it felt it carried a positive and negative connotation that unveiled a hidden treasure we were all unaware of in the history of Ohio and the Northwest Territory of the United States dating back to the colonial days.

Revelation continued to build in our prophetic intercession and research time. We all knew that a Christian group called the Moravians had traveled from Germany to the United States in the 1700s. What we didn't know is that they also settled in the land of Ohio and the Northwest Territory of the new land. For those unaware, the Moravians are believers who initiated a round-the-clock prayer watch in 1727 that continued nonstop for over a hundred years. They experienced great moves of the Holy Spirit much like Pentecost. During this time, the leader of the movement, Zinzendorf, felt the Lord leading them to send missionaries to foreign lands. By 1791, sixty-five years after commencement of that prayer vigil, the small Moravian community had dispatched 300 missionaries to many foreign lands. They had arrived in the land of the United States in 1735 from their Herrnhut settlement in present-day Saxony, Germany. They came to minister to the scattered German immigrants, to the Native Americans, and to enslaved Africans. They established settlements to serve as home bases for these missionaries, one being Schoenbrunn village located in Ohio that was settled in 1772. Zinzendorf, the leader of the Moravian movement, came to Schoenbrunn with one of his spiritual mentees David Zeisberger. David remained even when Zinzendorf returned to Germany. He began to work among the Native Americans in the thirteen colonies. His work among the Delaware Indians proved to bear much fruit; there was a move of God with many saved. The Delaware were so impacted by David and the other Moravian missionaries that they also became known as the Moravian Indians. David as well as other Moravians lived with and among the Delaware in a town called Gnadenhutten, meaning "tents of grace." It was a beautiful move of God in the very early history of our nation.

In September 1781, a time leading into the Revolutionary War, the British-allied Indians forced the Christian Delaware, now known as the Moravian Indians, to leave their settlements. They took them northwest to a place called Captive Town on the Sandusky River. The British took the Moravian missionaries David Zeisberger and John Heckewelder to Detroit, where they were kept under guard and tried under charges of treason. They suspected them of giving information concerning the British forces to the American military base, Fort Pitt. They were acquitted. The following is the sad story of what then transpired for the Christian Delaware.

Due to the insufficient rations in Captive Town, the Delaware were going hungry. In February of 1782, 98 were given permission to return to the Moravian village to collect the stored food and to harvest the crops in the field that they were initially forced to leave behind. There was still great unrest in the region, so safety was a concern.

On March 8 and 9, 1782, a group of Pennsylvania militiamen under the command of Captain David Williamson, engaged in a surprise raid on the Delaware at Gnadenhutten. The militia accused the Christian Indians for the deaths and kidnappings of several white Pennsylvanians, although they had not been involved in the previous incidents and truthfully denied the accusation. The militiamen refused to listen to or believe the truth.

In retaliation, the soldiers rounded them up and placed the men and women, along with the children, in separate cabins overnight. The militiamen then voted to execute their captives the following morning. Informed of their impending deaths, the Moravian Delaware spent the night shouting out to one another from the two cabins and joining in a night-long time of intercession, singing hymns and prayers to forgive their executioners. The next morning, the soldiers took the Delaware one at a time and murdered them. In all, Williamson's men murdered 28 men, 29 women, and 39 children. The militia piled the bodies in the mission buildings and burned the village down. They also burned the other abandoned Moravian villages.

Two boys survived, one Moravian and one Delaware. The young Delaware was scalped in this tragic massacre, but he survived. The two were able to return to Sandusky to inform the Moravian missionaries and other Christian American Indians as to what had occurred.

Some of the militiamen refused to take part and left the area. One of those who opposed the killing of the Moravian Lenape was Obadiah Holmes, Jr. He later wrote of the incident:

> One Nathan Rollins & brother [who] had had a father & uncle killed took the lead in murdering the Indians, ...&

Nathan Rollins had tomahawked nineteen of the poor Moravians, & after it was over he sat down & cried, & said it was no satisfaction for the loss of his father & uncle after all.[6]

In 1889, future president Theodore Roosevelt called the atrocity "a stain on frontier character that the lapse of time cannot wash away."[7]

As this was fully revealed and shared, the glory of the Lord filled the meeting room to such a degree all we could do was weep under the weight of His presence and the weight of this tragic wound that occurred to stop the harvest and revival move of God. We knew we must go there to pray for Ohio and the Northwest Territory and to see this "stain on frontier character" healed and cleansed.

We arrived the next afternoon and had the village to ourselves. It was a pleasant surprise as we walked the land and felt the tangible anointing and glory of His presence. So much so that we took our shoes off due to the overwhelming sense of holiness at this massacre site. As we began to pray, a gentleman appeared walking down one of the paths next to where we huddled. He kindly interrupted us, "Excuse me for interrupting you. My name is John and I am the caretaker of this village. I wasn't supposed to be here. I just came to see work that was done today on the rock paths. But if you would like, I will open up the museum and the cabins and share with you the full story of what transpired here."

The group responded with a resounding, "Yes!"

All that I have shared above is an abbreviated yet accurate portrayal of what occurred, but I will add one more revelation. When the Delaware and Moravians prayed the night before they were massacred, they also voiced out loud forgiveness to those who performed the horrific and evil act. Just wow. I still get moved to tears typing this. Thus, the resulting glory of His presence that is evident in the land. That all-night intentional time of worship, prayer, intercession, and forgiveness on the revival site by the Delaware and Moravians who would be massacred the next day left a mark of glory, revival, and awakening in the land.

John, the caretaker, shared with us that he was not a Christian when he first took the job at this historic site. One day, he was walking down the rock path and had an encounter with the Holy Spirit. He rushed to the nearest church he could find. The pastor at the church led him to the Lord, and John is now saved and filled with the Holy Spirit. We prophesied that he had been sent there to be the new apostle of the Indians to bring back the revival move that was killed by the militia men that sad day in 1782. He smiled and shared, "David Zeisberger was known as the apostle of the Indians."

I replied, "Yes, and now you will be that in this new era of awakening in this land."

Such a profound and powerful time. He has now invited us to come back anytime we want and has welcomed us to hold intercession, revival, and prophetic glory encounters in the Moravian Church in Gnadenhutten and the oldest Moravian settlement Schoenbrunn, which houses the first Moravian Church of the Northwest Territory. Our worship and prayer time on the land was life-altering and glorious. And John has already asked Mike and April Farris and me to return to lead a service in the church.

GOSPEL OF WORDS AND HOLY SPIRIT

In closing, I want to end with a powerful scriptural truth shared by Paul in First Thessalonians 1:5, "For our gospel came to you not merely in the form of words but in mighty power infused with the Holy Spirit and deep conviction." It is so imperative as we move in the anointing and power of the Holy Spirit that all we do is grounded in His Word—the Spirit and Word partnering together. Jesus spoke the Word to the disciples, and they were clean (see John 15:3), and yet later He breathed on them to receive the Holy Spirit (see John 20:22). This shows that both were needed. In the encounter at Pentecost, they were empowered with the *dunamis* power to fulfill the Kingdom exploits the Lord had destined for them to achieve. Stay grounded in His Word and empowered with the presence, anointing, and glory of the Holy Spirit.

NOTES

1. Jill Austin, *Dancing with Destiny: Awaken Your Heart to Dream, to Love, to War* (Grand Rapids, MI: Chosen Books, 2007), 72.

2. Ruth Ward Heflin, *Glory: Experiencing the Atmosphere of Heaven* (Hagerstown, MD: McDougal Publishing, 1990).

3. Austin, *Dancing with Destiny*, 71-72.

4. "I Surrender All," Judson W. Van deVenter (lyrics) and Winfield Scott Weeden (music), 1896. Public domain.

5. Kathryn Kuhlman, "Jerusalem Conference (1 of 2)," Fruitful Sermons, YouTube, March 01, 2015, https://www.youtube.com/watch?v=iL2xx9Jm7vE.

6. "Gnadenhutten massacre," Wikipedia, accessed July 2, 2020, https://en.wikipedia.org/wiki/Gnadenhutten_massacre.

7. Ibid.

PRAYER TO AWAKEN
DISCERNMENT IN YOU!

*I continue to pray for your love to grow and increase
beyond measure, bringing you into the rich revelation
of spiritual insight in all things. This will enable you
to choose the most excellent way of all—becoming pure
and without offense until the unveiling of Christ.*
—PHILIPPIANS 1:9-10

Here we end this message with one of the foundational scriptures used
in Chapter One. Friends, just as Paul prayed the above prayer for the
believers in Philippi, I pray this prayer for each of you—that you will have
eyes to see, ears to hear, feelings to feel, and a knowing revelation to know.
The Greek word for *insight* (*aisthēsis*) refers to practical understanding
linked to life. It is a word that implies walking out the truth that insight
reveals (Strong's #G144). Other translations of this word are *experience*
and *discernment*. You see, it is more than discerning something—it
means to experience the reality of something and apply it to life. This is
so powerful! It is my prayer for you that you discern and experience the

reality of the spirit realm and you are awakened and activated to be able to apply it to your life.

As we look to verse ten, we discover that the Greek word for *choose* is one that we introduced at the beginning of this discussion. It is *dokimazo*, which means to approve or also as the testing process that salvages the good and discards the useless. It signifies the ability to regard something as genuine or worthy on the basis of testing (Strong's #G1381). This truly lays out a wise Kingdom understanding. Discernment becomes the path to finding what God approves, not simply what God forbids. When love, revelation, and insight overflow into our discernment, we will always be looking for what is excellent and pleasing in our heavenly Father's eyes. We choose what is the most excellent or best, not by law or rules but by loving discernment. We see with the eyes of discernment as our heavenly Father sees.

In the closing of this journey, I would like to scribe a prayer that will inspire empowerment and faith for a new encounter and season to walk in discernment. Apply this in every area of your life so you walk in a most excellent way in all the Lord has called you to accomplish.

> *Lord, thank You for this journey of learning and discovery in discerning the spirit realm. I come before You now and welcome the awakening and increase of discernment in my spiritual walk. Lord, impart wisdom and keen insight as I grow and maneuver in the realities of the spirit realm. Lord, I say yes to hearing Your voice more clearly. Lord, bring me into the rich revelation of spiritual insight in all things.*
>
> *Lord, awaken dreams, visions, impressions, seeing, hearing, feeling, and sensing—all of those areas You have blessed us with in order to relate to You and to hear and partner with You. Cause me to see through Your eyes with Kingdom sight. Let me see from heaven's perspective and not man's*

perspective. Help me to see and discern through and from Your heart of love, wisdom, and truth. Lord, where I have been judgmental or critical, I ask that You forgive me. I welcome You to give me keen wisdom and an ability to carry burdens faithfully in intercession to victory. Open my eyes to see, my ears to hear, and my senses to know when You are speaking and revealing spiritual insight and truth. Cause me to be more sensitive to perceive Your promptings in the Spirit. Cause Your Word to come alive in me that I will discern with wisdom and truth from Your Word.

Lord, I thank You that there are more for us than against us. Cause me to perceive and know the activity of the angels You have sent to aid me in all You have called me to do. Lord, give me insight and maturity when discerning those spirits in operation in the demonic realm. Lord, I choose to focus on You and worship You and exalt You and to live above the principalities enthroned over regions. I ask for strategies from heaven to see these entities lose their demonic hold. Bless me with the understanding of times and seasons we are living in and sensitivity to Your anointing and moves of Your Spirit.

Lord, I desire to step into the fullness of what You are calling me to in this now time. Use me, Lord, to impact the lives of those I encounter in my everyday life, in my workplace, in my ministry, and in the spheres of influence where You have positioned me. Cause me to walk in Your anointing, to be supernaturally natural. Holy Spirit, fill me with a fresh fire and breathe into me Your ruach breath of life. I say yes to discerning the spirit realm, and as this gift is awakened and increased may the lives of those around me be impacted with Your love and for You and Your Kingdom. May captives be set free, may a harvest be realized, spheres of influence and regions set free, and great victories attained and transformation achieved. Fill me with boldness. Empower me to walk fearless. Awaken to me the warfare arsenal You have bestowed on me. Empower me to be a Kingdom glory carrier to impact the dark world, to see Your Kingdom come and Your will be done on earth as it is in heaven. And Jesus, I give You all the glory, all the honor, and all the praise. It is in Your name I pray! Amen!

APPARENT DEMONIC GROUPINGS LIST [1]

ALTAR MINISTRY RESOURCE: DEMONIC GROUPINGS

- Spirit of Antichrist
- Spirit of Bondage
- Deaf and Dumb Spirit
- Spirit of Death/Shadow of Death
- Familiar Spirit: Witchcraft, Spirit of Divination, Occult, Rebellion
- Spirit of Fear
- Haughty Spirit: Prideful Spirit
- Spirit of Heaviness/Depression
- Spirit of Infirmity
- Spirit of Jealousy
- Lying Spirit
- Spirit of Error
- Spirit of Perversion/Whoredom/Lust Sexual Sin
- Seducing Spirit
- Spirit of Slumber/Unbelief
- Spirit of Rejection
- Religious Spirit
- Spirit of Jezebel

SPIRIT OF ANTICHRIST

Everyone who does not acknowledge that Jesus is from God has the spirit of antichrist, which you heard was coming and is already active in the world (1 John 4:3).

Bind: *Spirit of Antichrist*

Plunder its house!

- Repentance for aligning with and operating under the influence of the spirit of antichrist
- Break attachments from the below listed activities and other partnering demonic spirits
- Renounce all of the following activities
- Cast out or evict all partnering evil spirits

Signs: *Self-Exalting, Humanism, Opposes Jesus, Critical, Confusion, Occult*

Attempts to Take Christ's Place

Blasphemes Holy Spirit

Displays Open Unbelief

Acts/Speaks Against

The miracles of God, Word of God, testimony of Jesus Christ and His teachings, God, Christians

Denies/Opposes

Atonement of Christ, deity of Christ, humanity of Christ, blood of Christ

Work of the Holy Spirit, ministry and victory of Christ miracles

Rationalizes

Christ, the Word, miracles

Disturbs Fellowship and Gathering of the Saints

Stirs up strife between believers

Harasses, persecutes the saints

Suppresses ministry

Doctrinal Error/Twisting of Doctrine

Humanism

Legalism

Cults, Occult

Note: For *Cults* see also Familiar Spirit

Closed-Minded

Confusion

Deceiver

Defensiveness

Self-Exalting

Worldliness

Critical, Mocking Attitude

Judgmentalism

Lawlessness

Mean-spirited

Violent

Once the house is plundered: command the antichrist to get out.

- Issue an eviction notice to this spirit (Speak it out loud)
- Loose and welcome in: a dynamic personal relationship with Jesus, a baptism in the Holy Spirit, grace, truth, awakening to the Word of God, awakening to the presence of God, a hunger and faith to know Him more, spirit of prophecy, gift of teaching and sharing the true word of God, gifts of the Spirit

SPIRIT OF BONDAGE

Stand fast therefore in the liberty by which Christ has made us free, and do not be entangled again with a yoke of bondage (Galatians 5:1).

Bind: *Spirit of Bondage*
Plunder its house!

- Repentance for aligning with and operating under the influence of the spirit of bondage
- Break attachments from the below listed activities and other partnering demonic spirits
- Renounce all of the following activities
- Cast out or evict all partnering evil spirits

Signs: *Unworthiness, Rejection, Fears, Performance, Control, Pride, Self-Pity, Poverty Mindset, Feeling Lost, Addictions, Compulsions, Infirmity, Spiritual Oppression, Thoughts of Death*
Unworthiness/Worthlessness
Embarrassment, Shame, Condemnation, Rejection
Bruised Spirit, Anguish of Spirit, Brokenhearted
Self-Condemnation, Self-Pity
Bitterness/Resentment
Critical Spirit, Fault Finding, Judgmentalism, Accusation, Strife (conflict)
Self-Deception (believing what is not true about yourself, positive or negative)
Spiritual Blindness (inability to see God's truth)
  Unrighteousness
  Doubting salvation, no assurance of salvation, fear of death
Performance

Perfectionism, drivenness

False responsibility, false burden (not your own), false guilt

False compassion (misplaced compassion)

Anxiety, nervousness, frustration

Feeling Lost (disconnected)

Vagabond Spirit, Restlessness

Fears/Paranoia/Fear of Death

MPD (multiple personality disorder), Schizophrenia

Pride, Superiority

Control, Dominance, Possessiveness, Compulsory Subjection and

Control, Slavery (enslavement, oppressed)

Poverty Mindset (never enough)/Coveting Wealth in Order

to Hoard

Self-Reward

Compulsions and Addictions

Substances: Caffeine, cigarettes, alcohol, drugs (legal or illegal) or medications (beyond prescribed use)

Behaviors: Overeating (gluttony), anorexia, bulimia, overspending, sexual activity

Unholy Soul Ties

Inability to Break Free/Bound

Helplessness, Hopelessness

Thoughts of Death, Death Wish, Thoughts/Attempts of Suicide

Phantom Pain (not due to loss of limb)

Infirmity

Stiffness

Chronic Fatigue

Idleness (sloth, sluggish)

Hyperactivity, ADD, ADHD

Tourette's Syndrome (involuntary activity, movements and vocalizations)

Spiritual Oppression

Mind Control

Witchcraft (rebellion)

Satanism

Once the house is plundered: command the spirit of bondage to get out.

- Issue an eviction notice to this spirit (Speak it out loud)
- Loose and welcome in: liberty, Spirit of Adoption, true kingdom identity, freedom and healing from all addictions, fresh infilling of the Holy Spirit

DEAF AND DUMB SPIRIT

Now when Jesus saw that the crowd was quickly growing larger, he commanded the demon, saying, "Deaf and mute spirit, I command you to come out of him and never enter him again!" (Mark 9:25)

Bind: *Deaf and Dumb Spirit*

Plunder its house!

- Repentance for aligning with and operating under the influence of the deaf and dumb spirit
- Break attachments from the below listed activities and other partnering demonic spirits
- Renounce all of the following activities
- Cast out or evict all partnering evil spirits

Signs: *Unforgiveness, Sorrow, Sleepiness, Confusion, Infirmity, Seizures, Accidents, Thoughts of Death*

Unforgiveness

Self-Pity/Wallowing/Pining Away

Uncontrolled Crying
Emotionless
Sleepiness
Confusion
Stuttering
Stupors (dazed)/Motionless Stupor
Lethargy (sluggish, slow)
Tourette's Syndrome
Chronic Infections
> Chronic ear infections, eye diseases
Deafness/Blindness
Seizures
> Convulsions, epilepsy, foaming at the mouth
Tearing Things, Gnashing of Teeth
Dumbness (insanity in the Greek)
> Madness, insanity, lunatic behavior, schizophrenia
Poverty
Accidents
> Burning accidents, drowning accidents, destruction
> Fear of fire, fear of water
Thoughts of Death
> Thoughts or acts of suicide, sensing approaching death
Death
Notes: For *Uncontrolled Crying* **see also Spirit of Heaviness**

Once the house is plundered: command the deaf and dumb spirit to get out.

- Issue an eviction notice to this spirit (Speak it out loud)
- Loose and welcome in: healing, hearing, boldness, peace, deep and peaceful sleep

SPIRIT OF DEATH/SHADOW OF DEATH

Even though I walk through the valley of the shadow of death, I fear no evil, for You are with me; Your rod and Your staff, they comfort me (Psalm 23:4).

Bind: *Spirit/Shadow of Death*

Plunder its house!

- Repentance for aligning with and operating under the influence of the spirit of death/shadow of death
- Break attachments from the below listed activities and other partnering demonic spirits
- Renounce all of the following activities
- Cast out or evict all partnering evil spirits

Signs: *Fears, Deception, Destruction, Seduction, Nightmares, Mental/Spiritual Torment, Hopelessness, Isolation, Sickness, Thoughts of Suicide/Death*

Unbelief

Fear

Deception

Blinded Heart and Mind

Seduction (luring)

Abortion (one or more)

Discouragement/Hopelessness/Despair/Depression

Sorrow/Aching Heart/Excessive Mourning or Grief

Lethargy

Isolation/Abandons Friends or Family

Occult Involvement involving

Lilith

Diana

Luciferian doctrines

Satan

Wicca practices and rituals

Worship of dead saints

Dedication to dead saints

Being named after dead saints

Prayers to dead saints

Ouija board

Occult, witchcraft rituals involving killing of animals or bloodshed

Oppression, Mental Torment

Something keeps whispering that he or she is going to die.

Dreams of:

Being attacked by animals, demons, grim reaper

Being chased by dead people

Being married to dead people

Walking in a graveyard

Being flogged

Being shot

Being hit by a vehicle

Falling into a pit and being unable to get out

Seeing Shadowy Dark Figures

Obsession with Blood, Death, Violence

Sickness or Disease (that does not respond to prayers or medical treatment)

Sharp pains in the body

Sudden loss of appetite

Self-Affliction

Death Wishes, Thoughts of Suicide/Attempts of Suicide

Thoughts of Murder/Murder

Once the house is plundered: command the spirit of death/shadow of death to get out.

- Issue an eviction notice to this spirit (Speak it out loud)
- Loose and welcome in: life and light, prosperity, healing, blessing, a fresh infilling of the Holy Spirit

FAMILIAR SPIRIT: WITCHCRAFT, SPIRIT OF DIVINATION, OCCULT, REBELLION

One day, as we were going to the house of prayer, we encountered a young slave girl who had an evil spirit of divination, the spirit of Python. She had earned great profits for her owners by being a fortune-teller (Acts 16:16 TPT).

Give no regard to mediums and familiar spirits; do not seek after them, to be defiled by them: I am the Lord your God (Leviticus 19:31 NKJV).

For rebellion is as the sin of divination, and insubordination is as iniquity and idolatry (1 Samuel 15:23 NASB).

Bind: *Familiar Spirit and Spirit of Divination/Occult/Rebellion*
Plunder its house!

- Repentance for aligning with and operating under the influence of the familiar spirit/witchcraft/spirit of divination/occult/rebellion
- Break attachments from the below listed activities and other partnering demonic spirits
- Renounce all of the following activities
- Cast out or evict all partnering evil spirits

Signs: *Independence, Control, Spiritual Error, Fears, OCD, Drugs, Infirmity, Sexual Sin*

Generational Iniquity, Family Curses

Self-Will (independence from God)

Stubbornness, disobedience, rebellion, blasphemy

Control, Manipulation

Lying, deception

Spiritual Error

Unhealthy fear of God or hell

Fear of losing salvation

Superficial spirituality

Religiosity, legalism, ritualism

Doctrinal obsession, doctrinal error

Spiritual adultery, spiritual unfaithfulness

Superstition

Fantasy

Hallucinations

Fears, Suspicions

Obsessions, Compulsion

Drugs (pharmakeia)

Easily Persuaded, Passive Mind

Victim, Lethargy

Poverty Mentality

Entry to Occult

Dungeons and Dragons and other dark games, Ouija board, Pokémon, horror and "supernatural" movies, music that defies, mocks or rejects god (hip-hop, rock), astrology, horoscope, tarot cards, tea leaves, fortune telling, palmistry, psychics, past life readings, psychic healing, pendulum divination, charms, fetishes (good luck piece), occult jewelry, yoga, I Ching, martial arts, Rieke (palm healing), video games and online games steeped in the occult, witchcraft, sexual perversion and killing

Occult Activity

Clairvoyance, dreamer (false), divination, channeling, automatic handwriting, mind reading, mental telepathy, false prophesies transcendental meditation, trance, spirit guides hypnosis, mind control, enchanter (spells), charmer, muttering, incantation, white magic, levitation-séance, necromancy (consulting the dead), medium, consulter of the dead, black magic (evil), sorcery (spells, black arts), witch, conjuring (summoning demons), soothsayer, ritualistic body piercing, occult and demonic tattoos, ritualistic flying and suspension by hooks for spiritual enlightenment, Ouija board, physical ritual abuse, death

Cults

Belial, Black Panthers, Buddhism, unbiblical Catholicism, Christian Science, Confucianism, Freemasonry, Eastern Star, Hinduism, Islam, Jehovah's Witnesses (Watchtower), KKK, Mind Control, Mormonism, New Age, Occultism, Rosicrucianism (secret society), Satanism, Scientology, Shintoism, Spiritism, Sufism (Islam-related), Taoism, Theosophy, Unitarianism, Unity, Universalism, Voodoo, Santeria, Wicca, Witchcraft, Lilith worship, Santa Muerte worship, Brujeria

Sexual

Incubus, Succubus (dreams of sexual activity with demon spirits)

Seduction

Incest

Ritual sex

Harlotry (prostitution)

Once the house is plundered: command the familiar spirit/witchcraft/ spirit of divination/occult/rebellion to get out.

- Issue an eviction notice to this spirit (Speak it out loud)

- Loose and welcome in: truth and revelation, humility, mercy, love, peace, joy, purity, a spirit of prophecy, awakening to the Word of God, awakening of the presence of the Lord, fresh infilling of the Holy Spirit

SPIRIT OF FEAR

For God will never give you the spirit of fear, but the Holy Spirit who gives you mighty power, love, and self-control (2 Timothy 1:7).

Bind: *Spirit of Fear*

Plunder its house!

- Repentance for aligning with and operating under the influence of the spirit of fear
- Break attachments from the below listed activities and other partnering demonic spirits
- Renounce all of the following activities
- Cast out or evict all partnering evil spirits

Signs: *Abandoned, Abused, Fear of Authority, Low Self-Esteem, Unbelief, Depression, Paranoia, Sleep Disorders, Illness, Escape, Addictions, Trauma or Repeated Traumas*

Abandonment

Orphaned

Abuse

Trauma

Fear of Touch

Fear of Giving or Receiving Love

Fear of Authority

Fear of Man

Fear of Confrontation/Correction/Disapproval/Judgment/
Accusation

Fear of Intimidation, Embarrassment

Fear of Failure

Passivity, Timidity, Compromising (conceding)

Frustration

Judging, Resentment

Jealousy

Excessively Self-Aware

    Low self-esteem, inadequacy, inferiority complex, insecurity

    Self-Rejection

Unbelief

    Faithlessness, no fellowship with the Father, cannot call upon
    God

    Spiritual blindness, fear of losing salvation, fear of God (in an
    unhealthy way)

Lack of Trust/Doubt/Distrust/Skepticism/Suspicion

Stress/Tension/Anxiety/Apprehension/Worry

Agitation/Vexation/Negativity/Dread

Moodiness, Sorrow, Continual Crying

Loneliness

Depression

Confusion, Ineptness, Paralysis (mental?)

Stuttering

Hyper Sensitivity, Unduly Cautious/Careful

Excitability/Panic/Hysteria

Fears of:

    Heights, closed-in places, darkness, germs, danger, death

Phobias, Paranoia, Terror, Torment, Trembling, Rejection

Sleep Disorders

    Insomnia, sleeplessness, sleepiness, teeth grinding, nightmares

Sickness

Hormonal imbalance, headaches, high blood pressure, heart attacks, migraines, chronic fatigue syndrome

Escapism

Procrastination

Daydreaming, fantasy, unreality, indifference

Pretension (posing, posturing), sophistication, playacting, theatrics, pouting, hypochondria, isolation, recluse

Restlessness, roving

Self-Reward

Mind Control

Schizophrenia

Insanity

For Fantasy, see also the Spirit of Whoredom

For *Headaches*, see also the Spirit of Infirmity

For *Resentment*, see also the Spirit of Jealousy

Once the house is plundered: command the spirit of fear to get out.

- Issue an eviction notice to this spirit (Speak it out loud)
- Loose and welcome in: humility, mercy, love, peace, joy, a spirit of truth, spirit of boldness, power, love, a sound mind, a spirit of adoption, true kingdom identity, awakening to the Word of God, awakening of the presence of the Lord, fresh infilling of the Holy Spirit

HAUGHTY SPIRIT: PRIDEFUL SPIRIT

An arrogant man is inflated with pride nothing but a snooty scoffer in love with his own opinion. Mr. Mocker is his name! (Proverbs 21:24)

Bind: *Haughty/Prideful Spirit*

Plunder its house!

- Repentance for aligning with and operating under the influence of the haughty/pride spirit
- Break attachments from the below listed activities and other partnering demonic spirits
- Renounce all of the following activities
- Cast out or evict all partnering evil spirits

Signs: *Independence, Intellectualism, Self-Centered, Pride, Control, Entitlement, Anger, Excessively Competitive, Racism*

Competitive (excessively)
> Perfectionist
> Pride in education, pride in position (excessive)

Entitlement
> Coveting, greed, self-pity, idleness

Frustration, Impatience, Agitation

Critical, Judgmental, Resentful, Intolerance, Gossip

Argumentative

Lying/Deception

Spiritual Pride (independence)
> Intellectualism (knowledge is from reason),
> Rationalism (reason is truth)
> Religious spirit, legalism
> Rebellion
> Rejection of God (atheism)

Ego-Centric
> Self-Importance, vanity, self-centered, self-righteous
> Self-Delusion, self-deception, selfishness

Pretension (posing or posturing)

False Humility, playacting, theatrics
Uncompassionate (emotionally hard)
Unforgiving
Pride
Superiority, egotism, arrogance, haughtiness, smugness
Stubborn, obstinate, stiff-necked
Boastful, bragging
Scornful (mocking)
Holier-than-thou attitude, lofty looks
Controlling
Overbearing, domineering, dictatorial
Anger/Bitterness, Bitter Root Judgment/Hatred
Irritability, unkindness
Insolence (rude), contentiousness (combative)
Wrath (anger), rage
Violence
Note: For *Wrath* see also Spirit of Jealousy

Once the house is plundered: command the spirit of pride/haughtiness to get out.

- Issue an eviction notice to this spirit (Speak it out loud)
- Loose and welcome in: humility, mercy, love, peace, joy, a spirit of truth, awakening to the Word of God, awakening of the presence of the Lord, fresh infilling of the Holy Spirit

SPIRIT OF HEAVINESS/DEPRESSION

To grant those who mourn in Zion, giving them a garland instead of ashes, the oil of gladness instead of mourning, the mantle of praise instead of a spirit of fainting. So they will be called oaks of righteousness, the planting of the Lord, that He may be glorified (Isaiah 61:3 NASB).

Bind: *Spirit of Heaviness/Depression*

Plunder its house!

- Repentance for aligning with and operating under the influence of the spirit of heaviness/depression
- Break attachments from the below listed activities and other partnering demonic spirits
- Renounce all of the following activities
- Cast out or evict all partnering evil spirits

Signs: *Abandonment, Rejection, Brokenhearted, Condemnation, Unworthiness, Self-Pity, Hopelessness, Insomnia, Torment, Passivity, Escape, Thoughts of Suicide, Trauma or Repeated Traumas*

Abandonment

    Rejection

    Bastard (to alienate)

    Abortion (having one, surviving one)

Brokenhearted

    Heartbreak, heartache, hurt, inner hurts

    Excessive mourning, grief, sorrow, continual sadness

    Continual crying

Condemnation/Guilt/False Guilt

Burdened/False Burden, Pressured

Introspection

    Critical, disgust

    Unworthiness, shame

Troubled Spirit, Wounded Spirit

Self-Pity

Lack, Poverty

Discouragement
> Dejection, defeatism
> Despair, despondency, gloom
> Hopelessness
> Dread

Passivity
> Weariness, sleepiness, tiredness, fatigue
> Lethargy, listless, laziness
> Indifference

Insomnia

Torment

Escape
> Isolation, loneliness
> Drivenness (excessive)
> Hyperactivity
> Restlessness, vagabond, wanderer
> Gluttony
> Disorder
> Cruelty
> Suicide

Morbidity (injury, illness)
> Pain, headache, sickness
> Death

Once the house is plundered: command the spirit of heaviness/depression to get out.

- Issue an eviction notice to this spirit (Speak it out loud)
- Loose and welcome in: The Comforter, a garment of praise, joy, love, peace, power, a sound mind, acceptance, true kingdom identity, a fresh infilling of the Holy Spirit, right brain alignment and thoughts

SPIRIT OF INFIRMITY

And behold, there was a woman who had a spirit of infirmity eighteen years and was bent over and could in no way raise herself up (Luke 13:11 NKJV).

Bind: *Spirit of Infirmity*

Plunder its house!

- Repentance for aligning with and operating under the influence of the spirit of infirmity
- Break attachments from the below listed activities and other partnering demonic spirits
- Renounce all of the following activities
- Cast out or evict all partnering evil spirits

Signs: *Unforgiveness, Allergies, Infections, Diseases, Disorders, Mental Illness, Oppression, Death*

Generational Curses

Wounded Spirit

Unforgiveness

Bitterness, hatred

Allergies

Hay fever, other allergies

Infections

Fever, inflammation

Colds, bronchitis

Fungus infections

Plague

Venereal disease

Diseases/Chronic Diseases

Arthritis

Asthma

Cancer

Epilepsy, seizures

Heart disorder, heart attack

Skin disorders

Ulcers

Lingering Disorders

ADD, ADHD

Bent body or spine

Bleeding

Blindness

Deafness

Chronic weakness, feebleness

Fainting

Headaches, migraines

Impotence

Lameness, paralysis

Lingering trauma

Mental Illness

Memory loss, senility

Tourette's syndrome

Hallucinations

Schizophrenia paranoia

Mania (obsession, hysteria)

Insanity, lunatic, madness

Spirit of Death

Oppression

Slavery (enslavement, bondage, oppression)

Torment

Death

Note: For *Oppression* see also Spirit of Heaviness

For occult activity and cults that lead to infirmity, see Familiar Spirit

| *Once the house is plundered: command the spirit of infirmity to get out.*

- Issue an eviction notice to this spirit (Speak it out loud)
- Loose and welcome in: wholeness, health, life, joy, power, love a sound mind, peace, fresh infilling of the Holy Spirit

SPIRIT OF JEALOUSY

And if a spirit (sense, attitude) of jealousy comes over him and he is jealous and angry at his wife who has defiled herself—or if a spirit of jealousy comes over him and he is jealous of his wife when she has not defiled herself (Numbers 5:14 AMP).

Bind: *Spirit of Jealousy*

Plunder its house!

- Repentance for aligning with and operating under the influence of the spirit of jealousy
- Break attachments from the below listed activities and other partnering demonic spirits
- Renounce all of the following activities
- Cast out or evict all partnering evil spirits

Signs: *Unworthiness, Insecurity, Self-Centered, Competitive, Critical, Anger, Unforgiveness, Argumentative, Gossip, Inability to Cry, Causing Division, Rebellion, Self-Hatred, Bitterness, Hatred, Racism*

Unworthiness, Inferiority

Insecurity

Materialistic/Covetous/Envy/Greed

Dreamer (imaginations)

Ego-Centric/Self-Centered (self-focused)

    Competitive (excessively)

    Discontent, dissatisfaction, restlessness

    Indifference, hardness of heart, inability to cry

    Selfish

Critical

    Judging, faultfinding

    Distrust, suspicion

    Gossip, accusations, backbiting, belittling

Anger

    Spite, (anger), strife (anger), temper, burn (anger), rage

    Bitterness, bitter root judgment, hatred, enmity (hatred)

Unforgiveness

Factiousness (division)

    Seeking to cause debates, causing divisions, disputes

    Contentious, argumentative, bickering, quarreling

    Mocking, dishonorable words, cursing, coarse jesting

    slander, lying

Deception (deceived, deceiving)

Rebellion

Blasphemy

Malice (evil intent, anger)

    Retaliation, revenge

    Stealing

    Fighting, gangs, violence

    Cruelty, hurt, sadism (inflicting pain)

    Wickedness

    Destruction

    Murder

Self-Hatred, Suicide

Once the house is plundered: command the spirit of jealousy to get out.

- Issue an eviction notice to this spirit (Speak it out loud)
- Loose and welcome in: love, acceptance, peace, joy, self-control, patience, contentment, fresh infilling of the Holy Spirit

LYING SPIRIT

There are six things which the Lord hates, yes, seven which are an abomination to Him: haughty eyes, a lying tongue, and hands that shed innocent blood, a heart that devises wicked plans, feet that run rapidly to evil, a false witness who utters lies, and one who spreads strife among brothers (Proverbs 6:16-19 NASB).

Bind: *Lying Spirit*

Plunder its house!

- Repentance for aligning with and operating under the influence of the lying spirit
- Break attachments from the below listed activities and other partnering demonic spirits
- Renounce all of the following activities
- Cast out or evict all partnering evil spirits

Signs: *Independence, Pride, Performance, Low Self-Image, Poverty, Emotionalism, Wickedness, Rationalization (excuse), False Spirituality Mind Control, Sexual Sin, Drugs, ADD*

Fear of Authority, Other Fears
Independence

Pride, arrogance, vanity

Entitlement

Self-Protection

Performance

Perfectionism, drivenness

Seeking approval

Insecurity, low self-image

False responsibility, false burden

Lying

Excessive talking

Flattery

False compassion

Exaggeration, insinuations (implying)

Gossip, accusations, slander

False witness

Deceit, cheating, manipulation

Stealing, robbery

Rationalization (excuse)

Hypocrisy

Poverty, Financial Problems (especially tithing)

Emotionalism

Passion (inordinate)

Crying

Arguments

Profanity

Wickedness

Vengeance

Religious Spirit

Jezebel Spirit

False Spirituality

False Prophet/False Prophecy

Dreamer, Vain Imaginations/Strong Delusions

Superstitions

False Oaths

Curses, Self-Inflicted Curses

False Teaching/False Doctrines/Heresy

Divination

Mind Control

Mental Bondage

Sexual

Fantasies, uncleanness, lust, pornography, compulsive masturbation, fornication, adultery, sodomy, lesbianism, homosexual behavior, transsexual behavior, transvestite, depraved desires

Drugs

Notes: For *False Prophecy,* see also Familiar Spirit.

For "homosexuality" and *Sodomy,* see also Spirit of Perversion, Whoredom.

Once the house is plundered: command the lying spirit to get out.

- Issue an eviction notice to this spirit (Speak it out loud)
- Loose and welcome in: honesty, goodness, truth, purity, joy, awakening to the Word of God, a fresh filling of the Holy Spirit

SPIRIT OF ERROR

We are of God. He who knows God hears us; he who is not of God does not hear us. By this we know the spirit of truth and the spirit of error (1 John 4:6 NKJV).

Bind: *Spirit of Error*

Plunder its house!

- Repentance for aligning with and operating under the influence of the spirit of error
- Break attachments from the below listed activities and other partnering demonic spirits
- Renounce all of the following activities
- Cast out or evict all partnering evil spirits

Signs: *Lack of Discernment, Easily Persuaded, False Beliefs, Pride, Anger, Competition, Lies*

Lack of Discernment

Easily Persuaded (toward error)

False Doctrines, New Age Beliefs

    Cults, occult, doctrines of devils

Pride/Haughtiness

    Always right, unsubmissive, unteachable

Angry

    Argumentative, defensive, contentious, (self-protection)

    Hatred

Competition (excessive)

Hypocrisy, Lies

Once the house is plundered: command the spirit of error to get out.

- Issue an eviction notice to this spirit (Speak it out loud)
- Loose and welcome in: Spirit of Truth, Spirit of Promise, patience, peace, self-control

SPIRIT OF PERVERSION/WHOREDOM/ LUST/SEXUAL SIN

The Lord has mingled a perverse spirit in her; so they have caused Egypt to err in her every work (Isaiah 19:14 MEV).

Bind: *Spirit of Perversion/Lust, Spirit of Whoredom/Sexual Sin*
Plunder its house!

- Repentance for aligning with and operating under the influence of the spirit of perversion/whoredom/lust/sexual sin
- Break attachments from the below listed activities and other partnering demonic spirits
- Renounce all of the following activities
- Cast out or evict all partnering evil spirits

Signs: *Lusts, Sexual Sin, Emotional Dissatisfaction, Wounded Spirit, Confusion, Unbelief, Deception, Worldliness, Evil Actions*

Wounded Spirit

Guilt, shame, chronic worry

Emotional weakness, weakness, dizziness

Emotional dissatisfaction

Unforgiveness

Hatred

Self-hatred, marking, cutting, suicidal thoughts, actions

Doubt, Unbelief

Atheism

Idolatry

False teachings

Doctrinal error (twisting the word of God)

Diviner (false prophet)

Confusion (spirit of Egypt)

Deception

Lover of Self

Arrogance, stubbornness, contentiousness, crankiness

Lust for Authority/Power/Position/Social Standing

Lust for Money, Greed, Hoarding, Poverty
Lust for Food
Lust for Activity (excessive)
Worldliness

Foolishness

Drunkard spirit

Tattoos

Evil actions

Cruelty

Lust for Sex

Uncontrollable sexual desires, perverse sexual acts, sensuality, lustful fantasy, filthy mindedness, adulterous fantasy pornography, self-gratification, compulsive masturbation, self-exposure, exhibitionism

Seduction

Fornication (sexual activity before marriage), Promiscuity, Unfaithfulness, Adultery, Rape

Harlotry, whoredom, prostitution of body, soul or spirit; illegitimate children, bastard spirit (unholy covenant)

Abortion

sexual deviation, perversion

Homosexuality (same sex), sodomy (anal, oral), lesbianism (same sex)

Bisexuality (with both sexes), Transvestite (cross-dressing+),

Sadomasochism (physical, mental suffering in sex)

Incest (family members)

Child abuse

Pedophilia (with children)

Incubus, Succubus (dreams of sex with spirits)

Chronic sexual dissatisfaction, frigidity

Seducing spirit, Spirits of Shame, Pride, Lust

Once the house is plundered: command the spirit of perversion/whore-dom/lust/sexual sin to get out.

- Issue an eviction notice to this spirit (Speak it out loud)
- Loose and welcome in: chastity, discernment, godliness, purity, Spirit of Truth, Spirit of Holiness, ability to abstain from sexual sin, self-control, healing from addiction and bondage

SEDUCING SPIRIT

But the [Holy] Spirit explicitly and unmistakably declares that in later times some will turn away from the faith, paying attention instead to deceitful and seductive spirits and doctrines of demons (1 Timothy 4:1 AMP).

Bind: *Seducing Spirit*

Plunder its house!

- Repentance for aligning with and operating under the influence of the seducing spirit
- Break attachments from the below listed activities and other partnering demonic spirits
- Renounce all of the following activities
- Cast out or evict all partnering evil spirits

Signs: *Fear of Man, Seeks Attention, Dulled Sense of Right and Wrong, Attracted to False Prophets, Evil Persons, Greed, Hypocrisy*

Fear of Man

Wanders from the Truth of God

Seared Conscience (dulled sense of right and wrong)

Emulation (imitates)

Gullible/Easily Swayed/Easily Deceived/Enticed/Seduced

Attracted to False Prophets, Signs and Wonders

Fascination with Evil Ways

    Evil objects, evil persons

    Music that defies, mocks or rejects God

    Trance

    Including fascination with evil television shows and movies steeped in the occult, vampires, dark angels, werewolves, etc.

Seeks Attention

Sensual in Dress, Actions

Greed, Exploitation

Hypocritical Lies

Once the house is plundered: command the seducing spirit to get out.

- Issue an eviction notice to this spirit (Speak it out loud)

- Loose and welcome in: Spirit of Truth, Spirit of Holiness, purity, awakening to the truth and Word of God, true gift of prophecy

SPIRIT OF SLUMBER/UNBELIEF

God granted them a spirit of deep slumber. He closed their eyes to the truth and prevented their ears from hearing up to this day (Romans 11:8).

Bind: *Spirit of Slumber/Unbelief*

Plunder its house!

- Repentance for aligning with and operating under the influence of the spirit of slumber/unbelief

- Break attachments from the below listed activities and other partnering demonic spirits

- Renounce all of the following activities
- Cast out or evict all partnering evil spirits

Signs: *Can't Hear or Understand the Word of God, Unbelief, Confusion, Distracted, Mental Slowness, Sleep Disorders, Sickness, Sexual Sin*

Can't Hear the Word of God

Can't Stay Awake in Church

Confusion

Distracted Easily

ADD, ADHD

Dizziness

Mental Slowness

Lethargy

Lazy

Sleep Disorders

Sleepiness, chronic fatigue syndrome, sleeplessness

Unbelief, Blasphemer

Fear, Torment, Terror

Sexual Sin, Perversions

Sickness

Eye disorders, blindness

Hearing problems

Arthritis

Asthma

Anemia

Circulatory problems

Palpitations

Note: For *Sickness* see also Spirit of Infirmity

Once the house is plundered: command the spirit of slumber/unbelief to get out.

- Issue an eviction notice to this spirit (Speak it out loud)
- Loose and welcome in: being filled with the Spirit, spiritual eyes open, healing, awakening to the Word of God, awakening to the presence of God

SPIRIT OF REJECTION

Bind: *Spirit of Rejection*

Plunder its house!

- Repentance for aligning with and operating under the influence of the spirit of rejection
- Break attachments from the below listed activities and other partnering demonic spirits
- Renounce all of the following activities
- Cast out or evict all partnering evil spirits

Signs: *Self-Rejection, Overly Aggressive Reactions, Independence, Self-Idolatry, Covetousness, Pride, Sabotaging of Relationships, Fears, Rebellion, Emotional Immaturity, Trauma or Repeated Traumas*

Aggressive Reactions

Refusing comfort

Rejections of others

Harshness, hardness

Skepticism, unbelief

Aggressive attitudes

Swearing, foul language

Argumentative

Stubborn, defiance

Rebellion

Fighting

Self-Rejection

Low self-image

Inferiorities

Insecurity

Inadequacy

Sadness, grief, sorrow

Self-accusation, self-condemnation

Inability or refusal to communicate

Fear of failure

Fear of other's opinions

Anxiety, worry, depression

Negativity, pessimism

Hopelessness, despair

| *Measures to Counter Fear of Rejection*

Striving, Achievement

Performance, Competition

Withdrawal, Aloneness

Independence:

Isolation

Self-protection

Self-centeredness

Selfishness

Self-justification

Self-righteousness

Self-Idolatry:

Criticism

Judgment

Envy, jealousy

Covetousness

Self-pity

Pride:

Egotism

Haughtiness

Arrogance

Manipulation

Possessiveness

Emotional immaturity

Perfectionism

Once the house is plundered: command the spirit of rejection to get out.

- Issue an eviction notice to this spirit (Speak it out loud)
- Loose and welcome in: love, acceptance, true kingdom identity, spirit of adoption, awakening to the Father heart of God

RELIGIOUS SPIRIT

Jesus spoke up and said, "Watch out for the yeast of the Pharisees and the Sadducees" (Matthew 16:6 TPT).

Bind: *Religious Spirit*

Plunder its house!

- Repentance for aligning with and operating under the influence of the religious spirit
- Break attachments from the below listed activities and other partnering demonic spirits
- Renounce all of the following activities
- Cast out or evict all partnering evil spirits

Signs: *Legalism, Pride, Holier-Than-Thou Attitude, Ritual over Relationship, Fear, Judgment, Against New Moves of God*

Overemphasis on Outward Form

Have to say the right word

Have to do the right things

Have to have the right look

Fear of what others think

Dresses to attract attention on oneself

Dresses like Jesus, an angel, in a manner that draws attention to the person and not to Jesus

Acts otherworldly

Always quoting scripture, cannot engage in conversation without making everything spiritual, acting above others

False tongues

Condemnation and Fear

Condemns when things aren't done "just right"

Perfectionism

Fear of failure

Fear of losing man's approval

Pride

Judgmental

Critical

Holier-than-thou attitude

Self-righteous

Self-exalting or great false humility

Functions closely with a political mindset and spirit

Resists New Moves of God

Jealousy

Steeped in tradition

Speaks out against moves of the Lord

Their tradition and movement is the most spiritual and elite

Elitist thinking about their traditions

Superstition

With using the Word

With their rituals

All tradition works and fear based

Oppressive Legalism

No flexibility

Rigid dogma

Required and method-based prayers

Required and method-based services

No freedom for gifts or the Holy Spirit to move freely

No thriving relationship with Jesus or the Holy Spirit

Driven Need to Figure Out God

Intellectualism

Driven to make God predictable

Cannot relate to the supernatural

Places God in a box

Much doctrinal error

Deception

Lying spirit

Dependence on Self-Effort

Achieves righteousness through works of the flesh

Striving

Cannot experience peace separate from works

Perfectionist

Undue Emphasis on Tradition

Turning tradition into an idol

Idol worship

Worship focused toward an object or person and not to Jesus

No spiritual life or presence on the tradition

Spiritually dead

Accuses and condemns those who do not embrace tradition

Falsely honoring God with words, but not in heart and action

Spirit of Unbelief

Spirit of Slumber

Spirit of Bondage

Spirit of Fear

Once the house is plundered: command the religious spirit to get out.

- Issue an eviction notice to this spirit (Speak it out loud)
- Loose and welcome in: Spirit of Truth, freedom, relationship with Jesus, awakening to His Word, awakening to His presence, fresh infilling of the Holy Spirit

SPIRIT OF JEZEBEL

But I have this against you: you tolerate that woman Jezebel, who calls herself a prophetess and is seducing my loving servants. She is teaching that it is permissible to indulge in sexual immorality and to eat food sacrificed to idols. I have waited for her to repent from her vile immorality, but she refuses to do so. Now I will lay her low with terrible distress along with all her adulterous partners if they do not repent (Revelation 2:20-22).

Bind: *The Spirit of Jezebel (This spirit can operate in both men and women)*

Plunder its house!

- Repentance for aligning with and operating under the influence of the Jezebel spirit
- Break attachments from the below listed activities and other partnering demonic spirits

- Renounce all of the following activities
- Cast out or evict all partnering evil spirits

Signs: *Prophetic, (but wants to control those who are truly prophetic); Gets Close to Leadership, Defensive, Not Teachable, Bypasses Proper Authority, Deceptive, Spiritual Pride, Desires Control; In the World: Seductive, Power Hungry (makes evil deals for power, will say one thing to gain favor will do the exact opposite to get power)*

Prophetic Assignment

Appears prophetic

Threatened by true prophets

Speaks soulish prophecies to entice people

Controls those who are true prophets

Silences the voice of the true prophet

Steals favor from the true prophet

False Favor

Establishes relationship with leader

Finds weakness and uses against others, leaders

Usurps authority for complete control

Seduction with words

Seduction with actions

Seeks to gain pastoral, leadership endorsement

Manipulation

Seeks recognition impurely

Will deceive and lie to gain favor (lying spirit)

Operates in false humility (for the sake of favor)

Will look for the weak link (someone to become the Ahab)

Appears Very Spiritual

Uses flattery to appeal to others

Their word is the final word even over leaders

Operates in a religious spirit

Quick to point out faults of others while appearing sad about those faults

Doctrinal error, subtle twisting of the Word of God

Impure motives

Seek sdisciples to lead

Very secretive when praying for others (usually in isolated places)

Says to be able to impart a higher spiritual impartation than anyone else

Control

Controls prayer, church, Christian meetings

Business meetings

Governmental meetings

In the world wants media attention

Will engage in evil deeds to control

Sexual acts

Sexual perversion

Mammon, greed/illegal money dealings for wealth

Lies and Defames for Power/Control

Kills

Robs Inheritance

Pride

Control

False humility

Actually, has poor self- esteem, wears religious mask to hide it

Will engage in very overt "spiritual acts" to gain attention

Wailing, crying, mourning, warring, contending, prophesying

Families Life Is Shaky

When in the World, Often Involved in Occult Activity

Once the house is plundered: command the spirit of Jezebel to get out.

- Issue an eviction notice to this spirit (Speak it out loud)

- Loose and welcome in: Spirit of Truth, love, spirit of prophecy, holiness, purity, new infilling of the Holy Spirit, awakening to His Word and awakening to His presence

NOTE

1. Alice Smith, *Delivering the Captives* (Bloomington, MN: Bethany House Publishers, 2006), 96-118, Used by permission of publisher.

ABOUT REBECCA GREENWOOD

Rebecca Greenwood co-founded Christian Harvest International, Strategic Prayer Apostolic Network and Christian Harvest Training Center which ministers to the nations through teaching at Christian conferences, schools and gatherings and travels extensively releasing prophetic words and strategies for cities, regions, nations, and spheres of influence. Over the past 30 years, she has mobilized and led prophetic intercession and transformational spiritual warfare prayer journeys to over 45 nations which have resulted in effective transformational breakthrough. She is the author of ten books. And is the host of *Reigning in Life,* which appears on It's Supernatural Network (ISN). Rebecca and her husband, Greg, reside in Colorado Springs, CO and they have three beautiful daughters and three wonderful sons-in-law.

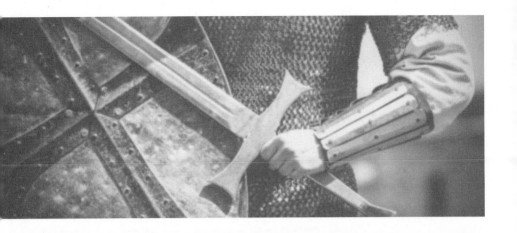

Are you ready to join the Army of the Lord?

Enroll in our Spiritual Warfare Online School taught
by Becca Greenwood!

Go to: spanprayer.org/spiritual-warfare-online-school

Christian Harvest
INTERNATIONAL